A Heart Promptly Offered

OTHER BOOKS IN THE LEADERS IN ACTION SERIES

A Heart Promptly Offered

THE REVOLUTIONARY LEADERSHIP OF JOHN CALVIN

LEADERS
IN
ACTION

DAVID W. HALL

DAVID VAUGHAN, GENERAL EDITOR

CUMBERLAND HOUSE
NASHVILLE, TENNESSEE

A Heart Promptly Offered
Published by Cumberland House Publishing, Inc.
431 Harding Industrial Drive
Nashville, Tennessee 37211

Copyright © 2006 by David W. Hall

All rights reserved. No part of this book may be reproduced or transmitted in any form or by any means, electronic or mechanical, including photocopying and recording, or by any information storage and retrieval system, without permission in writing from the publisher, except for brief quotations in critical reviews and articles.

All Scripture quotations are taken from the New King James Version. Copyright © 1979, 1980, 1982, Thomas Nelson, Inc., Publishers.

Cover design by Gore Studio, Inc., Nashville, Tennessee

Library of Congress Cataloging-in-Publication Data

Hall, David W., 1955–
    A heart promptly offered : the revolutionary leadership of John
Calvin / David W. Hall ; David Vaughan, general editor.
        p.   cm. — (Leaders in action series)
    ISBN-13: 978-1-58182-505-3 (hardcover : alk. paper)
    ISBN-10: 1-58182-505-6 (hardcover : alk. paper)
    1. Calvin, Jean, 1509–1564. I. Vaughan, David J., 1955– . II. Title.
III. Series.
    BX9418.H27 2006
    284'.2092—dc22
    [B]   2006015630

Printed in the United States of America
1 2 3 4 5 6—09 08 07 06

To Megan, Devon, and Andrew Hall
with thanks for you and with your parents'
prayers for you to be leaders in action.

Contents

PART 3: THE LEGACY OF JOHN CALVIN

FOREWORD

*K*NOWLEDGE OF the great Reformer John Calvin is perhaps at an all-time low, as illustrated by these two personal anecdotes.

Years ago, when I was working on my undergraduate degree, I took a course on colonial American history. Throughout the course, the professor talked about such things as the Pilgrims, the Puritans, Jonathan Edwards, George Whitefield, revivalism, and the Great Awakening. Of course, anyone who knows their church history will recall that all these were Calvinists to the core. In other words, it's not really possible to understand the motivation and worldview that shaped our nation apart from understanding Calvin. It just so happened that at the time I was reading Calvin's *Institutes* for my own edification. So one day after class I asked the professor if he had ever read the *Institutes.* To my surprise and dismay he had not. Shortly afterward I gave him a copy—and aced the class.

Another anecdote, closer to home, further illustrates the need for a renewed study of Calvin. A dear friend of mine recently graduated with an MDiv degree from one of the nation's premier conservative Presbyterian seminaries.

Certainly here, in a Reformed seminary—an institution devoted to the Calvinistic conception of Christianity—certainly here one would have to study Calvin. With this naive assumption, I perchance asked my friend how much Calvin he had read during seminary. "None," he said. A different friend, who happens to head a Reformed institution, recently lamented to me that many seminary students are leaving school because they are no longer being taught the Reformed faith. Sad but true. Many of today's "reformed" pastors have little or no knowledge of Calvin and the Reformation he helped shape.

What makes this ignorance so alarming is that Calvin, along with only a few other great men of the church, such as Augustine and Luther, not only shaped the Reformation but also changed the course of history. This may sound like a grandiose claim, but both friend and foe agree.

Calvin's influence was mainly the result of his writings. Though he was a pastor, a reformer, and a church leader, Calvin was first and foremost a thinker and a writer. The collected critical edition of his works fills fifty-nine volumes. These contain tracts, pamphlets, sermons, catechisms, church manuals, biblical commentary, letters, and of course, his renowned *Institutes of the Christian Religion.* The last of these has gained for Calvin an immemorial place in church history, and this work may rightly be considered his life's work.

Roman Catholic historian F. W. Kampschulte described the *Institutes* as "without doubt the most outstanding and most influential production in the sphere of dogmatics which the Reformation literature of the sixteenth century presents." M. Buisson, the French biographer, concurred:

Such a book is equally removed from a pamphlet to Ulrich von Hutten, from the satire of Erasmus, from the popular preaching, mystical and violent, of Luther: it is a work of a theologian in the most learned sense of the term, a religious work undoubtedly, penetrated with an ethical inspiration, but before all, a work of organization and concentration, a code of doctrine for the minister, and arsenal of arguments for simple believers: it is the Summa of Reformed Christianity.

What began in 1536 as a small handbook outlining (and defending) the new Reformed faith grew by 1559 into a dense, well-organized system of Protestant theology. Indeed, it was almost immediately recognized as the definitive defense of Protestantism against Rome. Well-known theologian Albrecht Ritschl once pointed to a copy of the *Institutes* and said, "There is the masterpiece of Protestant theology."

Indeed it is, or so think the editors of the Library of Christian Classics edition of Calvin's *Institutes*. They asserted:

The celebrated treatise here presented in a new English translation holds a place in the short list of books that have notably affected the course of history, molding the beliefs and behavior of generations of mankind. Perhaps no other theological work has so consistently retained for four centuries a place on the reading list of studious Christians. In a wider circle, its title has been familiar, and vague ideas of its content have been in circulation. It has, from time to time, called forth an extensive literature of

controversy. . . . Even in time when it was least esteemed, its influence remained potent in the life of active
churches and in the habits of men. To many Christians
whose worship was proscribed under hostile governments, this book has supplied the courage to endure.
Wherever in the crises of history social foundations are
shaken and men's hearts quail, the pages of this classic
are searched with fresh respect.

The famous church historian Philip Schaff said of the
Institutes: "This book is the masterpiece of a precocious
genius of commanding intellectual and spiritual depth and
power. It is one of the few truly classical productions in
the history of theology, and has given its author the double title of the Aristotle and Thomas Aquinas of the Reformed Church."

Assuming all this to be true (and there is no reason to
doubt it), then why are fewer Evangelicals reading Calvin?
Several reasons could be offered: (1) an overall decline in
reading; (2) the dumbing-down of the pulpit; (3) the
changing view of the pastorate (the pastor is now an exec-
utive and not a teacher-scholar); (4) the cultural bias in
favor of novelty—the "old is mold" mentality; (5) the prejudice against doctrine ("doctrine divides, while love
unites"); and many others.

All this may be true, but I must add that one of the main
obstacles to Calvin for many is a prejudice born of conjec-
ture and hearsay. In particular, many Christians know
nothing of Calvin other than that he was a predestinarian,
which to them means he believed in some kind of blind
fate. In fact, according to this common characterization,

Calvin believed in a capricious, tyrannical, and even bar-
barous God who delights to create men for damnation—a
God who, in fact, enjoys sending men to hell against their
will. Anyone who takes the time to study Calvin's teaching
on this subject will see that this is a cheap perversion—a
straw man, if you will, that does not hold up under close
scrutiny. Whether one agrees with Calvin's position on predestination or not, it is a simple fact of history that nearly
all the early Reformers—Bucer, Bullinger, Beza, Luther,
Oecolompadius, Vermigli, Zwingli, and others—held a
similar position. In a sense this aspect of Calvinism was not
peculiar to Calvin.

John Calvin has also been strenuously criticized for the
execution in Geneva of Michael Servetus. When all the
facts are known, it possible to understand why Calvin
consented to Servetus's death without at the same time
condoning persecution. Servetus was a renowned blas-
phemer and heretic who was troubling many of the Reformed churches. When he came to Geneva, the city
council had him arrested and tried for heresy. Calvin himself was called as an expert witness. While the trial was
under way, Calvin privately pleaded with Servetus to
change his position, knowing that if he were condemned,
he would be sent to the flames. Indeed, as soon as Servetus was convicted he was sentenced to death by burning.
Calvin, however, attempted to intervene to have the
mode of execution changed, but to no avail. Also, before
the proceedings, Calvin had contacted many of the other
Reformers to get their opinions on the matter; all agreed
that Servetus was worthy of death.

Though it is difficult for us to understand that sentiment, both Catholics and Protestants at the time conceded that heresy was punishable by the civil magistrate. According to this view, heresy was worse than murder; for in murder one kills a body, but in heresy one kills a soul and sends it to hell. Since truth, especially theological truth, was the foundation of the social order, heresy led to anarchy, chaos, and bloodshed. For men of the sixteenth century, heresy was an attack on the foundation of the social order.

In judging Calvin on this issue, not to mention our general evaluation of his life, we must keep two factors in mind. First, men must be judged in light of their times. This does not mean that right and wrong are relative. What it does mean is that most men imbibe the principles and prejudices of their age. Great men may be "ahead of their time" in some respects, but they are never so in all respects. Familiarity has a way of blunting the senses. For instance, most of us are horrified today at the execution of Servetus, but we view abortion as an issue to be debated rather than as a horrific reality in America every day. We can, if we exercise enough historical imagination, understand the sixteenth-century worldview without endorsing religious persecution. Universal toleration was an idea whose time had not yet come, but it was coming—in part due to Calvin's own ideas.

The second factor to keep in mind while evaluating a leader's life and legacy is that all leaders—even the greatest leaders—are imperfect. All leaders fail and sin. And some that lead greatly also sin greatly. One has only to remember David, the man after God's own heart. Calvin is no exception to the rule here. What follows is biography, not hagiography. If we are looking for perfection, we will not find it in our history, for that is a record of our failures, foibles, and follies. The wisdom of God can be seen, however, in how he uses such frail and fallen creatures for the blessing of mankind as well as his own glory.

David W. Hall's treatment of Calvin as a leader will no doubt become the definitive work on the subject. His style is lucid and his research impeccable. No one knows Calvin better. Here you will see Calvin as he was, not as his enemies have tried to portray him. You will come to understand the significance of Calvin's theology and to appreciate Calvin's profound history-altering legacy. And better yet, you will be inspired by Calvin's leadership and by his vision of the majesty of God. That vision, which is at the heart of Calvinism, is also the secret of great Christian leadership.

David J. Vaughan

Prologue

*T*HIS BOOK follows the long-standing pattern of the Leaders in Action series by first providing a short biography of John Calvin. Admittedly this biographical sketch is related to what follows and provides instructive lessons of its own as well as important cultural-social context. The second section compiles leadership lessons that exemplify the heart and soul of Calvinism with an emphasis on original sources. The final section of this work summarizes his enduring legacy. Each chapter illustrates how Calvin's life or thought can be applied to leadership in all ages.

Along the way are numerous excerpts from Calvin's own pen. Such exposure not only honors the Genevan Reformer's style but also best represents him to those who frequently begin with a bias against Calvin. Allowing him to speak for himself, as it were, is the best defense of his work. In these pages, one will not only see summaries of Calvin through his letters, commentaries, and sermons but also receive an adequate overview of the main topics of Calvin's *Institutes.* In addition, this work also delves into Calvin's political theory and his impact on unfolding political customs. Furthermore, this work seeks to treat

Calvin in context, not as an individual only; thus, by design it traces the development of a movement, giving needed attention to the embodiment of Calvin's ideas through his disciples as one of the surest tests of a theory.

I have particularly been aided by the following who have met with me, read the manuscript, and counseled me on crucial improvements to this volume. I am happy to acknowledge my debt of gratitude to Matthew Burton, Patrick Conner, Paul Fish, Lewis Godwin, Kip Howard, Mark Jennings, James Jordan, Paul Keel, Robbie Langston, David Meyer, Paul Meyer, B. B. "Bobby" Negron, Peter Neumeier, Jeff O'Hara, Brady Pritchett, Nathan Redding, Mike Snider, Timothy Verner, Paul Wagoner, and Mac Worley. Each of them wishes to give public acknowledgment for their wives' wisdom and insight as greater than their own.

As always, I could not contribute without the love and support of my wife, Ann, and my three growing covenant children: Megan, Devon, and Andrew. I am more grateful for each of them with every passing day.

Our prayer for this offering is that it might engender wise, well-rounded, scriptural, and impactful leadership. Until other leaders are produced who had a better or longer-lasting impact than Calvin, we will settle for reacquainting readers with a superb model of character and legacy.

CHRONOLOGY

1543	Received a home near St. Peter's from Genevan civic leaders
1543	Published *The Bondage and Liberation of the Will; On the Necessity for Reforming the Church*
1544	Published a *Brief Instruction . . . Against the Anabaptists*
1549	Death of Idelette de Bure; Theodore Beza relocated to Geneva
1550	Published *Concerning Scandals*
1558	Founded the Academy of Geneva (dedication service in June 1559)
1559	Revised and completed final edition of the *Institutes of the Christian Religion*
1564	Death of Calvin (May 27)

PART 1

THE LIFE OF JOHN CALVIN

It is into Calvinism that the modern world plunges its roots. For it is Calvinism which first reveals the dignity and worth of man. Called of God, heir of heaven, the merchant in his shop and the peasant in his field suddenly become the equal of noble and king.

—JOHN RICHARD GREEN

He that will not honor the memory and respect the influence of Calvin knows but little of the origin of American liberty. The fanatic for Calvinism was a fanatic for liberty; and, in the moral warfare for freedom, his creed was his most faithful counselor and his never-failing support. The Puritans . . . planted . . . the undying principles of democratic liberty.

—GEORGE BANCROFT

CALVIN'S CULTURAL CONTEXT

A LEADER IN ACTION is rarely esteemed and seldom celebrated if his accomplishments are minuscule. If John Calvin's accomplishments had been diminutive, provincial, or short-lived, a volume on imitating the lessons that we can learn from him would be of little value at best. But with this short work I am pleased to join the chorus of many who have observed the incredible influence of Calvin on the modern world. This volume seeks to highlight his leadership, which tackled some of the most entrenched traditions and challenging institutions of his or anyone's day. Calvin was indeed a theologian of action.

It is admittedly difficult for most contemporaries to relate to John Calvin or to his times. He lived a half millennium ago chronologically (b. 1509), but in terms of experience and culture, he may seem closer to the Paleolithic period than to a coming decade. Thus, it is understandable that for folks to relate to him, he must be personalized and contextualized. That is a fair challenge for an author, and this small work seeks to ease that burden and close that gap. We obviously believe that if we can build such bridges to the past, then this Genevan theologian can serve as a helpful exemplar for leaders in many different fields.

One of the first books on leadership that I read as an adult was the whimsically titled *The Leadership Lessons from Attila the Hun.* While that book was part fiction, it also contained some very fine snippets, such as, "Be careful of the enemies you make; and make sure that you select them well." Whether Attila actually uttered that aphorism or not, it does have its value in certain contexts. So, while modern leaders might benefit from the leadership secrets of a notorious fifth-century Hun, and while others learn from historical figures ranging from Mao or Confucius (and the recent *The Wisdom of Alexander the Great* by Lance B. Kurke) to recent best sellers like *Good to Great* by Jim Collins or *Seven Habits of Highly Effective People* by Stephen Covey or Rudolph Giuliani's insightful *Leadership,* certainly the gap of a few centuries should not preclude learning from one who I have suggested elsewhere is to be considered as "the man of the millennium."[1]

An obvious question, though, is, Should Calvin be logically disqualified as a mentor for leaders, since he lived in such a radically different cultural context? Here, we answer in the negative for this reason: change all the tools and culture you wish, but human beings remain little changed over long periods of history. The supposed evolutionary spiral is not nearly so steep as to require that we forfeit learning from our grandparents. Hence, this study assumes that we can learn from history, and we do have much in common with previous leaders who are worthy of imitation.

I do not, however, want to minimize the differences between our time and Calvin's. There are many dissimilarities, but I wish to begin by noting three macro variations between his culture and ours. These merely serve to further magnify Calvin's accomplishments.

First, Calvin's period was principally antidemocratic. Prior to his day, the two major forms of government had been tribalism and monarchism. In the first form—customarily invoked only in small social groups and at early phases of their history—small groups, frequently patriarchal, ordered themselves without the help of any external government. Correspondingly, there were few benefits or aids from the government, and there was little individual say-so, except for elite leaders. When nations and cities began to grow and thrive, they turned to that second type of government: monarchy. All of the East was persistently monarchical prior to Calvin's time, there was no American experiment as of yet, and the only republics that offered any semblance of popular franchise were the city-states of Venice and Holland (even though we date the Dutch Declaration of Independence to 1581, which was seventeen years after Calvin's death and largely due to his Dutch Calvinist followers instigating a semirepublican form of government). To most modern leaders, in strong contrast, democracy in at least some elements is a corporate or social given; it is virtually unthinkable today not to presuppose some forms or customs of democracy. But to Calvin and his contemporaries not only was such level of participation not a given but it also was hardly imaginable. Calvin's leadership in this area and the subsequent triumph of democratic impulses over the past half millennium are a heroic change to be credited in no small part to Calvin and not minimized.

A second profound difference between Calvin's time and ours was religious. Prior to Calvin, most of the West was Roman Catholic. Despite a few radical groups a century before him, before the time of Luther and Calvin, there were virtually no Protestants. Church members relied on the clergy for information, and the church was not exactly an open society prior to the Reformation. It was hierarchical, paralleling the secular government as essentially monarchical, and in some places it ruled with an iron fist. This was hardly a pluralistic age. The church had also become corrupt, and its priesthood—as Luther exposed—at times cared more about money than about mortification of sin. The church prior to Calvin was also heavily centralized, education was restricted to the few, and free markets were seldom widespread. Calvin would effect change in all those areas.

Third, the spread of information was drastically different in Calvin's day. Only a few universities predate the Protestant Reformation (Cambridge, Edinburgh, Oxford, Paris, Rome, for example)—obviously none of the great American colleges. But at lower levels, the situation was even more impoverished. Most people lacked any formal education—Calvin would change that in Geneva, providing for a robust and free public education. Moreover, information itself was often the property of the few. Things that we assume—like television news, newspapers, the

Internet, and radio—did not exist. Reliable information was not always available for leaders. Calvin and Calvinists would help change that forever.

Many of the things we take for granted were not present five hundred years ago. Calvin did not inherit the benefits of a free society, an unfettered church, freedom of the press, or the wide dissemination and availability of education, artistic expression, or information. He had to lend a hand to create a climate in which these and many other things would later flourish. A leader who could deliver such lasting societal change is certainly worthy of study.

As we study the life, leadership, and legacy of John Calvin, his accomplishments will be more impressive when seen as pioneering concepts instead of as imitations of preexisting models. He tackled some truly monumental issues and forces.

Europe was a quilt of various tribes, family alliances, and fiefdoms in Calvin's day. The most centralized power was the Roman Catholic Church that sought to hold Christendom together. The city of Geneva, which became important as the primary staging area of Calvin's action, was not removed from these greater trends. Whether priests or governors realized it, a Reformation was about to commence in the early decades of the sixteenth century, and human society would irrevocably change through the decisive leadership of men like a once-quaint academic.

Calvin stood at the beginning of modernity, and his ideas and actions would change history forever. As with most good leaders, Calvin would not permit the magnitude of the task to discourage him. In fact, he is an epitome of courage, which many leadership mentors think of as the prime leadership virtue from which all others follow. His courage was rooted in this: regardless of what reformation was needed, Calvin would turn to the inspired Scriptures for solutions, and his work succeeded in ways that are almost unrivaled.

Others—today, though, mainly forgotten voices—have previously recognized the influence of Calvin. The highly respected nineteenth-century Harvard historian George Bancroft was one of many who earlier asserted that Calvin's ideas buttressed liberty's cause. He and others noted the influence of this thought on the development of various freedoms in Western Europe and America.[2] Writing in the middle of the nineteenth century, Bancroft extolled Calvin as "the foremost of modern republican legislators," who was responsible for elevating the culture of Geneva into "the impregnable fortress of popular liberty, the fertile seed-plot of democracy."[3] Bancroft even credited the "free institutions of America" as derived "chiefly from Calvinism through the medium of Puritanism." Moreover, he traced the living legacy of Calvin among the Plymouth Pilgrims, the Huguenot settlers of South Carolina, and the Dutch colonists in Manhattan, concluding: "He that will not honor the memory and respect the influence of Calvin knows but little of the origin of American liberty."

Bancroft esteemed Calvin as one of the premier republican pioneers, at one point writing, "The fanatic for Calvinism was a fanatic for liberty; and, in the moral warfare for freedom, his creed was his most faithful counselor and his never-failing support. The Puritans . . . planted . . . the undying principles of democratic liberty."[4] During the nineteenth century, fairly widespread appreciation of the societal impact of Calvin was not limited solely to American scholars. The renowned German historian Leopold von Ranke, for example, reached a similar conclusion that "John Calvin was virtually the founder of America."[5]

Calvin, of course, had defects, and my goal is not to present unremitting praise of Calvin—nor to point only to his political contributions, although I confess I see those as some of his most congealed delicacies. His faults, as a man, were obvious and many. Nineteenth-century Swiss historian J. H. Merle d'Aubigne succinctly summarized a healthy way to view the limitations of those who lived in an earlier era: "We entertain no blind admiration [for Calvin]. We know that he sometimes used bitter language. We acknowledge that, sharing in the faults of his century or rather of ten centuries, he believed that whatever infringed on the respect due to God ought to be punished by the civil power, quite as much as anything that might be injurious to the honor or life of man. We deplore this error." But d'Aubigne added: "How can anyone study with discernment the reformer's letters and other writings, and not recognize in him one of the noblest intelligences, one of the most elevated minds, one of the most affectionate hearts, and in short, one of those true Christian souls who unreservedly devote themselves to duty?"[6]

Calvin and his disciples—the truly spiritual thinkers of their time—will be recognized as having made a more lasting and positive contribution to thought and culture than the likes of Karl Marx, Jean-Jacques Rousseau, or Niccolò Machiavelli. Time will tell if others join in appreciating them, but we would do well to consider him and his legacy before disregarding his insights. Accordingly, some background briefing is essential, for one cannot fully comprehend Calvin's contributions and leadership in a vacuum.

It is, notwithstanding, impossible to identify another uninspired theologian who had a wider influence on the arts, business, education, philosophy, and politics—in short, human culture—prior to John Calvin. If a leader in action is measured by effect, Calvin was the second (only to the apostle Paul) most influential theologian in history; since the conclusion of the New Testament canon, he was the most influential in terms of public effect and change.[7]

In view of the tremendous and sustained societal and political sea change that occurred during and after Calvin's time, careful students will want to evaluate if one of C. S. Lewis's challenging comments is correct, namely that modern observers need to comprehend "the freshness, the audacity, and [soon] the fashionableness of Calvinism."[8] That is a well-placed challenge. Moreover, that fashionableness may explain how and why even some of the most stridently anti-Calvinist thinkers of a later day—venomous enemies of Calvinism, actually—would employ mottoes from the Calvinistic Huguenots of old to justify resistance to tyrants on American shores. Even if contemporary researchers remain largely blind to Calvin's immense legacy, there may have been a day when his legacy was far more apparent. We can be forgiven if our sincere aim is to uncover it, dust it off, and polish it a little.

To test Lewis's observations and to further our own assertions, we must turn now to review the life and precursors of Calvin. Before we conclude the short tour of this volume, we will see that Calvin helped transform the world into one that was open, democratic, information-based, industrial, and communal. This theologian of action would not shy away from tasks that daunting.

There are two kinds of leaders: (1) those who predict future changes and (2) those who change future predictions. The first sees trends and claims a place on the leading edge, thereby fitting in with those trends. The second—Calvin was certainly one of these—observes the trajectory but determines that it needs correction.

In advance of President George W. Bush's 2005 State of the Union address, journalist Fred Barnes suggested that leaders could be classified as either "eventful" or "event-making."[9] The merely eventful leader, wrote Barnes (while admittedly borrowing from Sidney Hook), is comparable to the little Dutch boy who put his finger in the dike to stanch the dam burst. Virtually anyone could have plugged that hole; such leadership is largely a matter of being in the right place at the right time and acting dutifully. In contrast, the event-making leader, noted Barnes, "does what others couldn't or wouldn't do. . . . [He] leaves the positive imprint of his personality upon history—an imprint that is observable after he has disappeared from the scene."

By that standard, Calvin was an event-maker far more than a caretaker. He tackled the bold needs and projects of the day.

CALVIN'S THEOLOGICAL FATHERS AND PEERS

*C*ALVIN HAD TO REALIZE that massive change could occur only on strong foundations. He was also modest enough to avoid boasting that all good ideas percolated from his own mind. His admiration for those excellent theologians who had gone before him reflected his willingness to value the contributions of others. He frequently referred to classic writings, and he drew upon wisdom from the past. He did not believe that all new insights were necessarily correct or that he or his generation would be superior in wisdom to others. The thinker he relied on the most was, in fact, the dominant voice in the West for a millennium: St. Augustine. What Calvin seemed to admire so keenly about Augustine, particularly his culture-shaping views, was that he was eminently biblical in many areas. Calvin the leader was not hesitant to stand on the shoulders of the giants who had preceded him. The considerable agreement between Calvin and Augustine is apparent in many formulations—including the political, which is one of Calvin's understated contributions to the modern world, which I hope to document.

Augustine of Hippo (354–430) was *the* dominant Christian theologian for centuries. For more than a millennium after his death, his shadow still loomed large over discussions about culture, ethics, and politics. His classic work addressing these matters, *The City of God,* sought to illustrate the antithetical and competing strains that characterize belief or unbelief throughout the history of mankind. Early in his life, Calvin read Augustine's work as part of his educational curriculum. For Augustine, the City of Man was infatuated with the prowess and pride of humanity, complete with its materialism, violence, unbelief, lust for domination . . . and oppression. In contrast, the *civitatis dei* (City of God) was characterized by a profound love for God, the valuation of the eternal over the temporal, high ethical standards, and the equitable treatment of neighbors. Calvin would certainly explore these themes further in his own work.

Calvin also agreed with Augustine on the subjects of human depravity and the inherent limitations of the goodness of man. Augustine viewed a tight civic order as a needed restraining apparatus for the good society. He did not expect unbelief to spawn virtuous culture or liberty on its own, noting: "Sinful man [actually] hates the equality of all men under God and, as though he were God, loves to impose his sovereignty on his fellow men. He hates the peace of God which is just and prefers his own peace which is unjust. However, he is powerless not to love peace of some sort. For, no man's sin is so unnatural as to wipe out all traces whatsoever of human nature."[10] One can see from these early aphorisms why Calvin thought of himself as Augustinian.

One scholar found that, of the sources Calvin quoted in the *Institutes,* Augustine is in a class of his own, being cited 228 times. The next most frequently cited authorities were Gregory I (39 times), John Chrysostom (27 times), Bernard of Clairveaux (23 times), Ambrose (18 times), and Cyprian (14 times). The number of citations from Augustine (228) compares to 9 from Cicero, 7 from Plato, 5 from Aristotle, and 3 from Seneca.[11] The Reformation itself was, in the main, a return to Augustinianism, and Calvin's thought can hardly be seen as an imitation of previous, secular models.[12]

Augustine was a pioneer in arguing that the divine will was more foundational in human affairs than even the greatest of human governments. According to him, "Divine Providence alone explains the establishment of kingdoms among men."[13] Calvin would certainly echo him at this point. Even the Roman Empire, as a concrete example of inhumane regimes in Augustine's own time, did not rise and fall apart from the sovereignty of God. Accordingly, those attempting to account for the rise and fall of governments should factor in the active outworking of God's providence in nations: "God allows nothing to remain unordered and he knows all things before they come to pass. He is the Cause of causes, although not of all choices."[14] Calvin would sound similar notes a millennium later. Contrary to the notion of human government as unaffected by the spiritual, Augustine contended that the sovereign God toppled and raised rulers at his own pleasure. Nothing escapes God's purview, as the Calvinist Reformers would later reiterate.

Augustine also provided an early form of resistance theory, which was later associated with Calvin's disciples, if a civil ruler lapsed into tyranny: "But if the prince is unjust or a tyrant, or if the aristocrats are unjust (in which case their group is merely a faction), or if the people themselves are unjust (and must be called, for lack of a better word, a tyrant also), then the commonwealth is not merely bad . . . but is no commonwealth at all. The reason for that is that there is no longer the welfare [the weal] of the people, once a tyrant or a faction seizes it."[15] Augustine, like Calvin later, was ahead of his time in these notions, and Calvin would avail himself to the best of the past before moving toward the future.

As a leader, Calvin knew better than to seek to re-create all parts of the wheel. He happily drew upon Augustine and built on him. A host of other intellectual mentors to Calvin also laid the foundation for his work. For example, the Magna Carta (1215),[16] the formation of the Helvetic Confederation (1291), and the Scottish independence movement offered further instances of premodern republicanism. With an Augustinian plow, these events tilled the soil for Calvin's work.[17]

Notwithstanding, such theology did not gain general approval—and representative governments were not begun on a widespread basis—until the advances during the age of the Reformation. Calvin's circle would take these small points of light and focus them into a floodlight of reform that would leave human culture radically altered. He stood on the shoulders of his ancient fathers, but he also stepped ahead courageously. He was not too proud to learn from the past, nor too timid to advance it.

If Calvin built on the foundations of Augustine and other medieval thinkers, his training and education were also steeped in the intellectual grounds of his day. Moreover, he stood on the shoulders of all who embraced biblical teachings. Some of the most helpful in his own day would form a chorus, a fellowship of Reformers. Another lesson to learn from Calvin's leadership is this: leaders of movements seldom lead alone—they customarily work in concert with and inspire other leaders to forge a lasting movement.

The Protestant Reformation began in the early sixteenth century, when a number of well-known leaders united to change the West. Men like the compelling German pastor Martin Luther, the brilliant Italian scholar-refugee Peter Martyr Vermigli, and Swiss patriots Huldrych Zwingli and William Farel would serve as chain links between Calvin and Augustine, but it was all one chain.[18] Calvin saw himself as returning the church and the faith to earlier norms, not so much as creating new theology or ethics. That conservative revolutionary posture is important in understanding Calvin, for he did not suddenly pop into existence in Geneva in 1536 devoid of context. In fact, his own life, education, and conversion intersected with key junctures of the blooming Protestant Reformation. Some acquaintance with the fellow Reformers of his day—William Farel, Martin Luther, and Huldrych Zwingli—illumines Calvin's life.

For example, even though differing with the later Calvinistic developments, Luther (1483–1546) believed that God had ordained both church and state as separate but legitimate spheres. Luther believed that both of these basic institutions properly wielded its own God-given power (or sword): the church wielded the sword of church discipline; the state wielded the sword of civil force. As long as each tended to its assigned sphere, all would work well. While acknowledging Luther's seminal role in the progress of freedom of conscience, Karl Holl nevertheless noted that it was Calvin's "Reformation that first set a rigid limit to the absolute power of the state."

Like Calvin, Luther's first aim was to demonstrate that the state had its origin in the will of God and was not founded upon a purely secular basis. Centuries before America's James Madison would echo similar sentiments, Luther proceeded to explain that if the world were a perfect place, secular government would be unnecessary ("And if all the world were true Christians, that is, if everyone truly believed, there would be neither need nor use for princes, kings, lords, the Sword or law, what would there be for them to do?"). The necessity for civil order, therefore, rested in the corruption of human nature. "Where all wrongs are endured willingly and what is right is done freely," wrote Luther, "there is no place for quarreling, disputes, courts, punishments, laws or the Sword."

One nineteenth-century historian, however, noted certain crucial differences between Luther and Calvin. Luther labored for the right relationship of the soul and did not seek to reform the sacraments or the liturgy of Catholicism; Calvin attacked the practices he thought were unsupported by Scripture. Luther "acknowledged princes as his protectors . . . Calvin was the guide of the

Swiss republics. . . . Luther resisted the Roman church for its immorality; Calvin for its idolatry."[19] American Pilgrims and many of their children were Calvinists; yet we should not underestimate the following claim from another nineteenth-century historian: "But for the Reformation led by Luther, there had been no Revolution led by Washington."[20]

Another historian asserted: "If the Swiss Reformation had been only a feeble copy of the German, there would have been uniformity, but no duration. . . . The regeneration of Christianity in these mountains proceeded from forces peculiar to the Helvetic Church, and received an organization in conformity with the ecclesiastical and political condition of that country."[21] Two other leaders, in addition to Calvin, would pioneer those paths.

Huldrych Zwingli (1484–1531), a Swiss Reformer immediately prior to Calvin, also recognized that resistance was legitimate if a secular leader sought to suppress true religion. But Zwingli also believed such resistance should occur only with the support of a large majority and without bloodshed.[22]

Just prior to the emergence of Calvin, Zwingli began his ministry at Zurich's *Grossmunster* church in 1519, making him one of the earliest declared Protestants in the world. Throughout his tenure, Zwingli labored for political structures that conformed both religion and politics to the precepts of the Bible.[23] Historian Robert Walton summarizes Zwingli's argument in his 1522 *Godly Admonition* as follows: "The cantons of the Confederacy stand in a covenant relationship with God; they are the Israel of the present. Political stability and national freedom depend upon the proper obedience to the Lord."[24] Leaders like this were not afraid to tether the fates of nations to the rule of God.

It would remain, however, for the mercurial Frenchman William Farel to establish another major beachhead in southern Switzerland and eventually lure Calvin there. Farel (1489–1565), originally from the south of France, arrived in Paris in 1509 and studied (as did Calvin) under Jacques Le Fevre at the University of Paris, then known as the "mother of all learning, the true lamp of the church."

Having been reared in a Catholic home, his conversion to Protestantism was gradual ("fallen little by little from my head; for it did not tumble down at first shock") and well tested, making him all the more zealous to the end. He once wrote, "I had my Pantheon in my heart, and such a troop of mediators, saviors, and gods that I might well have passed for a papal register."[25] Farel began to read the Bible for himself as Luther would later, and with similar results. Farel became one of the first Protestants (his conversion in 1512 predates Luther's, a fact often overlooked), and as the pioneer of reform in southern Europe, he was somewhat like Luther in temperament—quick to lay the ax to the root[26] while Calvin was normally more deliberative.

Farel fled Parisian persecution and eventually came into contact with the Reformers in Basel in 1523. During this time, Erasmus of Rotterdam, the leading humanist of the day, was in Basel and once described Farel as the "Elijah of the French Reformation."[27] Though less revered at the time and less recognized today, Farel was a near-match to Erasmus in debating Scripture. At a dispute at the University of Basel, with Erasmus present, Farel impressed scholars and citizens alike. One onlooker said of Farel's performance: "He is strong enough to destroy the whole Sorbonne single-handed." Theodore Beza later assessed his gifts: "Farel excelled in a certain sublimity of mind, so that nobody could either hear his thunders without trembling, or listen to his most fervent prayers without feeling almost as it were carried up into heaven."[28]

Farel came to Geneva in 1532 as a missionary, protected by the Bern government. He gained some success initially but was later exiled and returned for safety to Bern. He returned to Geneva in 1535 and was instrumental in convincing many citizens to embrace Reformed Christianity.

Shortly thereafter, Calvin arrived on a midsummer's night in 1536 and was strong-armed by Farel to join the reformation of religion and politics in Switzerland. Farel already knew of Calvin's recently published book, the *Institutes of the Christian Religion*. When he learned that Calvin was in the area, this warrior-poet of the Swiss Reformation could not resist urging young Calvin to enlist in the work of Reformation. The theater was then prepared for the entrance of John Calvin onto the world's stage.

Prior to 1536, Farel had been the premier spokesman for the Reformation in French Switzerland; during Calvin's first residence in Geneva, the council honored Farel as a first among equals.[29] Yet, just as leaders don't stand alone, Farel joyfully embraced that it was necessary for Calvin to assume a more prominent role. Working diligently for Protestant unity, it was Farel who "pushed Calvin to write . . . it is he who made the negotiations succeed; and if the Swiss churches adopted this profession of faith, it is in large part to him the honor is due."[30]

Farel would prepare the way for a younger Reformer, a powerful scholar-theologian, whose skills and knowledge were particularly needed in Geneva. Although these two Reformers were exiled two years later—when the city council viewed them as insurgents because they would not offer the Eucharist to the numerous bickering factions—they eventually returned to Geneva and were provided with a forum to train scholars from England, Germany, Holland, and Scotland.[31] The companionship of these leaders in action is not only a principle for leaders today but also a partial explanation for why their movement would prove so irresistible.

Farel's and Calvin's ideas, particularly that citizens should freely deliberate and that governors were servants of the people—first kindled in Geneva but later burgeoning into an international forest fire—ignited a veritable tradition.[32] The disciples of these two giants would further clarify and extend the principles of limited government, suspicion of authoritarian power, the need for checks and balances, and the necessity of separation of powers while at the same time permitting faith and federalism to grow symbiotically.

Education

*T*O MANY, JOHN CALVIN may be thought of as an emotionless technician in a sterile theological laboratory, removed from normalcy, oblivious to his own and others' humanity, impervious to feeling, and intent only on perfecting a rigorous Puritanism. But he was far more interested in integrity in action than in pursuing an idealistic agenda. The real Calvin was a rather different figure from the joyless caricature often stenciled in popular thought. Whether he is blamed or credited as a patron of advancements in science, education, and the revolutionary politics of democracy, it is remarkable that one of the greatest figures of modern history is "virtually unknown, except perhaps as a reminder of the crimes and follies of the past."[33]

A sound understanding of Calvin must take into account the comprehensive whole of his thought, contained in his sermons, commentaries, and his magnum opus, the *Institutes of the Christian Religion* (1559).[34] The *Institutes of the Christian Religion,* which is the most systematic of Calvin's works, is often considered by a skeptical public to be the least compassionate and humane of his works. Yet a careful examination of his writings actually disproves many of the myths, allegations, and stereotypes. Of course, a proper understanding of Calvin will also take into account the man, not just the thinker. An acquaintance with Calvin's life and his role in enhancing political freedom will help us assess his contributions to the structures of the free societies we know today.

Calvin serves as an encouragement to many who may not have been nurtured in a traditional family. Little is known about his mother, Jeanne la France of Cambrai (due to her early death), and his father was quite a dominant presence in Calvin's early life and education.

John Calvin was born on July 10, 1509,[35] in Noyon, a small town in Picardy, France. He was the middle son in a family with five children—three sons and two daughters. His father, Gerard, was an administrative assistant in the nearby cathedral complex, and his mother died when Calvin was only five.[36] His first biographer, his friend and colleague Professor Theodore Beza, later described him as "of middle stature, sallow features, and whose piercing eye and animated looks announced a mind of no common sagacity."[37]

Calvin's father enrolled him in one of the colleges of the University of Paris in 1521, intending for him to enter the priesthood. While at that university, Calvin studied rhetoric, logic, and the arts—common topics for the day—and received a classical education. He was also influenced by the work of the leading Roman Catholic progressive, John Major[38]—a towering intellect—and Peter of Spain.[39] The major theological assumptions during his education at the University of Paris included a hearty concurrence with Augustine on human nature, a pessimistic view of humanity flowing from the Fall and original sin, and rejection of salvation by human merit.[40] According to one historian, "Calvin's powers of reasoning and analysis may be traced to his rigorous training" under such Parisian masters. He also could not avoid the deluge of intellectual currents swirling through Paris at the time.

His instruction included training in three classic languages: Latin, Greek (learned from Melchior Wolmar at Orleans, to whom Calvin dedicated his commentary on 2 Corinthians), and Hebrew. Calvin's "humanist" education[41] included enrollments at key educational institutions at Paris,[42] Orleans, Bourges, Basel, and familiarization with other learning centers of the day. He was exposed to the thought of Erasmus, Jacques Le Fevre, Melchior Wolmar, and Francois Rabelais: a veritable *Who's Who* of Western European education for his day. Calvin would later complete the equivalent of a master's degree at the University of Paris, which ranked with or surpassed Cambridge and Oxford at the time. A free market of new ideas and Protestantism (originally thought of as "Lutheranism") surged in Paris while Calvin was a student.

His education was a bold one that sought to appreciate the classics of the past and also accorded less reverence to the traditions of Roman Catholicism. Calvin was a modern scholar who understood the role of criticism in arriving at truth. His first published work, a commentary on Seneca's *De Clementia* (1532), affirmed the radical notion that "the prince is not above the laws, but the laws above the prince."[43] Later, his published works would concentrate on a wide array of theological subjects.

Calvin's father played a dominant role in his early education at Paris, and Gerard eventually persuaded his son to train for the legal profession, which he considered a surer path to wealth than the priesthood. Since France was a monarchy, and the king was above the law, it was too much cognitive dissonance to house a law school in Paris—as if the king might ever be subject to a constitution; thus France's leading law school was in Orleans. From 1528 to 1533, Calvin studied law in Bourges and Orleans,[44] a preparation that would assist him in later endeavors, including laying the foundation for subsequent political ideas. He was later licensed to practice law, and his legal training ultimately aided him as he mentored Geneva's developing republic.

From this short listing, one can sense about young Calvin, whether the guiding hand was his father's or that of providence, that he was exposed to the best teachers of the day. He learned to absorb the good, as excellent leaders know. His education would serve him well all his life, and his exposure to master teachers was of great value.

CONVERSION

*I*F IT HAD BEEN left up to his wishes, John Calvin would have continued to pursue a comfortable academic career. He did not intend either to serve as a pastor or to work in Geneva, but God had other plans for him.

Calvin's only autobiographical account of his spiritual conversion appears in the 1557 preface to his *Commentary on Psalms*.[45] He did not wear his conversion on his sleeve but took many opportunities to practice what he preached. From Calvin's own testimony, he rarely saw himself as breaking new ground, and he described the book of Psalms as "an Anatomy of all the parts of the Soul." No sterile scholastic, as often maligned, he claimed that "there is not an emotion of which any one can be conscious that is not here [in the Psalms] represented as in a mirror." All the "lurking places" of the heart were illumined in these devotional poems.

He prefaces his spiritual testimony by stating his appreciation for other Reformed teachers of the time, particularly praising Martin Bucer and Wolfgang Musculus. He was happy to acknowledge his indebtedness to others, once praising Luther in this fashion: "It was a great miracle of God that Luther and those who worked with him at the beginning in restoring the pure truth were able to emerge from it little by little."[46] Although Calvin would differ significantly with Luther on several issues, he retained a lifelong admiration for his work and saw himself as building on a shared foundation. Calvin stated that, should Doctor Martin call him a devil, he would "nevertheless hold him in such honor [and] acknowledge him to be a distinguished servant of God."[47] While exiled in Strasbourg (1538–41), Calvin also forged a strong relationship with Luther's understudy, Philipp Melanchthon.

In his clearest spiritual autobiography, Calvin likened himself to David, as one who had been taken from a pastoral venue and thrust into a position of public responsibility. He reviewed for his readers how his father had destined him for the priesthood, but when Gerard considered the legal profession more lucrative, he enrolled young Calvin in legal studies. Calvin reflected on his early education, noting even there that providence was guiding him despite his father's urgings toward law for ignoble reasons.

Calvin's religious upbringing (he later called it "superstitious") was not abandoned easily. Even though he was plunged into a profound spiritual abyss, according to his own account, Calvin was found by God, who used a sudden conversion to "subdue and bring my mind to a teachable frame, which was more hardened in such matters than might have been expected from one at my early period in life." Apparently Calvin continued traditional Roman Catholic practices until his conversion in 1533–34.

After this "sudden conversion," the Parisian student found himself "inflamed with an intense desire," and he fervently pursued Protestant teachings. After a year of diligent study (so intense perhaps because Protestantism was new and also because Calvin studied under some of the finest teachers in the pristine movement), he was surprised that numerous people began to treat him like an expert on these matters. He humbly viewed himself as unpolished, bashful, retiring, and preferring seclusion. Yet, like the author of the Psalms, he sensed that he was inevitably being thrust into the role of a public leader. Instead of successfully living in scholarly quiescence, all his retreats became public debating forums. He wrote, "In short, while my one great object was to live in seclusion without being known, God so led me about through different turnings and changes that he never permitted me to rest in any place, until in spite of my natural disposition, he brought me forth to public notice."

In the early sixteenth century, Paris had become a hotbed of reform movements that had been particularly influenced by the Italian reformers Savonarola and Peter Martyr Vermigli. But in the fall of 1533, French monarch Francis I cracked down on the burgeoning Protestantism, which was causing considerable commotion in Paris.

The immediate cause of this crackdown was the installation of Nicholas Cop, a Protestant sympathizer, to lead the university. Some theorize that Calvin perhaps lent his literary expertise to help draft Cop's inaugural address.

True or not, Calvin himself believed it necessary to leave Paris immediately after its delivery. His escape from Paris was none too soon, as police seized his personal papers within hours of his departure.[48]

Although not as dramatic as Luther's,[49] Calvin's conversion was nonetheless absolute: he left Paris a committed Protestant in 1533. One recent scholar (Alister McGrath) emphasizes its suddenness, the term Calvin himself preferred. Calvin had severed his relationship entirely with the Roman Catholic Church by spring 1534.[50] Later he would rendezvous with his mentor, Nicholas Cop, the ousted rector of the University of Paris, in Basel, where both made their Protestant sympathies public. Much of the 1534–35 period was devoted to searching for an environment where the Reformation would be welcomed. Calvin had contacts with Geneva as early as 1535. While in Basel, he observed the development of the Reformation, monitoring both the ongoing debates and the resulting attacks on Protestants.[51] After 1536, Calvin no longer considered himself a Parisian.

Calvin recounts how he left his native France and wandered in Germany in search of obscurity (at various times, Calvin had to resort to using aliases, including Charles d'Esperville, Martianus Lucanius, Carolus Passelius, Alcuin, Depercan, and Calpurnius),[52] only to settle temporarily in Basel. It was at Basel that he learned of numerous French Protestants being burned alive, which provoked passionate disapproval from Calvin and the other German-speaking Protestants, "whose indignation was kindled against such tyranny." Thus Calvin developed an antipathy to state tyranny from an early age.

Calvin wanted to avoid the fray. His own spiritual pilgrimage indicates that he resolved to devote himself to quiet scholarly obscurity until William Farel detained him in Geneva, "not so much by counsel and exhortation as by a dreadful imprecation, which I felt to be as if God had from heaven laid his mighty hand upon me to arrest me." The myths about Farel's imprecation are numerous. Even though the exact words are lost, it is clear that Farel applied some fiery threats to Calvin's conscience.

Since the direct highway to Strasbourg was dangerous, Calvin sought another path, intending to spend no more than a single night in Geneva. He expected Geneva to be relatively safe in 1536, crediting the partial triumph of Protestantism there largely to Peter Viret—a fellow Reformer who would remain a close friend for years. Although the conflicts in Geneva were by no means over—"the city was divided into unholy and dangerous factions"—Calvin nevertheless thought it safer than the Strasbourg route. While he expected only a short stay in Geneva, someone conveyed his itinerary to Farel, whom Calvin described as burning "with an extraordinary zeal to advance the gospel." Farel then "strained every nerve to detain" Calvin. After Calvin initially rejected Farel's summons, Farel resorted to calling down curses on Calvin's plans for a life of tranquil academic pursuits. These curses terrorized Calvin to the point that he acceded to Farel's demand, despite his natural timidity and reticence.

Thus Calvin the reluctant and shy Reformer began his work in Geneva with the unostentatious title of lecturer on the Holy Scriptures in the church of Geneva. That city and the world would not be the same thereafter.

The psychological self-portrait seen in his commentary on the Psalms is contrary to the malicious profiles compiled later by biased or hostile critics. Calvin's disciple and eventual biographer, Theodore Beza, noted the following traits of Calvin: he was modest, temperate, thin (he normally ate only one daily meal because of an intestinal ailment), possessed an astonishing memory, was unusually attentive, and of clear judgment and counsel. Beza recorded how he "despised mere eloquence, and was sparing in the use of words. No theologian of this period wrote more purely. . . . With regard to his manners, although nature had formed him for gravity, yet . . . there was no man who was more pleasant."[53] Moreover, Beza was not surprised that "one endowed with so great and so many virtues should have had numerous enemies." His disciple even had the foresight to deny that Calvin "reigned at Geneva, both in church and state, so as to supplant the ordinary tribunals"[54]—an early hint about Calvin's belief in the separation of jurisdictions.

But even with such a promising beginning, Calvin would learn—as many other leaders have—that success is seldom easy or rapid. He would soon suffer a setback that would have terminated lesser leaders, but his consuming passion for eternal truths kept him persevering. As a leader, Calvin would neither shy away from the spiritual nor deny the reality of his own conversion. His spiritual rebirth was, in fact, the key to his theology and his activity. His genuine spirituality would be needed to sustain him through difficulties as soon as his short-lived honeymoon in Geneva was over.

First Geneva Residence

*W*ILLIAM FAREL HAD BEEN the leader of Genevan independence from 1535 until the time the Genevans officially accepted the Protestant Reformation on May 21, 1536.[55] Calvin settled in Geneva in July 1536. By the fall of 1536, Genevans initiated their new political culture with a large public debate and the presentation of a Confession of Faith by Calvin.[56] The four syndics (chief assemblymen) elected in February 1537 were all Farel sympathizers, and reorganization progressed steadily until a 1538 electoral backlash.

By this time, the combined powers of certain patrician families, residual Catholic sympathies, and internal political pressure within Geneva led to Calvin's and Farel's exile to Strasbourg.[57] New elections took effect in early 1538 in Geneva, and the new officials were less zealous for the Reformation; indeed, some openly opposed the combined efforts of Calvin and Farel.[58] After the change of administrations, Calvin and many Genevans found themselves at odds with certain factions and leaders within the city. Due to the extraordinary infighting among the citizens at the time, Calvin and Farel (pastoring the churches of St. Pierre and St. Gervais respectively) declined to offer Communion to the feuding citizenry, lest they heap judgment on themselves.[59] In return, the city council exiled them for insubordination two days later, on April 18, 1538—less than two years after Calvin's arrival.[60] Some leaders would have considered this a crushing blow.

Beza's biography, however, viewed this exile to Strasbourg as part of "Divine providence," enabling Calvin to train for greater effectiveness while employing his gifts to strengthen another city. It also allowed for the "over-throwing [of] those seditious persons . . . to purge the city of Geneva of much pollution." Accordingly, "Satan was disappointed" and "saw Calvin received elsewhere, and, as a substitute for the Genevan Church, another Church forthwith erected."[61]

After this initial brush with defeat, Calvin once again resolved to retreat from the public eye only later to be urged to return to Geneva by the esteemed Martin Bucer in tones similar to Farel's earlier summons. Calvin's humility, which is often underappreciated, is evident from many parts of the written record. He refers in the conclusion of his only autobiographical explanation of his conversion to his wishing to "avoid celebrity" while inexorably being pushed to the fore of "imperial assemblies, where, willing or unwilling, I was under the necessity of appearing before the eyes of many."

His three years in Strasbourg, however, would be essential for his future. Calvin's exile ended in 1541 when he returned to Geneva "contrary to [his] desire and inclination." What motivated him to return to the place where he had been so rudely treated only a few years earlier? "The welfare of this church . . . lay so near my heart," he stated, "that for its sake I would not have hesitated to lay down my life." Competing with his natural diffidence, the weight of "solemn and conscientious duty" was greater than his personal comfort. Still, it was with considerable grief, tears, anxiety, and distress (not to mention "a remarkable act of social pragmatism and religious realism"[62]) that he returned to Geneva.

Calvin's biographer sheds light on his trepidation about returning to Geneva in 1541. After "the Lord had determined to take pity on the Church of Geneva," all four of the anti-Calvin chief elected officials had either been removed, executed for civil crimes, or condemned. The city "being thus rid of its filth and froth," wrote Beza, "began to long for its Farel and its Calvin." Beza explained that, since neither Farel (now in Neuchatel) nor Calvin wanted to return, it took arm-twisting from Zurich to convince them to do so. Beza also noted Calvin's aversion to conflict and his sense that his ministry in the church of Strasbourg was going well as reasons not to return. Moreover, Bucer and others initially declared that they had great objections to losing his services in Strasbourg.[63]

One of Calvin's demands before returning to Geneva in September 1541 was that a collegial governing body of pastors and church elders from the area be established.[64] When it came time to replace ineffective centralized structures, rather than opting for an institution that strengthened his own hand, this visionary Reformer lobbied for decentralized authority lodged with many officers. He also insisted that the church be free from political interference—separation of jurisdictions helped to solidify the integrity of the church too—and his 1541 *Ecclesiastical Ordinances* specifically required such a separation.

These clues indicate that moving Geneva into the Protestant column did not come easily, quickly, or without repeated accusations against the Reformers.

Calvin's sojourn in Strasbourg from 1538 to 1541, however, proved providential, as he later claimed. It was in Strasbourg, a city that had already traveled farther down the path of Reformation than had Geneva, that Calvin saw the full potential of Reformed religion and politics. Under the powerful example of such leading educators of the Reformation as Johann Sturm (1507–89) and Martin Bucer, Calvin received sound mentoring there. He accompanied Bucer on diplomatic missions, taught in Sturm's freshly minted academy that became a model for Geneva's own, and observed a harmonious relationship between church and state.[65] Calvin also pastored four hundred to five hundred French Protestant refugees.[66] Just prior to returning to Geneva, he became a citizen of Strasbourg and met a widow, Idelette de Bure, who became his wife. Calvin's only son with Idelette (Jacques, born on July 28, 1542) died in infancy, and he inherited Idelette's two daughters by a previous marriage, becoming solely responsible to care for them after his wife's death in 1549.

When Idelette died, Calvin faced an unparalleled grief. His letters to Farel and Viret reveal both his faith in God and his love for her. This was a "grief observed," and those watching developed admiration. He paid high tribute to Idelette after her death, extolling her as one who was an excellent companion in either exile, sorrow, or death.

Leaders have to learn to be productive after setbacks. In Calvin's case, his abiding confidence in the providence of God fueled his passion during exile and defeat. By using his time well during his Strasbourg residency, he not only added to his portfolio of experience, but he was also used of the Lord in that period. When it came to an end, he was more prepared—precisely because of this providential detour—to lead the Reformation from Geneva. Calvin is a superb historical example of a leader who rose . . . then fell . . . but he also recovered from his defeats and learned to use the time as well as he could in the interim. Like Winston Churchill in the twentieth century, he would learn to make the most even of defeats. Leaders understand that success is not always without its setbacks or interruptions. And if they don't at first succeed, with God's blessing, they try, try again.

Return from Exile

*I*N 1541, AFTER A three-year absence from Geneva and following the demise of some of their political opponents, Calvin and Farel[67] returned triumphantly to Geneva in what one historian called a miracle "beyond human conception."[68] The chief official of Geneva, Louis Dufour, delivered an invitation cosigned by all three elected councils of Geneva imploring Calvin to return; Dufour even traveled to Strasbourg to woo the exiled Calvin (who, at that time, was participating in a colloquy at Worms).[69] The citizens of Lac Leman urged him to resume his unfinished work, and the council forwarded moving expenses and an honorarium. In addition, they promised to pay Calvin a salary higher than the syndics' own if he returned! Later, in 1543, they also provided him with a home near St. Peter's Church.

Calvin's and Farel's first priority upon their reengagement was the establishment of the protocols in Calvin's

Ecclesiastical Ordinances, a procedural manual that pre-scribed how the area churches would supervise the morals and teaching of its own pastors without hindrance from any other authorities. The priority that Calvin assigned to this work shows how important it was for him that the church be free to carry out its own affairs, unimpeded by the state. The sovereignty of the ministerial council (Consistory)[70] to monitor the faith and practice of the church was codified in these 1541 *Ordinances.* Obviously, this arrangement marked a departure from the traditional union of church and state under Roman Catholic auspices. The Genevan innovation also differed from practices in Bern and Lausanne, both of which were also Protestant. With the publication of the *Ordinances,* "Geneva created a unique Christian commonwealth whereby church and state cooperated in preserving religion as the key to their new identity. Geneva was not the first city to develop a radically Reformed theology and polity. Much of Calvin's theological thinking was indebted to his early contact with Martin Bucer and his residence in Strasbourg."[71] Strasbourg may have been "the New Jerusalem" and the cradle of the Reformation's new understanding on government, but Geneva, with its innovative reforms and political distillation of Protestant theology under Calvin's guidance, would eventually surpass Strasbourg and become known as the "Protestant Rome."

Of interest to historians, both sympathetic and unsympathetic to Calvin, whatever Calvin was doing during this time transformed Geneva into a visible and bustling forum for economic development. With a growing intellectual ferment, evidenced by the founding of Calvin's Academy and the presence of modern financial institutions (e.g., a Medici bank), Geneva became an ideal center for perfecting and exporting reform.[72]

Despite the rise of commerce, however, the story of Calvin's leadership and impact on the region was not primarily economic. "What is special about Geneva," notes John B. Roney, "is the assumption that both the church and the state conformed to the will of God, and each had its proper sphere in the Christian commonwealth."[73] The translation of her faith into practice is witnessed by the creation of telltale social structures that emerged from the leadership of Farel and Calvin. A hospital was launched in 1535, and a fund for French refugees (*Bourse Francaise*) was established by church deacons in 1541. Calvin's Academy was founded in 1558. Eventually, thousands of refugees (mainly English, French, and Italian) came to Geneva for shelter, and many later returned to their own lands with fresh ideas about the relationship of citizens to government.[74]

Historian William Naphy views the rise of a competent class of elders and senators as instrumental in establishing Calvinism as a lasting political force in Geneva and Europe. Leading their procession, he writes, "stood Calvin, a figure increasingly famous throughout Europe; as Calvin increased in importance, Geneva gained international prominence. This new-found fame may well have aided Geneva in fending off the intentions of neighboring states desirous of controlling the city."[75] Moreover, as the electoral base stabilized in Geneva after the 1540s, along with solidarity among its church leaders, Calvin was able to expand the role of the Genevan ministers both at home and abroad. He was also sufficiently popular and insulated enough from internal opposition to devote the final decade of his life to implementing his social and political views. The later success of Calvin in Geneva illustrates the value of tenacity for leaders. The longevity of Calvin's influence is decidedly different after the return from his exile. What made that influence enduring was, to the surprise of many planners, a private, charitable institution—the church.

While Calvin's work has lasting influence in many sectors, it is important to recognize an oft-ignored truism about his work: his reforms began in the church and only then radiated outward. As a leader, Calvin practiced what he preached. A consistency of ideals, both in church and state, permeated his thought and action. He was prudent enough to realize that the best way to reform the culture was an indirect one, that is, to first reform the church. If "judgement began with the house of the Lord," then such integrity and dynamism would radiate outward, Calvin thought, and his actions over a long period of years proved his theory correct. His leadership, then, in the church is crucial to understand.

Leaders today would do well to spend some of their best efforts in the charitable sector. Indeed, long before the time of governmental assumption of benevolent tasks, Calvin believed the church to be ideally constituted to provide for many areas in society. He also knew that reform required patience, extending even to a dramatic setback like a forced exile if need be, and that societal change was seldom permanent if imposed on an unwilling populace. Better, Calvin knew, to win and change the hearts of people before seeking to legislate in certain areas. The church was crucial toward this lasting end, and upon his return from exile, Calvin set his hand to reforming what would become the reforming agency.

CALVIN THE PASTOR

*W*HEN CALVIN RETURNED TO St. Peter's Cathedral in 1541, he unceremoniously but symbolically resumed his pulpit activity by expounding the Scriptures at the exact verse where he had left off prior to his exile. Several days earlier, he had consulted with the Small Council, the real political powerhouse of the day, and encouraged it to make important reforms. The members were so willing to help him in the Reformation of Geneva that they not only approved his proposals to revise the protocols for church order, but they also appointed him to a committee to design a constitution for the Republic of Geneva.[76] The drafts of the constitution indicate that Calvin paid close attention to the minute details of administrative matters and municipal functions, and he made some suggestions for judicial reform.[77] (See "Calvin as Legislator" for more on his role in revising the Genevan constitution.) Philip Schaff recorded that Calvin was awarded a cask of old wine as payment for his efforts in revising the city constitution, and that "many of his regulations continued in legal force down to the eighteenth century." His legal training at Orleans would prove valuable over the course of his life. Occasionally, he was thus called on to divert attention away from church matters to assist in this constitutional role or other civic matters.

One of the procedural safeguards of the 1543 civic reform—a hallmark of Calvinistic ethos—was that the various branches of local government (councils) could no longer act unilaterally; henceforth, at least two councils were required to approve measures before ratification.[78] This early mechanism, which prevented consolidation of all governmental power into a single body of leaders, predated Montesquieu's separation-of-powers doctrine by two centuries, a Calvinistic contribution that is not always recognized. The driving rationale for this was a simple scriptural idea: even the best of leaders could think blindly and selfishly, so they needed a format for mutual correction and accountability. This kind of thinking, already incorporated into Geneva's ecclesiastical sphere (embedded in the 1541 *Ecclesiastical Ordinances*) and essentially derived from biblical sources, anticipated many later instances of political federalism. The structure of Genevan Presbyterianism began to influence Genevan politics; in turn, that also furthered the separation of powers and provided protection from oligarchy. The result was a far more open and stable society than previously, and Calvin's orientation toward the practical is obvious in these areas.

Recalling once again that this was a pre-information

age, it would also be a challenge to find ways to convey his ideas. The earliest and broadest method of disseminating Calvin's thought to those around him was through preaching, a decidedly oral medium. This method would surely be discounted by most cultural critics today but proved to be greatly beneficial to the Reformation. Calvin spoke to the masses in clear, forceful language, and with regularity he instructed and reached the leading minds of his day.

Contrary to the stereotype that Calvin was a dry or uninteresting Puritan, his sermons attracted large and consistent audiences. By the mid-1550s, one eyewitness reported that most Genevans, "even the hypocrites," heard these Calvinistic sermons.[79] Preaching might be thought of as the mass communication of the time, and Genevans received a considerable portion of their information from regular sermons. During most of Calvin's tenure, sermons were preached daily from all four of Geneva's churches. Stressing simplicity and clarity, Calvin's preaching was ideally designed to persuade the masses and to shape their expectations. In one such exhortation just before a citywide election, Calvin warned about civic dangers and called on the listeners to "think carefully and to take God as our president and governor in our elections, and to make our choice with a pure conscience without regard to anything except the honor and glory of God in the security and defense of this republic."[80] His preaching was pervasive, and one of Theodore Beza's 1561 letters to William Farel claimed that more than one thousand people heard Calvin's lectures on a daily basis—quite a mass communication accomplishment for the day.[81]

Calvin worked at reforming on numerous fronts, not with a coercive and dictatorial spirit, but through discourse, persuasion, and forceful rhetoric. One modern study recognizes the role that Calvin's preaching played in interpreting his significance. William Naphy provides examples of how Calvin confronted even elected officials in his congregation and concludes that Calvin's preaching was at times direct, confrontational, and "politically informed." One 1552 sermon so irritated the council that members inquired just why it was that he spoke of the senators and other civil rulers in a particular sermon as "arguing against God," "mocking him," "rejecting all the Holy Scriptures [to] vomit forth their blasphemies as supreme decrees," and as "gargoyle monkeys [who] have become so proud."[82] Calvin's rhetoric was certainly not so academic or technical as to elude his audience.

Calvin preached regularly in Geneva and Strasbourg, and his sermons provide rich amplification of his thought, which might otherwise be considered arid if his leadership were evaluated apart from these homilies. The theologian of action was just that: active and practical but always rooted in theological truth. Thousands regularly listened to him expound such notions, and Genevans could scarcely avoid exposure to his thoughts. This leader knew the value of communication that was practical in orientation. One can be academically correct in many different fields, but if he does not distill the information for the masses, his work will be less effective.

Although Calvin enjoyed preaching *extempore,* his adherents quickly realized the value of recording his expositions. In 1549, mainly at the encouragement of French refugees in Geneva, a recording secretary was appointed to take down Calvin's sermons. These sermons, which were later either lost or sold by the pound for scrap paper after the French Revolution, eventually yielded forty-four volumes in manuscript form—a prolific achievement considering Calvin had so many other duties.

During his final residence in Geneva, Calvin regularly preached expositions in the three Sunday services. By 1549 these messages were so popular that they were increased to daily expositions. Calvin's rotation allowed him to preach twice on Sunday and every day in alternating weeks. On average, Calvin thus prepared 20 sermons per month, normally drawing on New Testament texts on Sunday mornings, Old Testament texts during the week, and the Psalms on Sunday afternoons. His fertile mind could not be limited only to writing. Calvin preached 200 sermons on Deuteronomy, 159 on Job, 110 on 1 Corinthians, and 43 on Galatians—intellectual achievements in their own right. By these free and spirited orations, the common man was enlightened and equipped to carry the ideas of reform for a long time.

Any valid assessment of Calvin as a leader in action will consult his sermons for a well-rounded portrait of his activity and also understand this: he was never satisfied to communicate with intellectuals only. He made sure that the message was broadcast to all classes of people. And much of his information was practical in orientation.

Optimizing one medium only inspired him to employ other means of mass communication as well.

CALVIN THE AUTHOR

*W*ITH THE RISE OF the Gutenberg press, the Reformers wholeheartedly utilized the new media to amplify their thoughts and action plans. Perhaps no first-generation Reformer seized the moment like John Calvin. Expressing his thoughts with clarity and regularity was part of his life.

He became engaged in these writing skirmishes early on in his life. Initially he learned the power of the press the hard way when anti-Reformation French leaders published a spate of pamphlets defending their oppression of Protestants in the 1530s. One of their immediate goals was to justify their burning of Anabaptists at the stake, supposedly because the Anabaptists threatened civil stability. Suspecting that such propaganda was more accurately attributable to royalist sympathizers, Calvin believed that unless he actively opposed these outrages, tyrants would be convinced that they could continue such oppression without consequences. Calvin's earliest writing from the early 1530s exhibited his ready engagement in theological politics. "Unless I opposed them to the utmost of my ability," he wrote, "my silence could not be vindicated from the charge of cowardice and treachery." Such was his burden and animus for composing the maiden version of his *Institutes of the Christian Religion* in 1536. Calvin explained that this small treatise, originally consisting of only six chapters, was drafted to answer the slander by these French Catholic opponents and to vindicate the slain Protestants. Calvin denied that his motivation for publishing the *Institutes* was self-seeking notoriety, evidenced as much by his immediate withdrawal from Basel as by the "fact that nobody there knew that I was the author."

Calvin's prolific writings span at least four different genres. The first to understand is his *Institutes,* which provides a systematic overview of his most important thought. That culture-shaping classic was written, according to its own explanation, to serve as a primer on biblical teaching for college and seminary students. It would serve as a short summary of his thought. The second class of writings is made up of his commentaries. Now published in twenty-two double volumes (about five hundred pages each), these commentaries cover most biblical books and expand on the *Institutes.* Importantly, by having several layers of writings, his consistency of mind is apparent, and one source should be interpreted to harmonize with the others. A third strata of writings was published posthumously: his sermons. Calvin preached many sermons, and these were recorded from the middle of his ministry (most of his sermons date from 1550) and yielded another large body of work. Finally, Calvin wrote many letters and tracts that offer colorful insights to the mind of the Reformer and the events of his day. Among some of his more important tracts are *On the Organization of the Church* and various "orders for visitation and supervision." His 1539 *Reply to Sadolet* and his treatise *On the Necessity of Reforming the Church* further illustrate his apologetic orientation to address the pressing needs of the church in his day. Calvin thus did not restrict his writing to a small, specialized domain, but he was broad in his scope and ability to counsel the church.

Calvin was not afforded the luxury of being a professional theologian. He was in the trenches of the Reform movement with the troops, as a captain leading the army. He did not serve as a tactical strategist, protected safely in the headquarters of the military and divorced from the vanguard assaults. He was in the fray itself and wrote these treatises out of his battlefield experience.

Many of Calvin's other writings reflect his actual experience. His letters serve as a window into his private world. The warm expressions of compassion are present in many of these epistles. There is abundant literature available to vindicate the portrait of Calvin as a caring, compassionate pastor and adviser. He also served his contemporaries by compiling formal statements of faith, such as the 1545 Geneva Catechism—the first confession for the Genevan churches presented by Calvin and Farel in 1536—and a brief confession about the Eucharist (1537).

Calvin's principal work, the *Institutes of the Christian Religion*,[83] shows considerable growth over two decades.

Of the first four chapters of the original edition composed in Basel in 1536,[84] three articulated the customary features of Christian catechisms. The first chapter was on "Law," an exposition of the moral law or the Ten Commandments. Another chapter was a detailed exposition of the Lord's Prayer. The final chapter was an explanation of the Protestant view of the sacraments. These first chapters were not filled with philosophical ruminations, intricate definitions, or theoretical arguments. They were structurally similar to Luther's (and many others', even Roman Catholic) catechism. What was intended to serve as a basic text displaying sound instruction (see Titus 1:9) for future ministers morphed and expanded over time into a classic for Western civilization—in both church and state.[85] This seminal work became a conduit of practical influence, first shaping hearts then actions.

Calvin's thought spread throughout Europe and sailed over the Atlantic with various colonists, cropping up frequently in sermons and pamphlets in various colonies. If English sermons in the seventeenth century were still referencing Calvin's *Institutes* as a robust source for opposing governmental abuse, American colonial sermons conveyed his sentiments even more. "Probably no other theological work," wrote Dartmouth historian Herbert Foster, "was so widely read and so influential from the Reformation to the American Revolution. . . . In England [it] was considered 'the best and perfectest system of divinity' by both Anglican and Puritan until [Archbishop William] Laud's supremacy in the 1630s. Oxford undergraduates were required to read Calvin's *Institutes* and his Catechism in 1578."[86] "Most colonial libraries seem to

contain some work by Calvin," and "scarcely a colonial
list of books from New Hampshire to South Carolina appears to lack books written by Calvinists."[87]

Other importers of Calvinism to the West were the
Geneva Bible and Beza's *New Testament Annotations,*
which inspired readers ranging from Shakespeare (in his
plays composed during the 1590s, the bard quoted from
the Geneva Bible)[88] to American colonists with "scores of
marginal notes on covenant, vocation . . . deposition of
kings, the supremacy of God's Word [over human tradi-
tion], and the duty of orderly resistance to tyranny."[89] Beza
and Marot's hymnbook of metrical psalms, which became
surprisingly popular, paved the way for acceptance of
other ideas championed by the enormously influential
Beza.[90] Herbert Foster further detailed that political
Calvinism was spread through Beza's *Annotations,* which
were published annually or semiannually for half a century while America was first being settled. Indeed, Beza's
works are in the libraries of four early American colleges
and were held by many influential leaders.

Even the Scottish philosopher David Hume, a fan of
neither Knox nor Calvin, admitted: "The republican
ideas of the origin of power from the people were at that
time [about 1607] esteemed as Puritan novelties."[91]
These novelties stemmed from Calvinism. Even closer to
the founding period of colonial America than Hume,
New Englander Cotton Mather wrote, "The best ministers of New-England have generally been Calvinists."[92]
Western society owes many of its best political advances
to Reformation theology, and the establishing of America
during the early 1600s owes more to Calvinism than to

many other influences. It is simply impossible to imagine such a broad impact apart from the literary explosion fueled by Calvin and his disciples.

Calvin's ideas, then, took on a life of their own and became the actions emulated by many others, due in no small measure to the printing press and Calvin's wise employment of the latest technology. Contemporary historian David Fisher concludes, "Of all the determinants which shaped the cultural character of British America, the most powerful was religion."[93] A strong case can be made that the most determinative religion at the time was Calvinism or one of its offshoots. And long after his 1564 death, Calvin would live on and continue to mentor many through his writings, which are still widely available today.

CALVIN THE EDUCATOR

*H*ISTORICALLY, EDUCATION, AS MUCH as any other single factor, has advanced cultural and political action plans. One of Calvin's most enduring contributions to society—a contribution that also secured the longevity of many Calvinistic reforms—was the establishment of the Academy in Geneva. Through his Academy, Calvin succeeded where others had failed. Worth noting, none of the other major Protestant Reformers are credited with founding a university that would last for centuries, even becoming a sought-after property by some surprising suitors.

Although Genevans had tried for two centuries to establish a university, initially receiving authorization as early as 1365 from Pope Charles IV, only after Calvin's settlement did a college finally succeed.[94] With a history of educational misfires, Calvin's relentless attempt to establish an academy in the late 1550s surely drew many skeptics. By the time of Calvin's arrival, city officials yearned for a premier educational institution, but most Genevans in 1536 thought this target too ambitious. Regardless of the unsuccessful starts in education that had occurred between Geneva's adoption of the Reformation in 1536 and Calvin's return from his Strasbourg exile in 1541, it is clear that success in establishing a lasting university did not occur until Calvin set his hand to the plow after Geneva became settled in its Protestant identity in the 1550s. Calvin the leader understood the necessity for an institutional method to ensure that the pedagogy of the Reformation would continue. Both his school and its students would perpetuate the notions expounded in his sermons and writings.

Calvin was prudent enough to draw on others and his past experiences—even his painful exile—for inspiration for the school. There were three dominant influences on Calvin as he established an enduring university. And various leaders from different parts of Protestant Switzerland each made distinct contributions. First, Calvin profited from Peter Viret's previously established Lausanne Academy, which actually had been founded two decades before Calvin's. In the 1540s, the Lausanne Academy (approximately forty miles from Geneva) was the leading French-speaking educational institution, featuring an all-star faculty. The Lausanne influence on the Genevan Academy increased when some of those professors (Theodore Beza, Francois Hotman, and Peter Viret) came to teach in Geneva after 1559.[95] Rival leaders in Bern even accused Calvin of a brain-drain, conspiring to steal an excellent faculty, but all this happened because of institutional disruption in Lausanne itself. Second, Calvin witnessed another excellent model in Johann Sturm's academy at Strasbourg during his exile from 1538 to 1541. Third, Calvin emphasized the Bible-centered, expository method of Huldrych Zwingli, elevating the original texts of Scripture to the most authoritative platform possible. Most of the leading voices of the Reformation also became leaders in educational reform in Geneva, Lausanne, Strasbourg, and Zurich—surely a local lesson with global implications for a perceptive leader. After its inception in 1558, however, Calvin's Academy soon far outpaced these other centers and subsequently remained at the forefront of Protestant educational ventures for more than two centuries.[96]

The Academy, which was adjacent to St. Peter's Cathedral, featured two levels of curricula: one for the public education of Geneva's youth (the college or *schola privata*) and the other a seminary to train ministers (*schola publica*).[97] One should hardly discount the impact that came from the public education of young people, especially in a day when education was normally reserved only for aristocratic scions or for members of Catholic societies. Begun in 1558,[98] with Calvin and Beza chairing the theological faculty, the Academy building was dedicated on June 5, 1559, with six hundred people in attendance at the dedication in the cathedral. Calvin collected money for the school himself, and many expatriates donated to help its formation. The public school, which had seven grades, enrolled 280 students during its inaugural year, and the Academy's seminary expanded to 162 students in just three years. By Calvin's death in 1564, there were 1,200 students in the college and 300 in the seminary. Both schools, as historians have observed, were tuition-free and "forerunners of modern public education."[99] Few European institutions had ever seen such rapid growth.

Moreover, the Academy provided excellent education for internationals. This Academy always had a large number of immigrant students. By 1691, French students constituted 40 percent of the student body, while French-speaking Swiss were 25 percent. Only 8.3 percent of students were Genevan. Enrollment crested near the time of Beza's death, with more than 60 graduates per year, and then declined to about 50 per year by 1665 and continually downward to about 20 per year throughout most of the eighteenth century.

A recent study points out that many of the French immigrants who supported the *Bourse Francaise* were also the main financial contributors to Calvin's Academy. Thus, an immigrant constituency may have had more lasting impact than previous studies have recognized.[100] In itself, that is also a hint of the mode in which Calvin was happy to cooperate with others, who were not necessarily longstanding citizens of Geneva.

To accommodate the flood of students, the Academy planned to add—in what would become characteristic of the Calvinistic view of Christian influence in all areas of life—departments of law and medicine. Henry Baird chronicled that Beza requested prayer for the new medical department as early as 1567, by which time the law school was established. After the St. Bartholomew's Day massacre (1572), Francois Hotman—one of the leading constitutional lawyers on the continents—taught at the Genevan law school. In addition, Denis Godefroy, who influenced Johannes Althusius, also was on the law faculty and was one of two Academy professors to become first syndic (akin to mayor) in Geneva while teaching. The presence of these two legal giants, Hotman (from 1573 to 1578) and Godefroy, gave Calvin's Academy one of the earliest Swiss legal faculties. The medical school, attempted shortly after Calvin's death, was not successfully established until the 1700s.[101]

The Academy did not confer degrees but was assuredly Calvin's most vital educational legacy[102] to Geneva—so much so that more than two centuries after Calvin's death, the Academy was coveted by a Virginian who harbored few Calvinistic sympathies.

From 1560 onward, the Genevan Academy also doubled as the ministerial training ground for France and other international centers. According to William Bouwsma, Calvin's Academy emphasized the trilingual approach (the "classical" model) fostered by Erasmus: "Its students were first thoroughly grounded in Latin grammar and rhetoric by the study of Virgil, Cicero, and other classical authors, and in the fourth year they began Greek. They learned history from Livy and Xenophon and dialectic from the arguments of Cicero rather than from medieval textbooks. . . . Calvin's ideal for both pastors and secular rulers resembled Quintilian's generally educated orator, the ideal of humanist educators everywhere."[103] This training prepared numerous students for professional service, including vocations in law, medicine, politics, and education, as well as the ministry.

Calvin's Academy became the standard-bearer for education in all major fields. Three days each week, professors in Hebrew, Greek, and the arts would give two hour-long lectures in a morning and an afternoon session; the alternating days would have a one-hour lecture.[104] In time, scholars from Paris and Lausanne flocked to this excellent educational center.[105] Those original students would graduate and lend their hands to drafting influential confessions of faith, serving as political advisers in England, Germany, France, Holland, and Scotland, and teaching at other leading universities. After education at Calvin's Academy, for example, Thomas Bodley returned to Oxford and established the Bodleian Library, perhaps the finest research library in the world. His action followed Calvin's educational mission.

Moreover, the Academy exported missionaries. The Genevan Church sent more than one hundred missionaries to Brazil, England, France, Holland, and Italy before 1562.[106] Many of these, including pastors from Geneva and Lausanne, went underground, hid in safe houses, and reappeared in French cities to minister from time to time.[107] Geneva became an energy source for reform, acting at times like the best of resistance movements. Its influence in Europe, England, and Scotland was enormous.[108]

After its founding, the Academy also helped nourish alternative power structures. As early as 1555, Geneva was unique in Switzerland in entrusting the power of excommunication to the Consistory (comprised of local ministers and elders), not the civil magistrate.[109] That was both progressive and restrictive of the civil power. That this structure was at the heart of Calvinism and its view of political reality is seen from the fact that wherever Calvinism spread, other "Venerable Companies of Pastors" cropped up, for example, in Potiers (1555), Orleans (1557), La Rochelle (1558), and Nimes (1561).[110] Perhaps the influence of the Academy helps explain these similarities. These ecclesiastical governing authorities precluded civil magistrates from acting as the only lawfully ordained governors; power had to be shared with the private sphere. In contrast to other municipalities, one thing that contributed to Geneva's unique adherence to a consistent Reformation was the creation of an institution that was rare for its day: the Consistory. The collegial religious body assumed numerous roles (that is, moral correction, corporate guidance, and censorship) that had once been the prerogatives of princely courts.[111]

However, it is doubtful that Calvin's ideas would have been exported as quickly or in a sustained fashion without his groundbreaking work in the Genevan Academy.

So enduring was Calvin's educational reform that, more than two centuries later, a leading opponent of Calvinism was eager to secure Calvin's Academy. The little-known story rehearsed below shows how long Calvin's educational shadow extended.

COMPARATIVELY FEW people know that Thomas Jefferson wanted to relocate the school Calvin founded—one of the world's foremost universities at the time—from Geneva to northern Virginia years before he founded his own University of Virginia. The brief flirtation (or aggressive courtship in Jefferson's case) with purchasing the universally renowned Genevan Academy in 1795 further reveals a Jefferson who sometimes failed to stack the bricks in the wall of separation high enough to preclude robust theology from influencing public education.

Jefferson's pursuit of Calvin's Academy illustrates the continued esteem in which Calvin's ideas were held both in America and internationally more than two centuries after his death in 1564. While Jefferson is customarily depicted as ardently opposed to any public influence by religion,[112] he actually lobbied long and hard to relocate Calvin's Academy to America. The offer of the Academy ("a splendid project" Jefferson called it) came from one of its patrons of Huguenot[113] descent, Francois D'Ivernois (1757–1842).[114] Even into the 1790s, Geneva was respected by many of the most cultured Americans who continued to revere that city as the font of their own spiritual heritage and civic life since it had been the incubator of the Protestant Reformation. Refined citizens of the day (such as Benjamin Franklin[115] and others) enrolled their children and grandchildren in Genevan institutions to receive a proper Protestant education.

Unless one wishes to view the Founding Fathers as on the verge of buying a colossal pig in a poke, it is difficult to think they were oblivious to the residual legacy of Calvinism still pulsing through the veins of the school founded by Calvin in 1559. D'Ivernois regretted that radicals targeted the school and its faculty in the summer of 1794, attempting to overthrow any strategic command center that might obstruct their revolution. One of their first tactical steps was to imprison faculty members and the most fervent Calvinist ministers.

This attempted takeover catapulted D'Ivernois into action. He quickly proposed a university immigration to several expatriate friends (including Albert Gallatin, a former senator from Pennsylvania). He also approached John Adams (the sitting vice president, who had earlier applauded Calvinist resistance theory in his *Defense of the Constitutions*) about the possibility, and finally he tried to sell Jefferson on the idea by letter. D'Ivernois volunteered to raise enough capital to relocate the entire university and permanently endow the faculty if the Americans could simply gain approval and sell some land to fund a private endowment for other expenses. He threw in this inducement if a partnership could be reached: these brilliant Calvinistic faculty members, in turn, could also help the new nation by carrying with them "truly Republican" habits, fully supportive of the new American setting.

Jefferson loved the idea, and many Americans grew enthusiastic about the possible immigration of Calvin's Academy. John Adams, for example, described the plan as an honor, and John Jay energetically supported the proposal, hoping D'Ivernois could quickly close the deal. Such a migration would have filled a "vast chasm in education," in the words of Secretary of State Edmund Randolph.

Jefferson not only appreciated this embodiment of Calvin's legacy but also lobbied for it in his own legislature. Although the Virginia Assembly declined D'Ivernois's offer, Jefferson would not surrender the idea. He even asked George Washington to lend his hand to raising funds for the venture, but it was ultimately unsuccessful. After Jefferson, Jay, and Adams failed to persuade their countrymen to liquidate acreage sufficient to endow the project, Jefferson retreated and began to form his own university instead of plucking up Calvin's Academy at a fire-sale price.

Still, the attempt to purchase such an overtly and particularly religious institution with public funds, if needed, indicates the respect that the earliest Americans retained for educational institutions of Calvin's Geneva. As Library of Congress historian James Hutson writes, "The first four presidents of the United States and other distinguished founding fathers like Jay and Randolph supported—some with great ardor—the plan to bring *L'Academie de Calvin* across the Atlantic."[116]

Even if Jefferson were a Deist, the idea promoted in his personal seal (used to authenticate his letters) is unmistakably Calvinistic, and the school he coveted was Calvin's.[117] The motto behind his personal seal's words, "Rebellion to Tyrants Is Obedience to God," had its origin in a peculiarly Calvinistic context and is intelligible only against that backdrop.

To be sure, Jefferson was *not* a Calvinist. He accused them variously of being fanatics, tyrants, intolerant, malignant, or delirious. Nevertheless, he was wise enough to recognize a worthy contribution by the Genevan Reformer. One need not, after all, embrace every aspect of Calvinism in order to pay tribute to some portion of it. Jefferson and others from the founding period of the republic recognized the educational excellence founded by Calvin. His considerable endeavor to acquire Calvin's own Academy during the mid-1790s and numerous acts of the Continental Congress approved by Jefferson and the other Founding Fathers indicate that Calvinism continued to have a momentous impact on the American founding.

The anecdote above provides an impressive epitaph to the strength of Calvinism. Whether it was in Geneva, Boston, Edinburgh, or London, there once was a powerful set of ideas that overturned the unlimited government either by an unaccountable monarch or through a political cabinet. That set of ideas won the day only through sacrifice (martyrdom for some), resistance to tyranny, and a reformulation of civil government utilizing a more lasting platform. For whatever reasons, the disciples of John Calvin turn out to be leaders in these nascent movements. And Jefferson was apparently not alone in wishing to imitate aspects of Calvin's legacy to a large degree because both leaders understood the value of education.

CALVIN AND PUBLISHING

*T*HE PRINTING INDUSTRY IN Geneva throughout Calvin's rise to prominence is a story that proved crucial for the longevity of Calvin's work. One recent study states, "No description of the international efforts of the Reform can omit to mention the contributions of the printer and scholar Robert Estienne, the printer and martyrologist Jean Crespin . . . or for that matter the lifelong and deliberate use of publication as a weapon on the part of Calvin and Theodore de Beze."[118] Estienne printed French editions from Geneva by Calvin's disciples Beza, Hotman, and Viret. Jean Crespin, a groomsman at Beza's secret marriage,[119] published popular devotional material; moreover, a wide array of educational material was produced for the burgeoning Academy. And Bibles and theological texts flew off Genevan printing presses.

Perhaps the largest single printing venture of the sixteenth century, Beza's French translation of the Psalms into metrical form, went to press in Geneva.[120] This Psalter, which became the international songbook of expansionistic Calvinism,[121] went through numerous editions (27,400 copies were printed in 1562 alone). Stanford Reid notes that to a greater degree than "all the fine theological reasoning, both the catechism and the Psalter entered into the very warp and woof of the humblest members' lives. For this the credit must largely go to the first pastor of Geneva." Hymns and songs powerfully lodged distinct ideas in the popular mind, especially aided by reading the Bible in the common language and sermons that were understood by the masses. The singing of psalms afforded these Protestants occasions to confess their beliefs. Some anti-Protestants even went so far as to view the singing of psalms as a subversive act![122]

The ability to defend the views of Calvin rapidly in print magnified the lasting impact of his thought.[123] The number of books published in Geneva rose from three volumes in 1536 to twenty-eight in 1554 and to forty-eight by 1561. The number of volumes printed in Geneva the five years prior to his death was a stunning average of thirty-eight volumes per year (a tenfold increase in twenty-five years). The average dropped to twenty per year after his death.[124] By 1563, there were at least thirty-four presses, many manned by immigrants.[125] Shortly after Calvin's death, a contemporary wrote: "The printed works flooding into the country could not be stopped by legal prohibition. The more edicts issued by the courts, the more the booklets and papers increased."[126]

The content of publications in Calvin's day was taken

seriously, and efforts were made to ensure that truth was committed to ink. In 1560 a commission on printing was established to coordinate the efforts of the various Genevan publishers. This three-member commission included Beza and Jean Bude. The area ministerial association (the Company of Pastors) had a strong voice in what was printed, and every manuscript published in Geneva first had to survive Beza's scrutiny.[127] Not unpredictably, of the forty-eight Genevan publications in 1561, thirteen were by Calvin, seven by Beza, and five by Viret. Of the thirty-six works published in 1562, more than one-third (thirteen) were by Calvin.[128]

Geneva also developed an extensive and efficient literary distribution system. A childhood friend of Calvin, Laurent de Normandie (who later became mayor of Noyon), developed a network of distributors who took Genevan Calvinist publications into France and other parts of Europe. Many of the books were compact, designed to be hidden quickly in one's clothing.[129] Thousands of contraband books were spread throughout Europe during Calvin's time, and several distributors became Protestant martyrs.[130]

So successful was Calvin's city at spreading the message that all books printed in Geneva were banned in France beginning in 1551. Calvin's *Institutes* (along with at least nine of his other writings) had been officially banned in France since 1542, but that could not halt circulation. As a result, Geneva was identified as a subversive center because of its publishing; the 1551 Edict of Chateaubriand forbade, among other things, importing or circulating Genevan books.[131] Distributing such works for sale could incur secular punishment. But many books still filtered across porous European borders. Some shrewd printers, unwilling to be thwarted by state censorship, cleverly responded by employing fonts commonly used by French printers and by using fictitious addresses.[132] This new medium and its energized distribution pipeline allowed Calvin's message to transcend Geneva's geographical limitations.

The effect of this publishing on morality was dramatic. Sins, such as immorality and blasphemy, could lead to social disorder. Thus, the city magistrates began to endorse the morality of Calvin in the 1550s. E. William Monter claims that the city "had no true police," and the generational effect of catechizing served to unite citizens around enduring mental and moral agreements.[133]

Geneva's transformation would not have been complete, however, without the rapid influx of a large number of immigrants. Many of these immigrants were either attracted to Geneva because of its publishing or actually involved in the publishing business. A cohort of refugees virtually the size of Geneva's population arrived in a single decade. The Protestant immigration and publishing irreversibly transfigured Geneva from a city dominated by a few aristocratic families to one guided by religious interests and subject to popular approval. From 1550 to 1562, between seven thousand and ten thousand refugees, mostly Protestant, came to Geneva.[134] They brought with them, in addition to their faith, a variety of occupations, eventually recasting Geneva into one of the first democratic melting pots. None of this would have happened without Calvin, and it provided a successful social experiment for many others to emulate. These newcomers, who were highly educated for their time, were publishers, merchants, physicians, and authors. A knowledge class, including many teachers who would lecture at the Academy, was drawn to Geneva by Calvin's Reformation,[135] which dramatically enhanced human freedom.

All of the early teachers at his Academy and most of his fellow pastors from the mid-1540s until his death in 1564 were French immigrants. Leading publishers were immigrants as well. Before his death, the "pastors, professors, the printers and even the doctors and lawyers in Geneva were overwhelmingly religious refugees from France." After his death most of the second-generation pastors were Genevan-born, an indication that many of the settlers did not return to France.[136] About one-third of the pre-refugee population arrived between 1557 and 1559,[137] and the deluge of new inhabitants made a lasting impact on Geneva during and after Calvin's life.[138] Meanwhile, Italian-, Dutch-, and English-speaking churches also came into being with the arrival of so many Calvinistic refugees from other countries. More Italians sought shelter in Geneva than the combined number of Dutch and English exiles.[139] In addition, Calvin's cousin, Robert Olivetan, who sympathized with the Waldensians (a precursor group to the Protestant Reformation, originating in the twelfth century in southern France), embarked on the first translation of the Bible into French.

So quick was the transformation in Geneva that by 1555 all four of Geneva's highest elected leaders were Calvinists, and a majority of the Small Council also endorsed Calvinism.[140] Under Calvin's patient, persistent leadership from 1536 to 1558, a fundamental change of allegiance occurred within the powerful Small Council.[141] A fine case of directed gradualism, none of the members of the 1536 council sat on the 1558 council. Some of the leading families in 1536 saw their children in exile by the late 1550s, and Monter writes: "They were being replaced, slowly but surely, by magistrates who believed in collective, orderly rule under Divine inspiration. A tenacious and devout type of Calvinist governor . . . had taken control."[142]

Silk, wine, books, and political and religious ideas became the main exports of Geneva as a result of Calvin's actions. Ultimately, thousands of refugees fled to Geneva, a city that was becoming an international host for freedom of movement, publishing, assembly, and ideas. Moreover, once Geneva's democratic transformation was completed, the city did not turn back.

The final five years of Calvin's life were gratifying, especially when contrasted with the valiant struggles in his early years. In the 1560s he saw the establishment and growth of the Academy, the astronomical rise in publishing, pastors being trained and sent into various locales, the stabilization of the city of Geneva, and the maturation of the church's presbytery. In addition, he began to be a sought-after adviser. But most important, his work would outlast him.

The final years of his life were characterized by chronic physical illness and an almost compulsive drive to write. The final edition of the *Institutes* was completed in 1559, and most of his writings in his final five years were commentaries on biblical books and treatises on particular topics. As his life's curtain began to drop, the continuation of his work would have the support of well-conceived measures in Geneva and wisely selected and trained disciples. Calvin had succeeded as much as any other person to that point in history in finding ways to establish and multiply the ideas that fired the soul.

Indeed, his own personal motto, "Here, Lord, I present my heart promptly and sincerely," with an icon of a heart aflame, was apt. His burning passion could not be extinguished, and his theology of action—once committed to writing—reached more people after his death than it did at the zenith of his popularity. His ideas were multiplied.

DEATH

$\mathcal{W}$HILE NOT ALL LEADERS are applauded for their contributions in their own lifetimes— some efforts simply need long stretches of history for vindication—Calvin was revered by many in his own lifetime. The plaudits of his peers were strong confirmation of his leadership.

On April 25, 1564, sensing the nearness of death, Calvin filed his final will. In it he pleaded his unworthiness ("Woe is me; my ardor and zeal have been so careless and languid, that I confess I have failed innumerable times"[143]) and thanked God for mercy. He appointed his brother, Anthony (whose reputation for divorcing an earlier wife due to adultery had been maliciously used to malign Calvin himself), to be his heir, and in his will he bequeathed equal amounts to the boys' school, the poor refugees, and his stepdaughters. He also left part of his meager estate to his nephews and their children. To vindicate Calvin against charges of greed, Beza reiterated what Calvin had stated earlier: "If some will not be persuaded while I am alive, my death, at all events will show that I have not been a money-making man."[144] When his will was notarized and brought to the attention of the Senate,[145] members of that council visited the declining Calvin to hear his final farewell personally.

Calvin's importance and relationship to the city leaders may be gleaned from his *Farewell Address to the Members of the Little Council.*[146] The members of this council had gone to his home to hear his advice and to express their appreciation for the "services he has performed for the Seigneurie and for that of which he has faithfully acquitted himself in his duty." A contemporary recorded his sentiments from April 27, 1564. In that chronicle, the dying Calvin first thanked these leaders for their support, cooperation, and friendship. Although they had engaged in numerous struggles, still their relationship was cordial. Even though he wished to accomplish more, Calvin humbly suggested that God might have "used him in the little he did." He urged the senators to honor God and to keep "hidden under the wings of God in whom all our confidence must be. And as much as we are hanging by a thread, nevertheless he will continue, as in the past, to keep us as we have already experienced that he saved us in several ways."

He concluded by encouraging each one to "walk according to his station and use faithfully that which God gave him in order to uphold this Republic. Regarding civil or criminal trials, one should reject all favor, hate, errors, commendations." He also advised leaders not to aspire to privilege as if rank were a benefit for governors. "And if one is tempted to deviate from this," Calvin added, "one should resist and be constant, considering the One who established us, asking him to conduct us by his Holy Spirit, and he will not desert us."

Calvin's farewell to these political leaders was followed by his *Farewell Address to the Ministers* on April 28, 1564. From his chamber, Calvin reminded them poignantly: "When I first came to this Church there was almost nothing. We preached and that was all. We searched out idols and burned them, but there was no reformation. Everything was in tumult. . . . I lived here through marvelous battles. I was welcomed with mockery one evening in front of my door by 50 or 60 rifle shots. Do you think that that could disturb a poor, timid student as I am, and as I have always been, I confess?" The address reviewed his Strasbourg exile, the tensions he faced upon return, and some of his experiences with various councils. Calvin concluded by predicting that the battles would not lessen in the days ahead, warning, "You will be busy after God takes me, even though I am nothing, still I know I prevented three thousand uproars that there might have been in Geneva. But take courage and strengthen yourselves, for God will use this Church and will maintain her, and be sure that God will keep her."

Calvin humbly confessed: "I say again that all that I did has no value, and that I am a miserable creature. But if I could say what I truly wanted to, that my vices always displeased me, and that the root of the fear of God was in my heart, and you can say that what I was subjected to was good, and I pray that you would forgive me of the bad, but if there is anything good, that you conform yourselves to it and follow it."

He denied that he had written hateful things about others, and he confirmed that the pastors had elected Beza to be his successor. "Watch that you help him [Beza]," exhorted the dying Calvin, "for the duty is large and troublesome, of such a sort that he may be overwhelmed under the burden. . . . As for him, I know that he has a good will and will do what he can." Further, he requested that the senators not change anything in Geneva's structures and urged them "not to innovate—we often ask for novelties—not that I desire for myself by ambition what remains mine, and that we retain it without wanting better, but because all change is hazardous, and sometimes harmful." The advice from this leader is filled with layers of wisdom.

Always sensitive to the calling to lead in many sectors of public life, he concluded with a plea for his fellow ministers to recall how they would affect matters outside the walls of the church: "Let each one consider the obligation he has, not only to this Church, but to the city, which has promised to serve in adversity as well as in prosperity, and likewise each one should continue in his vocation and not try to leave it or not practice it. For when one hides to escape the duty, he will say that he has neither thought about it nor sought this or that. But one should consider the obligation he has here before God."

When Calvin passed away almost a month after making these comments on May 27, 1564, "the whole State regretted" the death of "its wisest citizen . . . a common parent." He was interred in a common cemetery at Plein Palais, finally finding the anonymity he craved. That, one historian wrote, was characteristic of Calvin in life as in death.[147] The widespread notice and sadness at his death should serve to correct any faulty view that his contemporaries either despised him or underestimated his importance. He was mourned, and his large number of friends would keep his memory alive far more than contemporaries would have predicted.

VINDICATION

*P*OPULARITY MAY BE FLEETING; it may even elude a leader in this life. However, the measure of a leader's success is not confined to this life only but also includes how history may vindicate him.

From what we can read from diverse firsthand accounts, Calvin was compassionate, far less prone to violence than contemporaries, retiring, surrounded by friends, and a parent to his wife's children, even though he and Idelette were married less than a decade. In addition, he was brilliant and energetic. For decades he was celebrated as a hero of Geneva. For later generations, he represented the founding of modern civic freedom. Why then, one may ask, is he so consistently maligned?

Anyone who seeks to defend Calvin may agree with the hazard noted by an earlier biographer: "How shall the writer appear impartial? [especially regarding one whose] faults have often been exaggerated. . . . It is not our fault if it is becoming almost impossible to write about Calvin without appearing to be his advocate. But let no one expect to find here an apotheosis. 'There is none good but one, that is God.' We know this and will never forget it. But if Calvin was a man, he was none the less a great man, or still better, a great servant of God."[148]

Much of Calvin's objectionable reputation stems from faulty information or from humanistic biases that stubbornly refuse to consider the facts. The recurrent allegation that Calvin was a Genevan dictator owes more, says Alister McGrath, to "imagination and anti-authoritarian agenda, informed by and tempered with images" of Adolf Hitler and Joseph Stalin than to actual history.[149] Calvin was not even a Genevan citizen until 1559;[150] neither was he ever an elected official with legislative power. He certainly did not rule autocratically. To the contrary, it was Calvin himself who insisted on collegial and decentralized rule (the Consistory) as early as 1541. Others more egotistical or prone to autocracy might have lobbied for the concentration of power in a dictator, but not Calvin.

Instead of pining for a theocracy, it might be more accurate to view Calvin (with historian Josef Bohatec) as advocating a pneumatocracy (rule by the spirit).[151] J. T. McNeill even recognizes Calvin's political tendencies as exhibiting a preference for liberal institutions and as opposing a forcible disturbance of the status quo.[152] This peacemaking side of Calvin is seldom factored into modern appraisals. Calvin wrote in 1541, however, that he highly valued "public peace and cordial agreement." He strongly believed that self-restraint was necessary, and as a personal discipline he tried to avoid giving sharp, public reproof, even if deserved. His forbearance paid off when some of his former enemies became supporters, and Calvin sought to "conciliate by courtesy."[153]

Critics of Calvin are quick, of course, to focus on the 1553 Michael Servetus affair.[154] While few historians harbor any desire to justify the act of the city council[155] (Servetus's execution resulted from the civil magistrate's decision, not Calvin's decree), the tragic events should be put in context. Servetus was the only person executed for heresy during Calvin's time in Geneva, while nearby Toulouse arraigned 208 people for heresy in a single year.[156] Calvin also—even though seldom acknowledged—pleaded for leniency in Servetus's punishment;[157] one result of his plea was that, before acting, the Genevan council consulted with other Swiss cities and leading theologians, who unanimously concurred with its decision. It is also true that this notorious case was one of the last battles in control for Geneva, and Calvin's opponents happily slandered him as a tyrant.

In contrast to Calvin, Thomas Aquinas, the towering medieval thinker, had favored burning heretics at the stake. He wrote that certain heretics were not only to be excommunicated but also should be handed over to secular officials "to be exterminated from the world by death."[158] Aquinas also believed in slavery and gender inequality, as did Plato and many others, who do not have every idea they advocated rejected simply because of a few aberrant notions. We might wish to treat Calvin similarly.

Critics gleefully broadcast their own favorite tales—

true or not—of Calvin's defects. Jerome Bolsec (a Genevan convicted of heresy) maliciously accused Calvin of
foisting executions and purgings on Geneva as soon as he
returned from exile in 1541, but there is no evidence that
Calvin had the power to implement such decrees, even
had he wished to. A generation ago, Basil Hall wrote that
those who accuse Calvin of wielding a dictatorial sway fail
to recognize two major factors. "First, if Calvin was a
cruel man how did he attract so many, so varied, and so
warmly attached friends and associates who speak of his
sensitiveness and charm? . . . Secondly, if Calvin had dictatorial control over Genevan affairs, how is it that the
records of Geneva show him plainly to have been the servant of its Council which on many occasions rejected out
of hand Calvin's wishes for the religious life of Geneva,
and was always master in Genevan affairs? . . . To call
Calvin the 'dictator of a theocracy' is, in view of the evidence, mere phrase-making prejudice."[159]

Aldous Huxley's baseless allegation that Calvin ruled
theocratically from Geneva is equally absurd; certainly
Huxley never had documentation for the claim that a
child was beheaded who had assaulted his parents. This is
too mythical to deserve response, unless one is completely
unfamiliar with Genevan history, government, and Christian teaching.[160]

One other widespread criticism of Calvin should be addressed, namely his handling of church-and-state relations.
The amount of concerted interaction among Calvin, his
company of pastors, and the city council may appear unset-
tling. Although there was a purposeful separation of jurisdictions, these Reformers did not believe it was healthy for

the leading spheres of influence, church and state, to operate in strict isolation. The Genevan Senate and the Council of Two Hundred frequently consulted with the pastors. At times, the pastors suggested legislation or due processes that were approved by the civil council. While each power was to have "autonomy of function, the relationship envisaged was one of harmony in which church and state cooperated fruitfully with each other to the glory of God."[161]

The first act of this marriage was the council's adoption of the *Ecclesiastical Ordinances* in November 1541, shortly after Calvin's return from Strasbourg, which set the pattern for many cooperative acts between church and state. In 1547 the Council of Two Hundred approved an ordinance prescribing an orderly method of inspecting the surrounding parishes. According to the records of the Genevan pastors, the council requested a set of procedures, and the pastors submitted the *Ecclesiastical Ordinances* for approval.

In January 1549 the syndics (chief governors) of Geneva issued a lengthy statement criticizing the citizenry for not working diligently for continued reformation in church and state and bemoaning specific misfortunes and disorders, interpreting these as tokens of God's wrath. The aldermen saw themselves as following the time-tested example of earlier rulers. This particular resolution listed specific behavioral vices and called the people to attend more carefully the daily preaching of God's Word. The councillors were so intent on having maximum publicity for this message that they ordered it read in each church and sealed the proclamation with the seal of the city. In Calvin's time the syndics occasionally visited congregations to hear sermons by prospective teachers or pastors. But that close interaction never confused the spheres of government or sought to combine them into one agency.

Likewise, the pastors felt as free to express their opinions on civic affairs as the syndics did on religious affairs. During one particularly tense time in 1551, with the city at riot's edge because of political rivalries, Calvin and his pastors appeared before the council and warned about danger in the city and the need to restore justice. In civil trials of religious persons, the pastors were normally involved, for example, at one point supplying a draft of questions for the council to depose Jerome Bolsec, a theological adversary of Calvin. As was earlier noted, the city council—not an ecclesiastical body—presided over the trial of Michael Servetus in 1553.[162] All of these were acts of the civil governors, despite the fact that religious persons gave advice in these matters.

A valid measurement of leadership is its impact on its immediate environment. If that is a fair test, we might well compare Geneva before and after Calvin. Today's Geneva, of course, is known for its international diplomacy, urbane culture, technology, and banking, which is far removed from the Geneva of Calvin's day, with its compact shops and candlelit homes stacked upon one another in narrow cobblestoned streets. The few lingering physical reminders of Calvin's Geneva—the old city, the oft-renovated St. Pierre Cathedral, and later monuments—may be turning grayer, but his ideas still gleam in the city and in the West.

Geneva became a haven for political liberty. And Calvin's church was at the vanguard of that movement.

Greater freedom for the church also meant greater freedom for society. This Protestant Reformation, far from being hidden under ecclesiastical bushels, affected every area of European life. Eventually fanning out through Europe to North America, it encouraged a heightened sense of liberty that beckoned some to cross oceans in search of new lands.

The Geneva that attracted worldwide fame with the advances of Calvin and his followers (the Academy began classes in 1558) had been, before Calvin, a richly textured medieval city, filled with artisans and craftsmen—not a city, though, that one would expect to become a nursery for democracy, complete with a religion that impelled so many cultural changes. The socioeconomic difference between before and after Calvin may be noted by comparing three key occupational segments. Prior to Calvin's immigration (1536) Geneva had 50 merchants, 3 printers, and few, if any, nobles. It is a measure of the changes that occurred during Calvin's residence that by the late 1550s Geneva was home to 180 merchants, 113 printers and publishers, and at least 70 aristocratic refugees who claimed noble lineage.[163] Geneva would continue to be a sanctuary for French and Italian men of letters, publishers, and dignitaries well into the seventeenth century. Calvin magnetically attracted men of "learning and piety to live near him on the *rue des Chanoines* in the Upper City and to restore the balance between commerce and erudition in Geneva."[164]

There were a few Protestants in Geneva prior to William Farel's arrival, but Protestant dominance of the city actually began in 1536. In Geneva in May 1536,

Genevans agreed thereafter to live "according to the Law of the Gospel and the Word of God, and to abolish all Papal abuses." Calvin would arrive in Geneva within two months of this historic and peaceful revolution. William Monter summarized the groundbreaking political achievements of the republic: "Geneva's citizens had usurped one by one the various prerogatives of their Bishop: the right to summon the citizens together, the right to judge civil cases and to execute judgments in criminal cases, the right to regulate the form of religion, and last of all, the right to coin money."[165] An exemplary peaceful revolution had succeeded, and that revolution exemplified "the spirit of moderation and the respect for legality,"[166] a legacy retained for centuries.

During these years when thousands of French and Italian refugees flocked to Geneva, the most influential immigrant was John Calvin. What was distinctive, however, was not merely the political (republican) form that Calvinism endorsed but "the juxtaposition of the more direct rule of God through his Word" in all areas of life.[167] The Reformers who created the new Genevan public square believed that biblical episodes were authoritative as they sought models for a new style of governing. Leaders impact their communities.

It is difficult to disprove historian William Naphy's assertion that customarily only a fraction of the available material is considered before critics begin to repudiate Calvin. The remedy for such distortions is, in part, to expose people to less biased sources and more facts. Naphy also points out that Calvin's sermons reflect his perspective as a participant (not "above the mundane events of Geneva's factional fighting") in these crucial upheavals, since he was not merely an ivory-tower academic.[168]

In sum, Calvin does not deserve all the criticisms customarily hurled at him. Considerable hostility is directed at him for another reason: many people simply object to his faith and thought. John Calvin, at the least, deserves dispassionate understanding and evaluation. Even if one does not wish to defend his every action or concept, the impact of his thought is difficult to deny.

The theology tested in the laboratory of the Genevan Reformation had a powerful influence on the West and early America. Early American political discourse reverberated with the echoes of the ideas of Calvin, his prolific disciples—Beza, Knox, Althusius—and others who ingested the Genevan intellectual cuisine. It is almost as if the teachings of those theologians had so saturated the culture that anyone could understand and embrace that worldview. Consequently, some go so far as to consider Calvin the ideological father of the American Republic.[169]

PART 2

THE CHARACTER OF JOHN CALVIN

*If we call the American statesmen of the late
eighteenth century the Founding Fathers of the
United States, then the Pilgrims and Puritans were
the grandfathers and Calvin the great-grandfather.
. . . [T]hough the fashionable eighteenth century
Deism may have pervaded some intellectual
circles, the prevailing spirit of Americans before
and after the War of Independence was essentially
Calvinistic. . . . The history of the United States is
that of a battle between the two Johns of Geneva,
John Calvin and Jean-Jacques Rousseau, and it
seems that Rousseau is winning.*

—ERIK VON KUEHNELT-LEDDIHN

*[There is a] rather striking correlation, both in
time and in place, between the spread of Calvinist
Protestantism and the rise of democracy.*

—ROBERT KINGDON

Realism

The knowledge of God does not rest in cold speculation, but carries with it the honoring of him.

OFTEN THE REPUTATION OF John Calvin is besmirched by his secular and unsympathetic critics with charges that he was rationalistic and dispassionately theoretical. One earlier critic accused him of being rationalistic prior to rationalism and Cartesian even before Descartes. Calvin is occasionally portrayed by some modern critics as if he were a twentieth-century logical positivist—possessed only by the objective facts, the mechanistic urge, or unappreciative of any emotional or practical considerations. By some Calvin is represented as the cold theologian in the laboratory, removed from practicality, oblivious to his own and others' humanity, and impervious to feeling. By much of modern society he is consequently maligned with the unpardonable sins of rationality, logicality, and consistency. To a large degree, of course, much of this improper caricature (for it truly is a caricature) is promulgated by those who disagree not so much with Calvin's methodology as with the conclusions of his theology.

To exonerate him from the charge of impracticality, one need look no further than some of the immensely practical and warmly pastoral notes of Calvin's magnum opus, *Institutes of the Christian Religion* (1559). This most systematic of his works, alleged by the critical public to be the work with the least pathos, is chosen precisely to reprove the above contentions and allegations. If his practicality is emitted in his most theoretical work, then certainly coupled with his other practical and pastoral contributions, Calvin should be reassessed as an eminently practical theologian. The *Institutes,* rather than being a cold systematic theology textbook, is a book written during the Reformation *by* a practical Christian, *about* practical Christianity, *for* practical Christians (much like Abraham Lincoln's suggestion of a national motto: "of the people, by the people, for the people").

A certain practicality of mode is apparent in the very form of the *Institutes.* Calvin wanted to express the rudiments of Christian theology in clear language. The practical nature of this theological presentation can be observed from the following.

First, it should be remembered that the original edition of the *Institutes* (1539) was not four books with eighty chapters. It contained six chapters, only one of which was polemical, that is, chapter 5, which argued against the five false sacraments of the Roman Catholic Church. Furthermore, the second chapter was on faith—certainly not a theoretical or rationalistic chapter in either style or content. Calvin's original sixth chapter was concerned with other practical topics, such as Christian freedom and his incipient thoughts on the church. Thus, the original 1539 work was far from the ivory towers of academia; it was forged in the fires of practical Reformation Christianity. Calvin intended for this work to be a basic primer on elementary subjects germane to every Christian's life: obedience to the Commandments, how to pray, faith itself, and the benefits of the sacraments. It is important to note that Calvin did not begin his work with categories drafted from philosophy, science, or theology. Instead, he wrote a practical treatise much like Luther's catechism, which is seldom criticized. In further revisions, to stress practicality and familiarity, he even organized the *Institutes* around the major points of the Apostles' Creed. Any expansions of the first edition should be interpreted in harmony with the author's intent, unless explicitly or implicitly denied.

Second, it should be noted that his self-understanding of his work, as enunciated in his preface, was overtly practical. In his address to the French king Francis I, he proffered an apologetic for Protestant Christianity. What could be, by the very nature of the case, more practical than the defense of a persecuted faith? Certainly such an apologetic endeavor to a nonsympathizer would not lead the reader to truncated notions and intricate theological matrixes. Rather, Calvin was practical. Although the prefatory address was based on sound scholarship, Calvin did not try to impress the king by demonstrating his sophisticated expertise. The language is simple and nontechnical. In the preface to the reader in the 1559 edition, Calvin's last will and testament within the *Institutes,* he reaffirmed that he wrote as a theologian of the church of God when he spoke of his "effort to carry out this task for God's church."[1] He stated the animating purpose of the final edition in these practical words: "God has filled my mind with zeal to spread his kingdom and to further the public good."[2] This is hardly an impractical purpose. Calvin further stated four reasons why he was finalizing this edition:[3]

1. "I have had no other purpose than to benefit the church by maintaining the pure doctrine of godliness."
2. To squelch the "rumor . . . spread abroad of my defection to the papacy."
3. "To prepare and instruct candidates in sacred theology for the reading of the divine Word."
4. To lay down a manifesto for his forthcoming and published commentaries so that he will "have no need to undertake long doctrinal discussions and to digress" in future writings.

In his own words, the purposes of the *Institutes* were to benefit the church by presenting godliness, to deny false rumors, to be an introduction for ministerial candidates to be able to better read the Bible, and to avoid further repetition in his commentaries. Calvin is preeminently practical. He wished to be brief and economic in his words. He desired to help young theologians with an introductory primer on scriptural teaching. He wished to dispel falsities about his ecclesiastical sympathies. Foremost among his purposes, however, was to write, in simple and practical terms, the pure doctrine of godliness to benefit the members of the church. Calvin did not perceive his audience to be other theologians so much as average believers. Thus he is necessarily practical and clear.

Third, as to the practical form of the *Institutes,* the organization of the final edition should be observed. The final format of Calvin's tome is centered on the four major components of the Apostles' Creed. Often used in the liturgy and known to the memory of most everyday Christians were the divisions of the creed according to the persons of the Trinity and the church. Calvin, the practical catechist, took these four familiar points of common agreement from the creed of the church and organized his writing accordingly. Thus *Institutes of the Christian Religion* is divided into four books. The first book concerns itself with God the Father. The second is concerned with his Son, our Lord, God the Redeemer. The third book discusses the work of the Holy Spirit, who applies the practical benefits and effects stemming from the grace of Christ. Finally, the fourth book concerns itself with the church. Accordingly, Calvin orients himself toward the practical man, unschooled in systematic theology. He wrote for the proletariat of the Reformation and refrained from excessive scholasticism.

Fourth, to corroborate Calvin's practical intentionality, one could note the numerous times that this theologian declined to enter the stratosphere of theological thought. Repeatedly Calvin refrained from going further than God's counsel allowed in the exploration of the mysteries of the faith. He avoided drawing inferences and implications unless biblically warranted. He did not fill the gaps of the circle of his systematic theology simply for logical consistency.

Calvin was comfortable in responding "*Agnotio*" (I don't know) to many things. He did not oversystematize his thought or sacrifice biblical mystery at the altar of epistemological exhaustiveness. In fact, he abhorred "an inordinate desire to know more than is fitting" (1.4.1) and explained that "the knowledge of God does not rest in cold speculation, but carries with it the honoring of him" (1.12.1). Even in the discussion of the order of God's decrees, Calvin refused to inquire further because it is not lawful (2.12.5). Many times much more could have been said, but Calvin bridled his pen, turning away from speculation and systemic ordering. It is as if Calvin was convinced that the scriptural truths were ordered and systemic enough. No foreign system need be superimposed. His aim was to be practical and not lose his common audience.

A final verification of Calvin's practical goal is seen from his style: he repeatedly recapitulates, reviews, and defines. His work is filled with definition, replete with the phrase "in sum," and at the outset of nearly every chapter or main section is a review. Like the best pedagogues, Calvin went to great lengths to keep the practical, nontechnical reader with him. Calvin, like any good preacher, delivered his themes with repetition—conscious that he was teaching nontheologically educated Christians.

If Marshall McLuhan is right ("the medium is the message"), then along with this practical medium, Calvin's message must be practical. His abundant reference to Scripture and precise, succinct exegesis exemplified his aim.

KNOWLEDGE

*The final goal of the blessed life rests in the
knowledge of God [which] arouses us to the
worship of God . . . and encourages us to
the hope of the future life.*

K NOWLEDGE IS AN IMPORTANT commodity for
any success. Calvin turned his attention to
such related subjects at the very beginning of his *Institutes*.
In fact, some of the opening chapters contain wisdom that
is unsurpassed; it is also distinctive in its approach. Here
Calvin answered the questions: How can a person know
himself or God? And what is the truest authority in all of
life?

In book 1, Calvin's penchant for the useful comes to
the surface immediately. He discusses two main theological topics in this opening section: how we can know God
and who God is. In this first book, Calvin presents the
knowability of God (chapters 1–5), Scripture as the
revelation of the known God (chapters 6–9), the attributes of God the Creator (chapters 10–13), including a
digression against idolatry (chapters 11–12), and the

works of God—chiefly being creation (chapters 14–15) and providence (chapter 16). The final two chapters of book 1 may be classified as practical application of the above principles, again demonstrating that Calvin was application-centered.

Throughout book 1 especially, Calvin enumerated the limitations to human knowledge as part of man's fallen condition. He realized that the best applications of knowledge would come if people realized that they could not know everything. Accordingly, in the very first paragraph, Calvin admitted our "shameful nakedness" in character and confesses "our own ignorance, vanity, poverty, infirmity, and what is more—depravity and corruption" (1.1.1), which can be remedied only by "recognizing that the true light of wisdom . . . rests in the Lord alone" (1.1.1). This depravity and "pride [are] innate in all of us" and "inclined by nature to hypocrisy" (1.1.2). This depravity in intellect is crippling, for "until Christ the Mediator comes forward to reconcile him [God] to us, no one now experiences God as Father or Author of Salvation in a favorable way" (1.2.1). Thus, for Calvin, it is impossible for anyone to know God by unaided intellect alone. The true knowledge of God is one in which faith is "joined with our earnest fear of God" and willing reverence (1.2.2). It is not a "vague general veneration for God" (1.2.2) or nebulous impassionate cognition about the Supreme Being, but the knowledge of God in verity is real reverence for him (1.2.2).

The inborn sense of divinity (*sensus deitatis*[4]) that can never be effaced is engraved upon our minds (1.3.3). This sense of divinity (not a theoretical capacity, but a *sensum*) is "naturally inborn in all, and is fixed deep within, as it were in the very marrow." For Calvin, this artifact of Eden leaves all excuse-less (1.4.1) and should lead to "true religion [which] ought to be conformed to God's will as a universal rule" (1.4.3). Furthermore, Calvin said, "The final goal of the blessed life" was not abstract rationality but "rests in the knowledge of God" (1.5.1), who is revealed to us. The true knowledge of God is a study not of theoretical constructs and objective data but of his fatherly kindness (1.5.8). In the laboratory of God's works, he can "easily be observed with the eyes and pointed out with the finger" (1.5.9) by the illumined believer. This knowledge, accessible to every practical person, both mirrors our stupidity and depravity (1.5.11) and "arouses us to the worship of God . . . and encourages us to the hope of the future life" (1.5.10). Accordingly, the knowledge of God is unavailable to the proud, the sophisticated, or the well-schooled intellect if unaided by the Holy Spirit. Yet even the simplest person may know God with the spectacles of Scripture.

Calvin excoriates the mind's capacity when he claims that, in its depravity, each mind is like a labyrinth (1.5.12), contriving "basely corrupt religion" (1.5.12). Nature and human intellect could only teach us the "confused principles as to worship an unknown god" (1.5.12). The Holy Spirit razes all human inventions and puts all human intellect in depraved parity. Thus, no intellectual superiority grants the educated a preferential advantage over the uneducated. One notes a consistent democratizing of knowledge as one of Calvin's contributions to culture. Even the common, rather nontheoretical practical folk may know God as well as the clergy or the highly educated. All are depraved in mental ability, all are rendered inexcusable (1.5.14), and only those "illumined by the inner revelation of God through faith" (1.5.14) may know him. For Calvin, the initial premise of his theology was that God is knowable, and this knowability of God is not the exclusive domain of the scholar. To know God, Calvin points out, is not as difficult and enigmatic as some theologians make it appear. It merely takes submission to his Spirit and the bespectacling of that Holy Spirit.

Calvin's doctrine of Scripture is also very easy to understand, and it is the basis of life's truest information. Those who accuse Calvin of verbosity should note that his treatment of Scripture (chapters 6–9) consumes less than thirty pages—another indication of the brevity Calvin chose while writing to practical Christians.

That Calvin had the highest possible view of Scripture can be best ascertained by reading chapters 6–7 of book 1. In a nontechnical manner he argued for the necessity (1.6.1–3), full inspiration (1.6.1; 1.7.4; 1.8.10,12), authority (1.7.1; 1.8.9–10), and full accuracy (1.6.2; 1.8.8) of Scripture. The self-authentication of Scripture (1.7.1–2; 1.8.10,13; 1.9.3) is the final apologetic for acceptance of Scripture. Calvin's foundation for the final testimony of Scripture's truthfulness is open to any who will accept God's authority, regardless of educational accomplishments.

Calvin's doctrine of Scripture is fundamentally practical as evidenced by two of his unique concepts. The first unique contribution proffered by Calvin in this area was his teaching about "the spectacles of Scripture" (cf.

1.5.14; 1.6.1; 1.14.1). Calvin asserted that the human mind was so depraved with a "great tendency to every kind of error, how great the lust to fashion constantly new and artificial religions" (1.6.3) that apart from viewing things through the eye lenses of Holy Scripture, man could possess no true knowledge of God. Again intellectual hubris is axed at its root by this theory, and common people may know God with a simple optical grant.

Second, Calvin taught that the inner testimony of the Holy Spirit was the final effective proof of Scripture's rootedness in the human heart. This *testimonium spiritu sanctu* (1.7.4–5; 1.8.11–13; 1.9.1) is not derivable from abstract theorizing but from a teachable spirit (for example, 1.8.5). Nor does it lead to pride but to a "simplicity which arouses contempt" (1.8.11) from the proud. The Spirit brings effective confirmation of the Word (1.9.3), and matters of faith rest in God's authority, not so much in towering intellects. This produces humility to be sure.

While Calvin accepted that human knowledge was limited, he also inspired and fueled a growth in knowledge. He understood both the premium and the discount to be applied to the human intellect.

HUMAN NATURE

We miserably deceive and ever blind ourselves . . . there is in us nothing that man's nature seeks more eagerly than to be flattered . . . blind self-love is innate in all mortals. . . . Nothing pleases man more than the sort of alluring talk that tickles the pride that itches in his very marrow.

*J*UST AS KNOWLEDGE SHOULD be neither over-estimated nor underestimated, Calvin understood that human nature had both boundaries and excellencies. Few leaders were bold enough to state the truth about human nature and act accordingly on this thesis: human beings are radically and persistently flawed creatures. They carry around with them a bias from nature. Calvin called that depravity, meaning that every human being—grand though any person might be—was affected by the ravages of sin. Human perfection was not a Calvinistic expectation, either in business, politics, education, or the church. His thought consistently reflected that truism, which few today comprehend.

In book 2, Calvin commences to describe our human

depravity. Returning to book 1, chapter 15, for the introduction of human nature, Calvin argued that man is a bipartite creation with both an inner (soul) and outer (body) life. Being created in the *imago dei,* man's imageness can be derived only from original nature, not deformed nature (1.15.4). For Calvin, the human soul, immediately created by God, is composed of two main faculties—the understanding and the will (1.15.7). Then in book 2, for the first five chapters, Calvin delineates the effects of the Fall.

Maintaining a distinction between the pre-Fall *imago* and the post-Fall *imago* (2.1.1), he described the depravity present in all human beings in the following ways: "We miserably deceive and ever blind ourselves [2.1.1] ... there is in us nothing of our own [2.1.1] ... nothing that man's nature seeks more eagerly than to be flattered [2.1.2] ... more pleasing is that principle that invites us to weigh our good traits [2.1.2] ... blind self-love is innate in all mortals [2.1.2] ... they so divide the credit that the chief basis for boasting and confidence remains in themselves [2.1.2]. . . . Nothing pleases man more than the sort of alluring talk that tickles the pride that itches in his very marrow [2.1.2]." Calvin cuts our proud contentions to the bone. In many other sections his views on depravity are depicted in vivid detail, all to the chagrin of defenders of innate human goodness.[5]

Calvin's brief exposition of the Fall in the Garden of Eden (2.1.4) locates the detestable crime of "pride as the beginning of all evils." Disobedience or unfaithfulness was the beginning of the Fall. Such nontheoretical categories as these formed the cradle of sin's birth; "therefore ambition and pride, together with ungratefulness, arose because

Adam by seeking more than was granted him shamefully spurned by God's great bounty" (2.1.4).

Calvin's simple definition of original sin as "a hereditary depravity and corruption of our nature, diffused into all parts of the soul" (2.1.8) breathes a realistic, if not refreshing, clarity. He further noted two things about this original sin: it is in every part of our nature and it ceases only at glorification. Man's nature is "destitute and empty of good, but so fertile and fruitful of every evil that it cannot be idle" (2.1.8), and "it is pointless and foolish to restrict the corruption" (2.1.9) only to certain parts. What sinner could avoid these charges? In fine, "the whole man is overwhelmed—as by a deluge from head to foot, so that no part is immune from sin" (2.1.9).

So thorough was the Fall that even "the foundation of our philosophy is humility" (2.2.11). Further, Calvin affirmed that "the Christian philosophy bids reason give way to, submit and subject itself to, the Holy Spirit so that the man himself may no longer live but hear Christ living and reigning within him" (2.7.1). This philosophy, far from a humanistic or rationalistic enterprise, is "that secret and hidden philosophy which cannot be wrenched from syllogisms" (3.20.1). Thus Calvin concludes that not only is our will depraved but also that reason itself was "partly weakened and partly corrupted, so that its misshapen ruins appear" (2.2.12). The only recourse, then, away from "the disease of self-love and ambition" (2.2.11) is the pursuit of humility. Mankind, incapable of finding truth apart from God, is left to vanity and absurd curiosity (2.2.11). Even though there is a measure of common grace (paragraphs 13–17 of book 2, chapter 2), unregenerated humanity cannot know God or his will. For Calvin, the knowledge of God was not a bare theoretical cognition, but it was related to that assurance of God's benevolence toward us (2.2.18). Calvin insisted that prevenient grace must be the precursor to any illumination. In summary, since men's unrenewed "minds are incapable of sufficient understanding" (2.2.21), the knowledge of God is given "only to him whose mind has been made new by the illumination of the Holy Spirit" (2.2.20).

In chapters 3 and 4 of book 2, Calvin is careful to explicate the effects of depravity on human nature. In typically Calvinistic terms (similar to Augustine's), he explained that only evil flows from our corrupt nature whereas grace creates any godliness (2.3.10). Conversion, perseverance, good works, and freedom to please God are all predicated upon God's work in us. Calvin adroitly handled objections put forward as apologies for free will (2.5.1ff.) and explained how God, Satan, and an individual may all be fully active in the same event (2.4.2). Calvin demonstrated his sensitivity to legitimate questions, and as a good pastor, he expedited his answers with directness and clarity. One is struck by how nontheoretical Calvin is in his refutations. Particularly in chapter 5 of book 2, Calvin took time to deal with individual passages of Scripture and specific questions that parishioners still ask.

A discussion of the transition from our miserable state to the redemption that God offers is provided in chapter 6 of book 2. This short chapter clearly exhibits the inner logical connection of Calvin's thought. He did not presuppose that all readers would be professional systematic theologians, looking for internal logical consistency. Instead he wrote for general readers and provided the missing links in his reasoning. After a lengthy review (2.6.1), Calvin stated the centrality and necessity for a mediator even in the Old Testament (2.6.1). He concluded that "the hope of all the godly has ever reposed in Christ alone" (2.6.3) and that even "under the law, Christ was always set before the holy fathers as the end to which they should direct their faith" (2.6.2). To believe in God, then, is necessarily to believe in Christ, and apart from Christ the saving knowledge of God does not exist (2.6.4).

If leaders have this view of human nature, it will affect their expectations of what people can truly accomplish—on the job, in the culture, or in the community. As Calvin realized, that would call for altered projections in many realms of human planning and activity.

HUMILITY

> [Augustine said,] "When a certain rhetorician was asked what was the chief rule in eloquence, he replied, 'Delivery'; what was the second rule, 'Delivery'; what was the third rule, 'Delivery'; so if you ask me concerning the precepts of the Christian religion, first, second, third, and always I would answer, 'Humility.'"

*I*T MAY SURPRISE SOME that humility is listed as a chief virtue of Calvin's character. Some would not quickly identify that because Calvin has been so persistently (and wrongfully) vilified. However, the review of his life experiences shows Calvin's humility when:

- He acknowledged his admiration for Luther and other Reformers instead of viewing them as rivals to be criticized. He was not, in other words, the only leader on the block.
- He sought to serve out of the limelight instead of going on a lecture tour.
- He left Basel quietly after composing the *Institutes,* one of the classic pieces of literature.

- He humbly exited Geneva upon his first exile and did not hurl invectives at those who treated him so badly.
- He avoided seeking to be the only visible leader, often calling to his side those with equal or greater intellectual ability.
- He gladly served in the church and did not aspire to political or corporate power.
- When he was about to pass away, he evaluated his own accomplishments with considerable modesty.
- He did not design a system of corporate governance that gave him more authority than others.

Others might not associate humility as a first virtue of strong leaders, but that can only reflect a deep misunderstanding of good leadership. Whether it is the humble leadership of a president, the quiet inspiration of CEOs who prefer to cast the spotlight on others rather than their own accomplishments, or whether it is the modesty of religious leaders, those who move people and organizations the most are normally those who also know their place, realize their limitations, and understand that they who would be first shall be last, as Jesus taught. That thesis is confirmed in the latest management study of what makes a successful company, *Good to Great.* The secret is humble leadership.

Calvin understood humility well. Indeed, he followed Augustine in viewing this as the prime virtue—almost the polar opposite of the prime vice, which was pride. One cannot help but see Calvin's emphasis on humility throughout his writings.

From the opening of the *Institutes,* Calvin noted that

human beings could not know God or themselves apart from his gracious revelation to them in the Bible. It becomes very difficult to be proud if we confess that our very capacity to know is limited and dependent on God's telling us how things work. Moreover, if we factor in the debilitating effects of the Adamic Fall, we also see how necessary it is both to turn to God as the fountain of any knowledge and also to admit our own intellectual inadequacy. To do so inspires humility.

On several occasions Calvin spoke clearly about the need for humility. In book 3, he urged his followers to lay aside private regard for themselves. Instead, they were called to divest themselves of "ambition and thirst for worldly glory" (3.7.2). The self-denial that he suggested diverts itself from vanity when we look to God in all that we do.

As soon as this humble outlook seizes the mind, it leaves no room for "pride, show, or ostentation." Calvin urged leaders not to yearn for applause but instead to seek to reflect glory to God. He frequently criticized arrogance in its many forms. He was constantly on guard against self-flattery, which "sets up a kind of kingdom in his own breast." Arguing that we merely have what God gives, Calvin knew that there was no need to betray ingratitude by acting as though we have produced all goods ourselves. The knowledge that God is at work defines how much credit a human being can take. In fact, Calvin saw it as a rule of life that if "the hand of God is the ruler and arbiter of the fortunes of all," then "instead of rushing on with thoughtless violence," we accept "good and evil with perfect regularity" (3.7.10).

Calvin even explained that the elect, if they understood things correctly, would not take pride from their standing with God. In fact, the very idea that God does not have all people saved engenders humility (3.21.1). He contended: "If election precedes that divine grace by which we are made fit to obtain immortal life, what can God find in us to induce him to elect us?" (3.22.2). Calvin knew that divine sovereignty took away "all reference to worth." Moreover, he wrote, "It is just a clear declaration by the Lord that he finds nothing in men themselves to induce him to show kindness, that it is owing entirely to his own mercy, and, accordingly, that their salvation is his own work" (3.22.6).

The whole subject of human inability and limitations is only consistent with this emphasis on humility. While discussing the moral law, Calvin noted that natural law was definitely limited in how much information it would yield. Thus, the human mind was forced to turn to revealed law if it wished to find God's truths. Calvin emphasized the utter powerlessness of human ability and called on people to "distrust our own ability" (2.8.3).

In fact, Calvin's treatment of the law also called for humility. Since neither nature nor natural law yielded all the information needed to please God, Calvin noted that the very fact that God issued law signified that "we should learn true humility and self-abasement" (2.8.1). We, in other words, may not be as proficient as we think in several areas. When one properly understands the law of God that leads to reverence instead of pride, and when one sees how difficult this is to attain, the law humbles us by charging us with both impotence and unrighteousness.

The heart and soul of Calvin's theology requires and engenders humility if it is rightly understood. Arrogance, whether it pertains to human accomplishments or presumes that eternal election applies to one who lives contrary to the ethical standards of God's election, is not a by-product of true Calvinism. Sure, distortions of Calvin's thought may yield such, but a right understanding of how God works can only lead to human humility before the grand power of almighty God. Leaders will better serve their people and organizations if they keep this balance prominent in their own lives.

Calvin's teachings and character seem to yield a particular kind of lifestyle and ethic by those who follow him. One who absorbs the character of Calvinism will exhibit a similar humility in the office, in the church, in the government, and in the home. Humility is characteristic of this great system of thought, and it was exemplified in the life of Calvin.

Nowhere was it more evident than in his comments about political leadership. Calvin's commentary on Daniel 6 virtually enshrines all the principles we are seeking to document. He displayed his suspicion of aggregate power in that commentary, to wit: "In the palaces of kings we often see men of brutal dispositions holding high rank, and we need not go back to history for this." Of the low and contemptible character of some rulers, he wrote, "But now kings think of nothing else than preferring their own panders, buffoons, and flatterers; while they praise none but men of low character." A prime example of the character expected of leaders is seen below.

It will always be deserving of condemnation when we find men selfishly pursuing their own advantage without any regard for the public good. Whoever aspires to power and self-advancement, without regarding the welfare of others must necessarily be avaricious and rapacious, cruel and perfidious. . . . The nobles of the realm [in Daniel's time] had no regard for the public good, but desired to seize upon all things for their own interests.

So, whatever the sphere, leadership should be humble and seek to serve rather than to be served. Calvin sounded the alarm about leadership that was interested in power, comfort, or self-aggrandizement. Learned humility was an antidote for those vices; it was also a virtue for leadership in general.

ETERNAL PERSPECTIVE

*To use this world as if he used it not. . . . Those
who are much occupied with the care of the body
usually give little care to the soul.*

$\mathcal{N}$OT ONLY DID CALVIN stress humility, but he
also emphasized the need to understand
the present in light of the eternal, the ultimate long-range
plan. Calvin urged his followers not to put all their hopes
in this world but constantly to compare their actions with
those that had eternal consequences. A unique advantage
is afforded to a leader with this outlook on life.

One of the sections where he does this with particular
clarity is in a part of the *Institutes* that became the first
"paperback" excerpt of his work. Chapters 6–10 of book
3 of the *Institutes* was quickly released as a freestanding
monograph as early as 1549 (a decade prior to the final
version of the *Institutes*). Englishman Thomas Broke first
translated this section into a booklet entitled *The Life and
Communication of a Christian Man.*[6] In these chapters of
practical living, the spirituality of the *Institutes* may have

reached its zenith as Calvin discussed typical Christian living. As he does so, he touches on the importance of viewing all of life from the perspective of eternity. If that distant future is allowed to define our present, things take on a different light.

It is important to observe, though, how Calvin calls for perspective in some of these chapters. This material was so important that it quickly became one of the most widely disseminated parts of his writing. After all, Calvin knew that a proper belief system (doctrine, as he called it) was not "an affair of the tongue but of the life; it is not apprehended by the intellect and memory merely . . . but is received only when it possesses the whole soul and finds its seat and habitation in the inmost recesses of the heart" (3.6.4).

He began this section by reminding his readers that one of the objects of God's saving power was to bring the ethics of believers into accord with the holiness of God (3.6.1). He also affirmed that one of the keys to life was the self-denial that could come only if people realized that they and all their abilities were owned by God. Calvin said that one "should not speak, design, or act without a view to God's glory. . . . We are not our own; therefore, neither is our reason or will to rule our acts and counsels" (3.7.1). That kind of trust in God necessarily calls for abandonment of self. For Calvin, the first step of Christian maturity was to abandon oneself and natural impulses and seek to have those replaced by a renewed mind that followed God in obedience. The "laying aside of private regard" for ourselves means that we are not our own persons but called to serve God. When we live and lead this way and learn "to look to God in everything," we are also "diverted from all vain thoughts" (3.7.2).

Once that view lodges itself in our habits, it "leaves no place for pride, show, or ostentation." On the other hand, Calvin realized that when people pursued selfishness first, they normally hit their target, and the result was vice or "a depraved longing for applause."

He also called disciples and leaders to exemplify forgiveness. Calvin thought it better to focus on people as God's creations instead of seeking to give them what we think they deserve (3.7.6). To walk in this forgiveness was also "altogether against nature." Accordingly, to love those who hate us would require God's working within us. Moreover, instead of the "frenzied desire, the infinite eagerness, to pursue wealth and honor, intrigue for power, we ought to resign the affections of our hearts" to be tamed by God.

Calvin also warned against collecting "all those frivolities which seem conducive to luxury and splendor" (3.7.8). He knew that if we pursued these pleasures, our minds would become restless and unfocused. Thus, a person should not hope for "any kind of prosperity apart from the blessing of God" (3.7.8) but must entrust all outcomes to the true Sovereign, who controls all and in whose goodness we should depend.

Leaders should learn from Calvin that the long range is always more important than the short range. Even if we have disruptions and all is not perfect in the short run, still we must trust God with all our affairs. Most would do better to trust God more than to flail mightily about trying to make things happen that never should.

That calls for self-denial, and it begins to view life as having very few accidents. If one knows that all of life is ordered by God, and that he is the kind of God who knows all, then we will "receive it with a placid and grateful mind, and will not . . . resist the government of him" who rules over all (3.7.10). This perspective of the eternal was critical for Calvin's action in so many areas.

He calls us to distrust any perfections we wish to ascribe to ourselves (3.8.2). Sometimes, the eternal perspective is needed to show us how weak and frail we are. Even prosperity can be a great challenge. When things go well, we tend to glide through life, not thinking so much about God as our own successes. To remedy that, Calvin believed that God would often bring a cross to bear. One result was that we would be weaned from focusing only on this life. Of course, hand in hand with that was the concurrent need to distrust oneself and also to "transfer your confidence to God" (3.8.3).

However, God also uses his providence to bring affliction and testing to us in order that we will trust him more and self less. Seasons of affliction are especially useful in reminding us not to store up treasures here on earth. Instead, we ought to ask ourselves often: Are my life and work giving glory to God?

Calvin realized that his disciples needed to trust in God's will and not so much their own. Nothing, whether it was poverty or exile (and he was an expert on the latter) would happen except by the will and providence of God (3.8.11). If one remembered that, he would be led to meditate more on the future.

In fact, Calvin recommended that whatever the trial before us, it would "train us to despise the present and thereby be stimulated to aspire to the future life" (3.9.1). This perspective certainly did not dampen the involvement of either Calvin or his disciples in many fields of human endeavor. Rather, it gave them a better perspective.

He warned against minds that were dazzled "with the glare of wealth, power, and honors" and called for us to be sensitive to the vanity of the present life (3.9.1). Consistency would never be achieved without this. Calvin wrote, "For we must hold that our mind never rises seriously to desire and aspire after the future, until it has learned to despise the present life" (3.9.1). That was an elementary lesson in leadership for him, and none could progress without it. We should not, in other words, be so infatuated with this life that we ignore eternity.

In one of his superb summaries, he put it this way: "If heaven is our country, what can the earth be but a place of exile. If departure from the world is entrance into life, what is the world but a sepulcher, and what is residence in it but immersion in death" (3.9.4). Rather than thinking that all of human contribution is made in one short lifetime, it would be better to view oneself as passing through, having been assigned a post or calling until the Lord transfers us.

Calvin also did not view death as the final enemy; the believer was to make "progress in the school of Christ . . . [and] look forward with joy to the day of" final resurrection (3.9.5). That is a powerful attitude adjustment, and such a worldview makes an enormous difference in the life of a leader.

Notwithstanding, Calvin did not call for his followers to

despise the present life. There was a balance to be found. We are to distrust this life but also to be thankful for it. The principle he advocated was this: we should use the gifts and things of this life for the purpose that "their author made and destined them" (3.10.1). We should neither overvalue nor undervalue what God gives. "To use this world as if he used it not," would keep us from overindulgence and vice. "Luxury," Calvin knew, could cause "great carelessness as to virtue. Those who are much occupied with the care of the body usually give little care to the soul" (3.10.4). Contentment, then, was a great indicator of good leadership and success.

Elsewhere, Calvin wisely expressed his sentiments while commenting on Luke 10:42: "Whatever believers may undertake to do, and in whatever employments they may engage, there is one object to which everything ought to be referred. In a word, we do but wander to no purpose, if we do not direct all our actions to a fixed object." Few mystics or devotional speakers will ever muster the depth of spirituality present in this paragon of Christian living. Calvin should no longer be vilified as a heartless rationalist by any reader of these chapters.

He knew that man did not live by bread alone. There was an eternity ahead, and that informed all that Calvin did and thought.

PROVIDENCE

Ignorance of providence is the ultimate of all miseries; the highest blessedness lies in the knowledge of it.

SOMETIMES LEADERS CAN EITHER perturb those around them needlessly or else drive themselves insane by taking on more than they should. One cure for that is to have leaders employ the humility explained in the previous chapter and then further apply that to accept some limitations. Logically, that makes sense only if one understands that human beings do not control their own destinies and if one embraces some theology of providence.

Providence has an original meaning that is often forgotten, namely, referring to what or how God has provided for his people. Some (particularly those who do not like the idea of God having control over their lives) think of God's providence as something that is constraining or limiting. It is, no doubt. But since it is God's providence, that must not be too bad.

Calvin certainly treated providence prominently. References to this vital truth are laced throughout nearly every chapter of the *Institutes.* Not only is it important for leaders to know that there is a power greater than their own, but this notion is so much a part of the heart of Calvin, that we cannot fully understand him if we ignore this idea.

From the outset, Calvin sought to clarify that providence was not to be confused with blind fate. Calvin viewed providence as "God's governance extended to all his works," which is "not the empty idle sort . . . but a watchful, effective active sort, engaged in ceaseless activity" (1.16.3). He denied that God idly observes from heaven, and he viewed providence as "that by which, as keeper of the keys, he governs all events. Therefore we must prove [that] God so attends to the regulation of individual events, and they all so proceed from his set plan, that nothing takes place by chance" (1.16.4). Later Calvin asserted that "nothing happens except from his command or permission" (1.16.8), and he even applies providence to an example of the death of a merchant, as he explains, "His death was not only foreseen by God's eye, but also determined by his decree. For it is not said that he foresaw how long the life of each man would extend, but that he determined and fixed the bounds that men cannot pass [Job 14:5]" (1.16.9). Thus Christians are to view "a death of this sort [as] God's providence exercised authority over fortune in directing its end" (1.16.9). For Calvin, providence is the determinative principle of all things (1.17.1), and indeed "the principal purpose of Biblical history is to teach that the Lord watches over the ways of the saints with such great diligence that they do not even stumble over a stone" (1.17.6). In sum, for Calvin, providence is essential, as well as practical, such that "ignorance of providence is the ultimate of all miseries; [whereas] the highest blessedness lies in the knowledge of it" (1.17.11).

Calvin noted the comfort of this doctrine: "Faith ought to penetrate more deeply, namely, having found him Creator of all . . . to conclude he is also everlasting Governor and Preserver—not only in that he drives the celestial frame . . . but also in that he sustains, nourishes, and cares for everything he has made, even to the least sparrow."

His view of God's providence is that it is a very practical "benefit" (1.18.1; 1.17.11). God's providence is determinative of all things (1.17.2,4,7,9), thus providing the security and confidence of the believer in the immutable decree of God (1.18.6). The final chapter of book 1 illustrates how Calvin saw the doctrine of providence as bearing immense comfort and application. He anticipated practical discrepancies (1.18.3–5) and answered those succinctly in those sections. He further spoke of the gratitude of mind, patience in adversity, and also incredible freedom from worry about the future, "which all necessarily flow from the knowledge" (1.18.7) of this providence.

Calvin was the preacher, not the rationalist, when he serially argued for providence with the rhetorical refrain, "If Joseph had stopped to dwell on his brothers' treachery. . . . If Job had turned his attention to the Chaldeans. . . . If David had fixed his eye upon Shimei" (1.17.8). Calvin argued that the absence of God's providence would leave us unbearable, hopeless, and with innumerable evils (1.17.10). Further he expected "relief" and "solace" to flow from learning to trust God's providence (1.17.11).

Book 1 concludes by extolling God's providence in these words:

> Let those for whom this seems harsh consider for a little while how bearable their squeamishness is in refusing a thing attested by clear Scriptural proofs because it exceeds their mental capacity, and find fault that things are put forth publicly, which if God had not judged useful for men to know, he would never have bidden his prophets and apostles to teach. For our wisdom ought to be nothing else than to embrace with humble teachableness, and at least without finding fault, whatever is taught in Sacred Scripture. Those who too insolently scoff, even though it is clear enough that they are prating against God, are not worthy of a longer refutation. (1.18.4)

Calvin, thus far on this subject, is assuredly not the cold logician some have caricatured him to be.

Not only did Calvin place a high emphasis on providence, but his disciples spoke of it often as well. Between the time of Calvin's Geneva and Jefferson's Virginia, one finds a consistent strand of this vocabulary. The covenantal argumentation in the Declaration of Independence shows how recurrent providence was in formulations removed centuries from Calvin.[7] Featuring a list similar to the grievance lists of earlier British Puritans, Americans confidently repudiated their English king in terms that reflected a theological tradition that was more than two centuries old.[8]

The Declaration of Independence illustrates several Calvinistic themes, not the least of which is divine providence. It refers to the transcendent basis for government in its two opening sections. As is well known, the Declaration not only roots itself in the providence of human events but also grounds the powers of government in transcultural and universal notions as provided by the "laws of Nature and of Nature's God." The phrase "of Nature's God," when coupled with the "the laws of Nature," signifies that the Declaration reaches beyond Deism and the glorification of reason. The authors could have—and many moderns likely would have—simply omitted any reference to theological notions. However, they believed such transcendent principles were essential for intelligibility by their countrymen and the best justification possible for armed resistance. A document so powerful, if its authors hoped for widespread approval, simply could not fail to reference the dominant theology of the day—thus the reference to nature's God.

The penultimate paragraph of the Declaration refers to God as "the Supreme Judge of the World," who had been frequently invoked in those terms by various American Calvinistic theologians and preachers. At the time, many sects could embrace similar language—one basis for its wide acceptance—but much of the theological phraseology in these documents is derived from Calvin's theology of providence.

The Declaration also alludes to derived powers, which stem from the consent of the governed. Many scholars now recognize that the "consent" motif was developed by Reformation advances to overthrow monopolistic powers.[9] In this context the Declaration refers to "the right of the People to alter or abolish" an existing government. It should be recalled that prior to the Reformation no such right to revolution was admitted. Despite a few medieval precursors, a full justification of the right to revolt did not arise until the writings of Calvin's disciples—Beza, Knox, Goodman, and the *Vindiciae.* Three times the Declaration referred to "tyrant" or "tyranny," leaving the clear impress of the 1579 *Vindication Against the Tyrants.* The language of biblical support for revolution did not become convincing until Calvin's disciples showed how necessary this was to resist tyranny. The American Declaration married that idea with providence.

The Declaration condemns "absolute Despotism" and reminds citizens of their duty to overthrow a king who would not submit to the law of the land. The call for George III to submit to the law was an echo of Samuel Rutherford's *Lex Rex.* Rutherford had earlier written that the king must be circumscribed by constitutions and other legal limits. The reiteration of the principle that the king is under the law, not over it, was widely accepted in early American culture because of the spread of that idea through the writings of Calvinists such as Rutherford and George Buchanan. Within Calvinism's long tradition, rebellion could never be taken up lightly. Resistance had to be intricately and exhaustively justified, and even then, it required nationwide repentance and fasting.

Separated powers and checks and balances were additional political pillars of the Declaration. Moreover, three theological ideas are stressed in its final paragraph as the moral basis for the independence of states: the "supreme Judge of the world," "divine providence," and "sacred" honor. God was not absent from the Declaration, and the understanding of God in 1776 had altered little from the theology of Calvin's Reformation.

Buttressing the Declaration, according to Douglas Kelly, are other "underlying Calvinist themes [which] permeate the founding documents." Among these are "the two-powers theory of church and state and the covenantal-conciliar thesis of limitation of governmental powers in terms of divine law. Throughout the carefully ordered separation of powers with checks and balances, deliberately restraining a more unified operation of government, we see a reflection of the Calvinist doctrine of the fallenness of human nature, with its inevitable tendency of an ascendant arm of government to abuse power in a tyrannical direction."[10]

When George Washington, who quickly became known as a leading spokesman for the principles of the Declaration, spoke of "providence," the theological history of this term cannot be ignored. Providence had been a major theme of the theological tracts and preaching by predominantly Calvinistic ministers in America for more than 150 years. Washington declared that no one had a stronger reliance on God as an "all-wise and powerful dispenser" of providence than he did. To those under his command, during the hard days of 1777, he preached hope based on providence: "A superintending Providence is ordering everything for the best. . . . [I]n due time all will end well." The next year, he ascribed credit for success thus far to "Providence," and in 1779 he wrote to his compatriots, "I look upon every dispensation of Providence as designed to answer some valuable purpose, and I," sounding almost as Calvinist as

Calvin, "hope I shall always possess a sufficient degree of fortitude to bear without murmuring any stroke which may happen."[11] This was the same Washington who uttered the sentiment that America could not be or remain a blessed nation if she jettisoned her piety.

The Calvinist rested his "political theories upon his faith in an almighty providence and found his actual institutions confirming his faith."[12] Whether appearing in Genevan edicts, English bills, colonial American charters, or New England covenants, Calvinism advanced liberty and prosperity at the same time. George Washington went so far as to ascribe, "Providence has at all times been my only dependence, for all other resources seem to have failed us."

God's providence is present in all events. His "invisible hand" indeed works in all things. He is truly sovereign over all of history. The best leaders depend on it, and Calvin knew long ago that to "avoid a senseless natural philosophy we must always start with this principle: that everything in nature depends upon the will of God, and that the whole course of nature is only the prompt carrying into effect of his orders."[13]

Calling, Work, and Labor

If we believe that all prosperous and desirable success depends entirely on the blessing of God, and that when it is wanting all kinds of misery and calamity await us, it follows that we should not eagerly contend for riches and honors; but should always have respect to the Lord, that under his auspice we may be conducted to whatever lot he has provided for us.

THE CALVINISTIC WORK ETHIC has been the subject of much study. At heart, certain historians and scholars have ascertained a historic and pervasive trend that suggests wherever the character of Calvinism roots, a resulting culture of industriousness and hard work ensues. Despite what some might think of as a divine disincentive to work (that is, salvation by grace alone), Calvinism actually encourages a very strong work ethic.

One of the societal overflows of Calvinism is the view its adherents derive about work. German social theorist Max Weber was partially correct in his analysis of this trend in his infamous 1905 work, *The Protestant Ethic and the Spirit of Capitalism*. In its baldest form, Weber argued that Calvinists confused earthly and heavenly prosperity. He interpreted them (wrongly!) as maintaining that prosperity could be interpreted as a sign of divine blessing. If true, then Calvinists would certainly be motivated to be the hardest workers. Labor and business would take on eternal significance, but one that was measured in this life by coins.

It is certainly erroneous to conclude, like Weber, that Calvinists believed material success proved they were the elect. To rebut that idea, simply consult Calvin's teaching on the eighth commandment. On the commandment that forbade stealing, he interpreted that the holding and protecting of personal property was by implication normal. In fact, that commandment, properly understood, called for believers to avoid being greedy for what others have, and it required every person to "exert himself honestly in preserving his own [property]" (2.8.45). He warned believers not to squander what God providentially gave and also to care for their neighbors' well-being. He also wrote: "This commandment, therefore, we shall duly obey if contented with our own lot, we study to acquire nothing but honest and lawful gain; if we long not to grow rich by injustice, nor to plunder our neighbor of his goods . . . if we hasten not to heap up wealth cruelly wrung from the blood of others; if we do not . . . with excessive eagerness scrape together whatever may glut our avarice or meet our prodigality. On the other hand, let it be our constant aim faithfully to lend our counsel and aid to all so as to assist them in retaining their property" (2.8.46). Had Weber factored those words into his theory, it might have been more accurate.

A prayer by Calvin stands in sharp contrast to Weber's confusion. The commonly mistaken caricature of Calvin as a crass capitalist should be contrasted with the prayer he suggested before beginning work, which is included in the 1562 Genevan Catechism. In that prayer, he led the people in asking God to bless their labor, noting that if God fails to bless it, "nothing goes well or can prosper." He prayed for the Holy Spirit to aid workers in this calling "without any fraud or deception, and so that we shall have regard more to follow their ordinances than to satisfy our appetite to make ourselves rich." Along with this, Calvin prayed that workers would also care for the indigent and that the prosperous would not become conceited. He prayed that God would diminish prosperity if he knew the people needed a dose of poverty to return them to their senses. Far from callousness toward the less fortunate, Calvin prayed that workers would "not fall into mistrust," would "wait patiently" on God to provide, and would "rest with entire assurance in thy pure goodness."[14]

He also asserted that any endeavor that ceased to have charity as its aim was diseased at its very root (2.8.50). Elsewhere, Calvin warned that luxury could incite great problems and produce "great carelessness as to virtue" (3.10.4).

Calvin clearly explains clearly his view of the relationship between prosperity and work:

> If we believe that all prosperous and desirable success depends entirely on the blessing of God, and that when it is wanting all kinds of misery and calamity await us, it follows that we should not eagerly contend for riches

and honors, trusting in our own dexterity and assiduity, or leaning on the favor of men, or confiding in any empty imagination of fortune; but should always have respect to the Lord, that under his auspice we may be conducted to whatever lot he has provided for us. (3.7.9)

In that same section, lest Calvin be misunderstood, he called for a "curb to be laid on us" to restrain "a too eager desire of becoming rich, or an ambitious striving after honor." Thus, Calvin's understanding of hard work did not necessarily equate success or prosperity with divine blessing. His views, though, did have a persistent tendency of ennobling various areas of human calling and labor. Business, commerce, and industry were all elevated by Calvin's principles, and those who adhered to them became leaders of modern enterprise. Weber and others are correct to identify that Calvinism dignified work and callings of many kinds.

One of the culture-shaping aspects of Calvin's leadership was his emphasis on the sacredness of ordinary vocations. Prior to his time, many workers felt little sense of calling unless entering the priesthood. Due primarily to the priestly emphasis of the Roman Catholic Church, prior to the Reformation, "calling" or vocation was restricted to ecclesiastical callings. Calvin taught that any area of work— farming, teaching, governing, business—could be a valid calling from God, every bit as sacred as serving as a minister. This was a radical change in worldview, which would ultimately alter the world's economies.

The formation of the Genevan Academy under Calvin called for general education (not only religious studies), and it provided for studies in law, medicine, history, and education. Calvin and other Reformers helped retire the sacred-secular distinction. He realized that a person could serve God in any area of labor and glorify him. Calvin counseled with many leaders, entrepreneurs, printers, and merchants, and he did not revile any lawful calling. The character of Calvinism ennobles all good work.

His comments on the fourth commandment underscores the dignity of work also. Just as God commanded people to rest on the seventh day, so the Lord expected them to work the rest of the days. Work was vital for all people made in God's image, and for Calvin, thus, all callings were important. His doctrine of work is further underscored—not to mention widely popularized—by his explanation of the fourth commandment: to rest on one day out of seven but work *the other six.*

For our own times, we can glean much about a right view of work if we explore Calvin's views on social welfare. Calvin and his colleagues believed that work should be required of all who received subsidy. Jeannine Olson comments:

There was an effort in Geneva to maintain the image of the Bourse Francaise as a fund to help people who were considered worthy, rather than as an institution that indiscriminately aided everyone. The funds were intended for those who were in genuine need, particularly those who were ill or handicapped. The deserving poor were numerous in this age before modern medicine or surgery, when a simple hernia or poorly aligned broken bone could render one unable to work. The limited funds of the Bourse were not

intended for derelict poor, those who are considered unwilling to work, lazy and slothful vagrants and vagabonds,
to use the popular English terminology of the era. The assumption that welfare recipients should be worthy of aid
had long been common in Europe, but the definition of
worthiness varied from one milieu to another.[15]

There were times and instances in the records of the
bourse (a fund for poor immigrants) when the deacons
would not give assistance to individuals because of lazi-
ness. Social relief did not call for subsidies that discouraged
personal industry and responsibility. Recipients of subsidies
from the church were expected to uphold Christian standards of morality; thus, the deacons attempted to use the
bourse as a means of discipline and encouragement.

In his *Commentaries,* Calvin set forth in greater detail
the work requirements for those being cared for by the
church's deacons. Of 2 Thessalonians 3:10, Calvin commented, "When, however, the Apostle commanded that
such persons should not eat, he does not mean that he
gave commandment to those persons, but forbade that the
Thessalonians should encourage their indolence by supplying them with food. . . . Paul censures those lazy drones
who lived by the sweat of others, while they contribute no
service in common for aiding the human race."[16]

In many respects, the experiment in welfare in Geneva
offers a clinic in what may happen when welfare is conformed to biblical impulses. Work is a necessary compo-
nent.

Moreover, Elsie McKee independently corroborates the
previously noted "work ethic" as she explains one differ-

ence between the Reformed and Romanist approaches to welfare: "From this Protestant viewpoint, Roman Catholic almsgiving to healthy beggars who could work seemed indiscriminate; it was not charity but irresponsible stewardship. The new valuation of work—not as a means of earning or even proving salvation but as an expression of gratitude and responsible use of God-given talents—was clearly a critical factor in the prohibition of begging among Protestants."[17]

In a sermon on 1 Timothy 3:8–10, Calvin suggested the early church's compassion was the canon by which to measure current Christianity: "When there were neither lands nor possessions nor what is called property of the church, it was necessary that each give his offering and from that the poor be supplied. If we want to be considered Christians and want it to be believed that there is some church among us, this organization must be demonstrated and maintained." Later in that same sermon he enjoined, "Now when that property has been distributed as it ought, if that still does not meet all needs, let each give alms privately and publicly, so that the poor may be aided as is fitting."

Calvin, whose name is not always immediately identified with compassionate advocacy for welfare to the poor, on one occasion rhetorically asserted, "Do we want to show that there is reformation among us? We must begin at this point, that is, there must be pastors who bear purely the doctrine of salvation, and then deacons who have the care of the poor."

From his writings on calling, the need for work, and the value of labor, the character of Calvinism shines clearly.

Calvin understood the "body of Christ" imagery of 1 Corinthians 12 very well and applied it to all vocations. He knew that church and society would be better off if people pursued different callings and did all work for the glory of God. Good leaders will remember this and seek to encourage workers to use their gifts wherever God calls them. And no lawful endeavor should be shunned. That calls for hard work, thorough preparation, and excellence in productivity. Calvin agreed with Paul in the New Testament: we do all to the glory of God. The great composer Johann Sebastian Bach signed each of his original scores with the initials "SDG," which stood for the Latin phrase *sola dei Gloria* ("to God alone be the glory"). He knew the character of Calvinism and applied it to his craft. Some of the finest Christians in history have also applied the lordship of Christ to their own vocations and served as leaders in fields for the glory of God.

History

*Indeed, the principal purpose of biblical history is
to teach that the Lord watches over the ways of
the saints with such great diligence that they do
not even stumble over a stone.*

I N THE FIRST PART of this work, we noted how
much Calvin depended on earlier scholars to
show support for his thoughts. Calvin, unlike many who
may think more highly of themselves than they ought, did
not seek to reinvent every wheel. In fact, even his innovations (such as the Company of Pastors or the Academy),
which seemed groundbreaking for the time, were virtually always informed by the best practices of the past.
Leaders who are most productive are normally those who
invoke the good and avoid the bad practices of the past.

Calvin relied heavily on the sound teaching that preceded him. Never afraid to associate with the likes of Augustine, he was also unafraid of challenging the preexisting
Roman Catholic tradition. What made the difference was
whether or not a source fully agreed with Scripture. If con-
sonant with God's Word and ways, Calvin was not hesitant to embrace an earlier historical figure. Not only did

this provide some amount of protection from various extremisms—since normally only sound ideas persist—but this was also an expression of humility; Calvin was not so proud as to believe that everything had to be original with him.

In his *Golden Booklet of the Christian Life,* Calvin referred to his respect for those Christian writers who had gone before him: "My intention, however, in the plan of life which I now propose to give . . . must be sought in the writings of others, and particularly in the Homilies of the Fathers" (3.6.1). While Augustine might be the first church father among equals, there were many others whom Calvin thought worthy of reference. Without a positive view of history as a worthy instructor, he never could have done this. Ever the practical thinker, he emphasized the proper role of history: "Indeed, the principal purpose of biblical history is to teach that the Lord watches over the ways of the saints with such great diligence that they do not even stumble over a stone" (1.17.6).

At one point in his commentary on Romans (for example, 4:23–24), he referred to the frequently cited dictum that "history is the teacher of life, as the gentiles truly say." Other leaders—ranging from Lord Bolingbroke, who said, "History is philosophy teaching by example," to Calvin's own disciple, Theodore Beza—affirmed the same important truth. In fact, Calvin's disciples developed a strong tendency toward viewing history itself as a teacher.

Widely esteemed as one of the premier commentators on Scripture in his day, Beza reflected Calvin's tutelage when he confessed in the preface to his commentary on

Job (1587): "I am minded to expound the *histories* of Job, in which . . . there are many dark and hard places, insomuch as I must here of necessity sail, as it were, among the rocks; and yet I hope I shall not make any shipwreck."[18]

Beza's awareness of the past, along with its complexity, led him to a humble assessment of his own ability as an exegete—a humility that is a proper part of a Calvinistic ethos. The two chief interpretive options for Beza on this ancient book were: (1) a historically informed hermeneutic ("the histories of Job"), or (2) a shipwreck resulting from an unawareness of the previous interpretations of Job. In this instance, Calvin's disciple saw the choice between a hermeneutic with history and a hermeneutic with a pride of discovery (hubris) but capable of shipwreck. He chose the former and, with an appreciation for the history of interpretation, not only found a sounder platform but also evidenced much more humility than many moderns. Many today would also profit from a history-induced humility.[19]

Calvin understood that many enterprises could be vastly strengthened by an improved working knowledge of history. Whether in the fields of science, religion, economics, or education, if one consults history, not only will sounder practices result, but humility will be a by-product as well. In terms of a recipe: history added to hermeneutic will yield more humility or less hubris.

Leaders who approach an issue or a challenge devoid of familiarity with what has gone before will invariably be less progressive—necessarily having to dedicate much time to basic rediscoveries that others have already documented.

They will also be prouder of their eventual discoveries. Such pride of discovery, while exhilarating and fulfilling, is also a fine fit with the self-centeredness and egotism that so often characterize our age and various managerial cultures. If, like Calvin, however, we adopt a humbler position (holding out the possibility that prior thinkers may have been equal to or greater than ourselves), then we can more readily benefit from their previous foundation. As a result, we will also arrive at a more sober assessment of our own originality. Progress and humility go hand in hand, but hubris and static conditions characterize the approach that arrogantly and automatically discounts those who have preceded us. A preferred model, therefore, will value history as an interpretive variable over the hubris associated with claims to original or novel discovery.

For those who seek to avoid replication, biblical interpretations need not be ignored by successive generations nor rediscovered by the alternating generations. We could profit by studying past interpretive efforts and attempting to mold our inchoate exegesis after the progress of our spiritual ancestors. The same may be true for scientific progress. Frequently, the greatest heuristic value is found in an approach that embraces the validity of history and does not limit scientific knowledge to individual scientists or their experiences. The better part of wisdom is to rule out inefficacious modes of interpreting, with the past showing which routes were dead ends.

We can either benefit from those who have already pioneered some of these paths for us or we can disregard their work, presuming that we are sufficient to discover all biblical truth by ourselves in our own generation. A rediscovery of the interpretations from good leaders of the past is needed in our own day. Such giants could teach us much. The choice, in the end, may be between hubris or humility.

As George Santayana would later aver—or Calvin might have if he'd written it first—leaders who fail to learn the errors of past are doomed to repeat them. That is especially true in any endeavor that involves human beings.

Calvin would likely agree with the modern philosopher Michael Oakeshott, who asserted in the political realm that it might be more profitable for us to "prefer the familiar to the unknown, to prefer the tried to the untried, fact to mystery, the actual to the possible, the limited to the unbounded, the near to the distant, the sufficient to the superabundant, the convenient to the perfect, present laughter to utopian bliss."[20] This is the humble option: a view of life with history, rather than the hubris of the Enlightenment.

This led Calvin and his disciples to value continuity and tradition. Although some who are not thoroughly familiar with Calvin perceive him to be a revolutionary, he was actually far too moderate in temperament and theory to be classified as a true revolutionary. He was more in favor of gradual change, not wishing to reject good notions or institutions from the past. He did not, for example, call for the overthrow of the church because it was moribund when he found it; he called for the reform of the Roman Catholic Church. Neither did he suggest the overthrow of most political structures, but instead he called for magistrates to rule justly and operate as God called them to govern. Calvin was more leery of radical overhauls than he was sure that lasting reform might take some time.

Because he valued the past, he also had a good view of tradition. Holding to existing customs brought considerable stability, and Calvin valued that. He was not interested in teaching by shock-value; at times, he was quite happy to allow reform to proceed at a slow pace. That, too, may be an example for today's leaders.

Calvin, though calling for changes in many areas, realized that providence-provoked patience and history-induced humility could only value continuity and tradition. He did not think it wise to change too much at once. His view of history helped him in that area.

SUCCESSION

*I never approved of deciding our cause by
violence and arms.*

$\mathcal{G}$ENEVA'S INTERNATIONAL MONUMENT TO the Reformation features a figure largely unknown to Americans and virtually uncredited for his contributions to Western political theory. This limestone figure, however, tells us much about the pulse of Calvinism. The chief lieutenant of Calvin, in both theology and polity, was Theodore Beza (1519–1605), often described as the most eloquent spokesman of the Reformation. His extension of the logic of Calvin's political views was accelerated by a crisis in 1572, which also became a vital turning point for subsequent republican theory. How Calvin groomed and prepared his successor is a part of the character of Calvin's work.

While it is true that some of Calvin's writings contained the seeds that would later bloom into resistance theory, it was only after his death that the writings of

Beza[21] and other Huguenot victims of oppression fully coalesced. When the fiery writings of John Knox and other Calvinistic Scots were added to the mix, a major political innovation resulted, namely, basing lawful resistance against totalitarianism on theological grounds.

One key ingredient of the success of Calvin was how he passed on his mantle to Beza, a person who was highly gifted and uniquely prepared to continue the work. The two worked closely together for fifteen years.

Beza was born on June 24, 1519, in Vezelay, France. He was the seventh child in the family and spent his formative years in Paris under the care of his father's brother, Nicholas. From 1522 to 1528, Nicholas Beza was one of the councillors in the Parisian Parliament, so Theodore was reared amid aristocratic wealth and privilege. In 1528 the young man was sent to Orleans to study with Melchior Wolmar, one of the leading classical teachers of his day. Wolmar had been Calvin's teacher at Orleans in 1532 and 1533, and Calvin dedicated his commentary on 2 Corinthians to this master teacher.

In 1539 Beza (at the age of twenty) completed his law degree at Orleans and moved to Paris to pursue a legal career. However, his interest in the classics led him to his first book, a plaudit-winning collection of poems dedicated to Wolmar. Beza's brilliance may have been superior to Calvin's, and his eloquence was an unmatched asset for the next generation of Reformation leadership. Even his adversaries extolled him as refined, attractive, polished, and cultured, a formidable opponent indeed.[22]

After Beza's conversion in 1548, he sought refuge in Geneva, arriving at a particularly trying juncture of Calvin's life, for Calvin's wife would die in 1549. Although few scholars have published studies of the role of Idelette in Calvin's life, one of his letters to a colleague exhibits his loss that Beza could not fill: "I have lost the excellent companion of my life, who, if misfortune had come upon us, would have gladly shared with me, not merely exile in wretchedness, but death itself. . . . She has always been a faithful helper in my work. Never have I suffered the least hindrance from her."[23]

Upon the urging of Peter Viret,[24] Beza accepted the call to become professor of Greek at the nearby academy in Lausanne. During his thirties he worked closely with Calvin, finally accepting a call to teach at the Geneva Academy in 1558. During his Lausanne years, with attendance at his academy skyrocketing to seven hundred,[25] Beza lectured on Romans and 1 and 2 Peter. He completed, at Calvin's urging, the translation of the Psalms begun by Clement Marot. With his strong background in poetry and classical languages, Beza was uniquely suited for this contribution to Reformation worship and doctrine. Calvin recognized an excellent heir. His cultured deportment and gentleness were among the reasons Calvin chose him to be his successor.

As an expert orator and perhaps the most noteworthy theologian other than Calvin, during the late 1550s, Beza began to be useful as a diplomat for the Calvinist movement. His eloquence and theological mastery proved to be a useful resource to the various Reformed assemblies during the 1560s as they responded to critics and formulated their own views.[26] His engaging and sophisticated expressions belie the caricature of Beza as a pedant.[27]

Of course, much of Beza's diplomatic career stemmed from Calvin's own efforts in this area. Few modern theologians have had the amount of political involvement that Calvin had. He consistently received briefings on affairs of state, regularly corresponded with officials at the highest levels, and tirelessly watched for opportunities to spread his political gospel.[28] Indicative of his correspondence, he dedicated his commentary on the Catholic epistles to the English king Edward VI, his commentary on Isaiah to Queen Elizabeth, and his commentary on Hebrews to the Polish king Sigismund. Some of his former students even briefed him on political developments after they left Geneva, and Calvin's advice extended throughout European Christendom. Calvin sought to provoke political change through his writings rather than through social upheaval. He pleaded in a letter on October 1, 1560: "I never approved of deciding our cause by violence and arms."[29] The result, as one non-Protestant scholar put it, is that "in the political domain, Calvinist ideas are at the origin of the revolution which from the eighteenth to the nineteenth centuries gave birth and growth to the parliamentary democracies of Anglo-Saxon type."[30] Beza would continue that political theology of action until his death in 1605.

Calvin began passing the baton five years before his death. In June 1559, Beza was installed as the founding rector of the Genevan Academy—another instance of Calvin's intentionally bypassing a position of prominence and providing a junior colleague with an opportunity to mature. After Calvin's death, Beza continued to teach Greek and biblical studies to the Geneva Academy's second-generation Reformers, who later carried the work of Calvin into the seventeenth century.

In addition to his responsibilities at the Academy, he also pastored one of the city's four churches, which flourished under his capable ministry. Moreover, Beza was fully involved in the Presbytery and was one of the Company of Venerable Pastors in Geneva from 1559 to 1564 while Calvin was its moderator.

Calvin took Beza into his confidence and discussed the most urgent matters and strategy for the Reformed movement's continued vitality. In his farewell to the Presbytery of Geneva in 1564, Calvin confirmed Beza's selection "to hold my place" and, after asking for support and counsel for his successor, Calvin said of Beza: "Of him I know that he has a good will and will do what he can."

Beza was immediately elected moderator of the Presbytery by the city council, a post that he maintained until 1580 when he voluntarily retired. During those sixteen years, he provided orderly leadership and transition for the Reformation in Geneva. He was a gracious host to the thousands of exiled Protestant scholars and leaders welcomed into Geneva's sanctuary.

Beza preached regularly and continued his lectures to students amid his other duties. His experience with the French church heightened his awareness of the political ramifications for the Christian faith. And he foresaw the need to extend Calvin's principles even further. His two primary political works were *Concerning the Punishment of Heretics by the Civil Magistrate* (1554) and *The Rights of Magistrates* (1574).[31] He was also widely published as a Bible commentator and was an early textual critic.

Beza's political impression was as lasting during the six-teenth century as any of Calvin's other disciples'.[32] His request was to be buried, like Calvin, in a nondescript grave at Geneva's Plain Palais, but a rumored plot to carry his bones to Rome as a Counter-Reformation trophy convinced the Genevan magistrates to order his body laid to rest in St. Pierre's cloister.[33]

When Beza died in 1605, although he had been a counselor to numerous governors[34] and "the incontestable head of a powerful party, and the spiritual director of a republic,"[35] he left behind little fortune. He had managed his family's wealth, which included rental quarters for students and boarders, but he occasionally had to liquidate assets from his library to pay his bills. When he died, Geneva's chief magistrate urged that "there might ever subsist a good understanding between Church and State. . . . All should walk in the footsteps of those two great men, John Calvin and Theodore Beza, who had so happily served the interests of the commonwealth."[36] If civic monuments are any reflection of abiding respect,[37] then respect for Beza is mirrored in both the 1857 Monument of the Escalade, featuring a relief of Beza praying,[38] and the 1917 International Monument to the Reformation in Geneva's old town.

Beza's writings had an impact far beyond the Lac Leman region. A well-known German Lutheran, Valentine Andreae, visiting Geneva after Beza's death and a half century after Calvin's, praised the city for "the perfect institut[ion] of a perfect republic." Armed with moral accountability, they had virtually eliminated the vices so characteristic of other places. Andreae claimed that, if not for his commitment to the Lutheran tradition, he "would have forever been chained to that place [Geneva] by the agreement in morals, and I have ever since tried to introduce something like it into our churches."[39]

Wherever the Huguenots immigrated, they bore Beza's strong Calvinism in their hearts as well as in their enterprise.[40] Shaped by the horrific massacre on St. Bartholomew's Day, this Bezan Calvinism blazed a trail of resistance to tyrants. At the same time, it frequently expressed its political theory in the language of Scripture, so esteemed in its day. Before Americans adopted Beza's themes, however, Europeans beyond Geneva extended and adapted his teachings.

Calvin's chosen successor continued the master's work well. Good leaders begin planning for their successions as soon as possible. And Beza had to be prepared to refine Calvin's work shortly after the Reformer's death in 1564. Calvin's care and foresight to make such preparations paid dividends for generations.

166 🙞

TRAGEDY AND OPPORTUNITY

For as often as the commandment of God and men are directly opposed one against another, this rule is to be perpetually observed; that it is better to obey God than men.

*C*ALVIN WOULD NEED TO have his successor well prepared because the challenges ahead would be daunting. One thing that Calvin's followers had to learn was to refine their political thought. Theodore Beza would be in the vanguard of that. Much of his political thought, in fact, was shaped by the 1572 St. Bartholomew's Day massacre of the Huguenots.[41] Two years after that genocide, Beza's *The Rights of Magistrates* (1574) justified armed resistance against a king if led by intermediating magistrates.

The 1572 *St. Bartholomewsnacht* was a turning point in the development of Western political thought and a summons for Calvinism to develop greater application than it had hitherto pioneered. After hearing of the brutal slaughter of the St. Bartholomew's Day massacre,[42] Beza, to degrees that Calvin never faced, was forced both to reconsider and also to refine the Calvinist doctrine of political resistance.[43]

Luring many Huguenot leaders to Paris for a wedding in August 1572, the French king Charles IX and Catherine de Medici initiated a gory massacre that began at 2:00 a.m. on Sunday, August 24. During the next three days alone, according to John Foxe (who sought refuge in Basel), rampaging marauders killed more than ten thousand people in Paris, their Protestant faith serving as the only indictment.[44] In addition to Paris, terrified Protestants throughout France sustained the following death tolls:

- 2,000 in Poitiers[45] in one day
- 1,000 at Orleans
- 800 at Lyon (300 in the archbishop's house)
- 500 at Rouen
- 264 at Boutdeauz
- 200 at Toulouse
- 100 at Main.[46]

The cold-blooded murder of sixty thousand French Huguenots[47] in a single month forced infant Calvinism to face the horror and, now, the inescapable menace of the very depravity that Calvin's writings had been implying. So if Beza extended the logic of Calvin's thought further than Calvin had, he was warranted in moving ahead with a more consistent version of resistance theory. Calvin had begun this shift after the early tensions in France (exhibited in his 1561 commentary on Daniel), but the devastation and cruelty a decade later unquestionably justified and prodded the thoughts of Beza and others.

Beza came to realize, after Calvin's death, that absolute submission to a governor, especially if that governor tyrannically slaughtered thousands, was not God's plan. Instead, he and others began to complete Calvin's earlier tenets. One result was that civil governors now had to be seen as deserving qualified submission. Their authority, in other words, was and must be limited.

Beza theologically defined the limited powers of government: a ruler's power was neither infinite nor unconditional. If a ruler was a tyrant, then resistance might be allowed. And in cases of such oppression, the intermediating magistrates were "duty-bound to repress these tyrants who act wildly and commit outrages. If they do not do so, then they shall answer for their disloyalty before the Lord, as traitors to their own country." For Beza, such an overthrow was never to be violent ("the rule is steadfast and perpetual"). He reminded his audience that, whenever they could not obey the commands of rulers without "offending the majesty and despising the authority of the King of kings and the Lord of lords," then they must not participate in revolution. A believer must obey God above all and not acquiesce to government-ordered ill behavior under the guise of civic obedience. This was a striking advance in political theory that radically shaped the modern world.

Beza, like Calvin, balanced these sentiments by noting that *private* citizens were not to overthrow the magistrate, even if the rulers were tyrants, "for that is a far different thing from refusing to yield obedience unto impious or unjust laws [edicts]." In addition, he called on Christians to avoid contentiousness while not forfeiting the right to defend themselves against a tyrant. He wrote that those who suggested that it was unlawful for Christians to seek and maintain their rights by civil pleas were deceived. He concluded: "As often as the Magistrate commands anything that is repugnant either to the worship which we owe unto God, or to the love which we owe unto our neighbor, we cannot yield obedience thereunto with a safe conscience. For as often as the commandment of God and men are directly opposed one against another, this rule is to be perpetually observed; that it is better to obey God than men."[48]

Others went so far as to urge that overthrow was mandatory in these cases.[49] Of course, most of these views, as in Scotland and England, depended on the notion that God had established a religious covenant with a nation, which implied a continuing corporate responsibility to a previous covenant.

If one senses progress in thought on the topic of restraining government by comparing this work with Calvin's earliest discussions, the likely explanation for the development resides in the reaction to the St. Bartholomew's Day massacre.[50] This stunning slaughter virtually extinguished a politico-religious movement—French Protestant churches had grown from zero to 2,150[51] in the generation prior to 1572—forcing Calvinists like Beza (who had close contacts and interaction with the French churches) to extend the logic of their principles.[52] The resulting evolution moved from the possibility of lawful resistance to the moral obligation to oppose evil rulers.

This massacre was both the coming of age and a fault point for Calvinistic political theory. Calvin and Beza had both discouraged rebellion and recommended support of one's rulers if at all possible. But with the treacherous slaughter and virtual extinction of Reformed religion in France, Beza led efforts to reassess the theory. In so doing, he proved that modifications within limits not only did not harm the theoretical foundations of Calvinism but rather improved its effectiveness. The result was that what once seemed radical (the suggestions of Knox, Peter Martyr Vermigli, and John Ponet) became the norm for Calvinists. Beza thus transformed Calvinism and normalized resistance to evil governments on biblical bases.

These developments went beyond situations that Calvin had faced; it is a tribute to Calvin's mentoring that Beza so ably addressed these life-and-death challenges. The resistance theory that grew out of this tragedy is an acknowledgment to the adaptability of Calvin's thought.

Preparation of one's successors, unless the movement is a personality cult, is essential. No leader in action should minimize its strategic value. In Beza's case, after serving so faithfully as Calvin's understudy, when crisis arose, he responded to tragedy by proposing better measures—ones that were consistent with the character of Calvinism.

FRIENDSHIP

There were few men who developed as many friendships as he and who knew how to retain not only the admiration, but also the personal affection of these friends.

ONE DEFENDER OF CALVIN noted that it would be impossible for a man to be so dearly loved at his death if he had been a monster all his life. Not only was Calvin praised at his death, but his many friends embraced similar ideas and sought to carry those on.

A study of Calvin's letters reveals a pattern of friendship and collegiality. He certainly did not view himself as the only individual involved in these matters of reform. One such study is *The Humanness of John Calvin* by Richard Stauffer.[53] For "the other side of the story," one should consult this small work. In the foreword to that monograph, J. T. McNeill chronicles how he had been led to question the "hearsay" about Calvin. As McNeill read Calvin's letters, he found that Calvin was vividly humane, associated with rich and poor alike, exhibited a sturdy loyalty to friends, and demonstrated gentleness, warmth, tenderness, generousness, hospitality, and other well-attested virtues.[54]

Stauffer describes the "calumny" Calvin has received from his enemies and also how he has "been misunderstood and misinterpreted by his great-grandchildren."[55] Another historian noted that no other Reformer generated more personal loyalty than Calvin. Emile Doumergue[56] expressed it this way: "There were few men who developed as many friendships as he and who knew how to retain not only the admiration, but also the personal affection of these friends."[57] Abel Lefranc articulated the same sentiment this way: "The friendships which he inspired . . . among his teachers as well as among his colleagues, are strong enough testimonies to the fact that he knew how to combine with his serious and intense commitment to work, an affability and graciousness which won everyone over to him."[58]

Calvin was a more sociable man than sometimes thought. He was a habitual letter writer, corresponding with jurists, governors, common people, and ministers. These letters provide glimpses into the real Calvin. In writing he could refer to the affection he had for his teacher Melchior Wolmar, and at the same time he could mourn the passing of a friend as so staggering as to be burdened with grief.

The character and impulse of Calvinism impacted the world through a fraternity of devoted and committed friends. American theologian Douglas Kelly confirms that the Calvinistic tradition wielded influence far beyond Switzerland and France. Perhaps its most enduring legacy is its emphasis on the derived sovereignty of the people and the right to resist tyranny, a teaching that "would pass (indirectly and combined with ideas of very different parentage) into late seventeenth-century English political theories of human rights . . . [and] American debates on law and government."[59] No individual could sow so many seeds; these victories were scored by a team of colleagues.

Calvin was the premier but certainly not the only Protestant theorist. Other Reformers in his circle of friendship briskly articulated theologies of the state, with the following seminal works appearing in rapid succession in less than thirty years: Martin Bucer's *De Regno Christi* (1551), John Ponet's *A Short Treatise of Political Power* (1556), Christopher Goodman's *How Superior Powers Ought to Be Obeyed of Their Subjects; And Wherein They May Lawfully by God's Word Be Disobeyed and Resisted* (1558), Peter Viret's *The World and the Empire* (1561), Francois Hotman's *Francogallia* (1573),[60] Theodore Beza's *De Jure Magisterium* (1574), George Buchanan's *De Jure Regni Apud Scotos* (1579), and Hubert Languet's *Vindiciae Contra Tyrannos* (1579). Each of these works legitimized the idea of citizen resistance against improper governmental expansion. Interestingly, this bulk of political thought emanated from a tight circle of friends, most of whom were in contact with Calvin. It is hard to attribute such robust similarity of thought to accident.

Calvin's friendship with Beza was a model of fraternity. With all the heady intellectual issues of the day, what greatly impressed Beza was Calvin's personal support and camaraderie. Thus Beza (and others) wrote about the friendship that Calvin shared with those around him. Calvin epitomized the modern notion of collegiality, and he was prudent enough to attract brilliant friends. Once when Beza was ill, Calvin wrote about the "fresh fear" that "overwhelmed him with deep sorrow" upon learning of his colleague's sickness. He was "staggered . . . already weeping for him . . . grieved" and afraid of the loss that might come to the church and to him personally.

There were many other friends besides Beza. The consensual strains of thought that flowed through the literary veins of Bullinger, Bucer, Viret, and Calvin—soon to be supplemented by Knox, Beza, Hotman, and Junius Brutus—formed an intellectual tradition with Geneva at its epicenter and Calvin as its father. His friendship with these scholars would prove to be the glue that held the movement together in its delicate infancy. J. H. Merle D'Aubigne noted this mutual interchange of ideas in these words: "The catholicity of the Reformation is a noble feature in its character. The Germans pass into Switzerland; the French into Germany; in latter times men from England and Scotland pass over to the Continent, and doctors from the Continent into Great Britain. The Reformers in the different countries spring up almost independently of one another, but no sooner are they born than they hold out the hand of fellowship. . . . It has been an error, in our opinion, to write as hitherto, the history of the Reformation for a single country; the work is one."[61] Calvin's associates served to stabilize and standardize an international movement.

Calvin, Farel, and Viret were called "the tripod" or "three patriarchs," so well known was their friendship. In Calvin's commentary on Titus, he wrote that he did "not believe that there have ever been such friends who have lived together in such a deep friendship in their everyday style of life in this world as we have in our ministry."[62] Even when there were strong disagreements, Calvin was a paradigm of friendship. When these Reformers experienced family struggles or joys, Calvin shared those in his letters. His letters to various Reformers are full of sympathy and quick to illustrate a healthy loyalty. Moreover, his correspondence with refugees shows his great compassion. He even built bridges to Luther's disciples after the German leader denounced him. Calvin also translated a theological work by Luther's chief disciple, Philipp Melanchthon.

What began in Geneva with a multinational cadre of colleagues, all seeking to extend the "republic of Christ," grew into a movement that featured theology, ideas, and a unique view of history far surpassing the city of Geneva alone.[63] With their confidence in God's providence and divine election, this circle of friends urged civil rulers to adopt their religious views and political practices "holding that no frontiers, no boundaries, no limits should confine the zeal of pious princes in the matter of God's glory and of the reign of Christ."[64] To some, their theology of resistance would appear politically subversive.

At times, as in any historic era, there were also disruptions of friendships. Calvin had to assist church members with broken relationships and deal with friction among the Protestant Reformers. Calvin learned to encourage others around him, and he delegated certain responsibilities to his associates.

Richard Stauffer concluded that Calvin was far from "the isolated hero or the lonely genius that has often been pictured. Throughout his career, he had relationships with friends who show him unfailing affection and indefatigable devotion. If he exerted such charm, it is certainly because he himself had been such an incomparable friend. . . . For the devotion which one showed him, he paid the tribute of unswerving loyalty."[65] After Calvin's death it would become the task of his colleagues to spread the word.

Many Counselors

Without mutual counsel, plans go awry,
But in the multitude of counselors they are
established.

—Proverbs 15:22

O NE OF THE DISTINGUISHING features of Calvin's life and work is the emphasis away from monarchism in all its forms. Whether it occurs in the modern boardroom or in the church, Calvin believed that—due to our fallen human nature—it would ordinarily be wise for crucial decisions to have the best insight and opinion of *many* informed leaders. Calvin knew that the Old Testament assertion "There is wisdom in many counselors" was applicable to leadership in the home, the church, and the state. He seemed to be constitutionally opposed to dictatorial rule. Consider these other proverbs, and much of Calvin's grasp of structure and decision making comes into clear view:

- "Where there is no counsel, the people fall; but in the multitude of counselors there is safety." (Proverbs 11:14)

- "Without counsel, plans go awry, but in the multitude of counselors they are established." (Proverbs 15:22)
- "For by wise counsel you will wage your own war, and in a multitude of counselors there is safety." (Proverbs 24:6)

Calvin circled his ministerial advisers around himself regularly and valued their collective input. And when it came to explaining the New Testament, Calvin developed a doctrine of "fraternal encouragement." He was one of the modern inventors of collegiality, standing out in an age of hierarchicalism. He went against the grain of much leadership theory in his day, heralding a new day of openness and collegiality. On 2 Thessalonians 3:15, he spoke of the need to admonish those who did not obey the church to keep people from being "aloof from" society. Social isolationism also tended to promote more sinfulness; thus collegial association and encouragement were needed. It is interesting to find him drawing this conclusion when many others do not. Calvin found evidence of the virtue of fraternal correction as an illustration of "brotherly love." In Calvin's thinking, J. T. McNeill pointed out, "Mutual admonition provides checks and balances against arrogance. . . . He [Calvin] has 'fraternal correction' incorporated into the constitution of the church at Geneva. Accordingly, in 1557 Calvin influenced the Little Council, the chief deliberative body for civil government, to admonish the recalcitrant in secret 'fraternal charity' sessions which met quarterly."[66] Clearly, then, Calvin found checks and balances helpful to church and state alike.

Calvin came to distrust the lone decision maker as

much as any earthly abuse. He knew that sinners, if unchecked, would act in accord with their nature. He anticipated the saying "Power corrupts; and absolute power corrupts absolutely." In place of an unchecked individual, Calvin recommended that spheres of power have multiple leaders and councils. He was averse to monarchies in any realm, fearing that they would abuse their power.

Harro Hopfl identifies these signatures of Calvinism— and these exhibit the heartbeat of Calvinism by negation:

- Calvin detested as much as anything rulers who acted as if their will made right.
- Because no single individual possessed "power and breadth of vision enough to govern" unilaterally, a council was needed.
- Even in a monarchy, a council was required.
- Tyranny was exhibited in a leader's unwillingness to tolerate restraint or live within the law. Any leader should be *sub Deo et sub lege* (under God and under law).[67]

These limitations on the ruling class shaped the resulting political practices approved by Calvinists. Hopfl views Calvin's notion of order as necessitating law. Law next required enforcement, and different agencies with differing gifts and tools must each "adhere to his station and perform its duties willingly." Hopfl summarized:

There is an unmistakable preference for an aristocratic form with popular admixtures of sorts, and for small territorial units. Monarchy is explicitly rejected for ecclesiastical polity on scriptural grounds; in civil polity no such outright rejection was possible because of the earlier *parti pris* in favor of the divine authorization of all forms of government and Calvin's almost inflexible opposition to political resistance. Nonetheless, the animus against monarchs is clear enough, and civil monarchy remains a discrepant and disturbing element in an otherwise carefully synchronized arrangement of mutual constraints.[68]

Calvin, thus, was a leader who advocated a collective approach to decision making in as many venues as possible.

This led to a definite ethos. The character of Calvinism may be seen by its persistent aversion to anarchy and self-appointedness. Calvin saw both of those as distinct threats to the peace and stability of society. He knew that anarchy would destroy the fragile fabric of the Genevan Reformation. As he watched Luther's Germany, he was not eager to repeat the overenthusiasms, which he could only compare to anarchy.

Neither was Calvin a fan of self-appointedness. His doctrine of ecclesiastical calling led him to emphasize that many partners act in concert to determine a call. If an individual alone decided, then either unqualified or tyrannical leaders could arise without hindrances. On the other hand, if various qualifying agencies and a popular vote were employed, there was less likelihood that a poor or dictatorial leader would rise to the top.

Calvin knew that the broader the spheres of influence and the less the chance for sole rule—even though creating encumbrances—the better off society would be. Most scholars can find his fingerprints all over American federalism. With three different branches of government, and one of those bicameral (the Senate and the House), new means of governing must pass numerous levels of scrutiny. While that entails that our government may not sprint ahead like some organizations, it also means that many counselors have callings to inspect ideas before they are approved. This Calvinistic distinctive—that is, that first readings require multiple readings—is based on the premise that an individual or the few will have more biases than larger, corporate groups. Thus, to the degree that one can involve legitimate accountability and inspection, that is a virtue.

His thought even demanded this application: mistrust yourself. Calvin understood that much evil could be done in the name of self-appointedness or insisting that one leader knew all. His practice as well as his theory worked together to limit the rule of the few (oligarchy) or the rule of one leader alone (monarchy). In both state and church, he sought to forge new structures to preserve these delicate balances.

Historians study the geographic spread of Calvinism to support this thesis: where the character of Calvinism was understood, councils arose to replace individual rulers. A strong confirmation of the sincerity of Calvin's commitment to collective decision-making models is that wherever his disciples planted churches, they formed corporate governing boards (the presbytery) or sought to elect a multiplicity of leaders. Calvin did not approve the establishment of churches without internal checks and balances. This is all the more noteworthy when it is seen as so highly unusual for the time and not necessitated by any other authority. Calvin voluntarily worked for reforms in church and state, and in each he vigorously labored for corporate structures that would limit the encroachments of human depravity.

To see how consistent Calvin was, his doubt about the perfectibility of human nature also extended this principle into the church. The genius of the Venerable Company of Pastors (some churches call this the fraternal, the presbytery, or the association, depending on denominational particularities) was that it did not entrust power solely to a chief minister or prevent others from giving advice.

Calvin's effect on Geneva and elsewhere was strong, and its trajectory favored the expansion of the civil franchise to produce more representation and less oligarchy in government. Herbert Foster correctly noted: "Before Calvin came to Geneva, there had been a natural tendency in time of war to centralize authority in the hands of the small and somewhat aristocratic council. On the whole, Calvin's influence tended to prevent this somewhat dangerous development of a political oligarchy and aided a gradual development of representative government."[69]

As a leader, Calvin did not believe that all good ideas resided within the mind of the leader or the few. He was humble enough to seek counsel from others, and any leadership structure with one individual at the top seemed mistaken to him.

CHRISTIAN LIBERTY

*Christian liberty is a proper appendix to
justification [which] gives peace to trembling
consciences.*

JOHN CALVIN LIVED IN a day when the freedoms
most of us cherish were uncommon. In two different spheres, he was challenged to work out an enduring view of liberty. First, in the civil sphere, he lived in a society that had only recently known monarchies. There was no long history of liberty, even in Geneva prior to Calvin's arrival. Before Calvin's time, most European cities were under the rule of a king and had few civil liberties. Much of his work would begin a tradition of civil liberty. The second area of authoritarianism that he inherited was in the sphere of church government. Prior to his time, under the dominance of the Roman Catholic Church, members were granted liberties only as the church recognized them. They were, at times, few and far between. As such, the idea that Christians could be truly free and at liberty to serve their own conscience was a new concept that Calvin aided substantially by his teaching.

In book 3 of the *Institutes,* he took up this subject of Christian liberty, and his insights are unsurpassed today. To begin with, a key distinction must be introduced from the conclusion of chapter 19 of that work.

Calvin spoke of two species of liberty: civil and spiritual (3.19.15). He taught that human government is twofold: (1) spiritual government is internal, and it trains the conscience in matters of piety and worship, and (2) civil government refers to external matters. The former has its seat in the soul; the outer government refers to external activity. The church is to teach and handle the spiritual order; the political rulers care for civil order. Calvin suggested that if we pay attention to this distinction, "We will not erroneously transfer the doctrine of the gospel concerning spiritual liberty to civil order." That division of labor would become an essential building block of stable societies; it would also supply ample protection for proper freedom.

With that in mind, it should be clearer that church and state each have a valuable role to play. However, they should not interfere with the proper jurisdiction of the other; God intended it to be that way.

As Calvin began his groundbreaking chapter on Christian liberty, he first sought to explain why it was so important. He argued that it was necessary for people to understand this, even if only on an elementary level, lest they have their consciences burdened by the threat of endless rules and stifling captivity. Indeed, he asserted, this topic was a "proper appendix to justification," meaning that if one knew how he was truly justified (by God alone), then he might also know that liberty would result only as one followed God. Thus, from the outset, Calvin's view of liberty is distinguished from any humanistic view of liberty. He believed that liberty was a gift, and one that should be used as God designed it.

For Calvin, this spiritual or Christian liberty consisted of three parts. First, believers were to have their consciences free in regard to the law of God. That is to say that if they were justified by God and freed from the demands of the law, then they would learn to look to the mercy of God continually and turn away from any thought of saving themselves by works. Not that the law was unimportant, but in terms of conscience, believers had to know that their assurance would come from looking only to Christ, not to human perfection or legal obedience. Freedom of conscience was as important as civil liberty, and it began with a right understanding of justification.

The second part of Christian liberty was that believers were to obey the law from a different motive. Being regenerated by God, they were to "voluntarily obey the will of God" (3.19.4), not so much obeying out of a servile fear. Instead of being in terror, the believer should know the love of God; liberty flowed from that. This also meant the end of various perfectionistic schemes. Calvin's followers were to be perfect in Christ, not in themselves. That also implied the end of legalism.

The third part of Christian liberty was that the believer was not obligated to observe external things only or keep the ceremonial customs of the Old Testament. Instead folks were permitted to use things as helpful or omit them, as long as they did not seek to overturn the moral law. Accordingly, there were many things in life that Calvin classified as "indifferent." To fail to make that distinction would, he thought, mean "no end of superstition" (3.19.7). God's Word was the authority for believers, but many things in life had to be decided in terms of principles and deduction. Believers were free to use the good things that God had created. They were to use them only as he had designed them and for his glory. As long as that was done, liberty was a good rule of thumb. The goal of this liberty was to "give peace to trembling consciences" (3.19.9). Of course, Calvin is not rightly understood as encouraging libertinism or using liberty as a "cloak for lust."

He also was aware that this was a volatile subject and that some could misuse liberty to confuse others. Thus he introduced a distinction that is highly useful still. Calvin drew a line between an "offense taken" and an "offense given." In the offense given, a person who was mature did something contrary to the law of God and caused confusion to less-mature onlookers. That was a misuse of Christian liberty, and it was out of order, a fault, and was wrong.

However, the "offense taken" (which he also called the offense of the Pharisees) occurred not so much when Scripture was violated as when the sensibilities of those who should be more mature were offended. This merely offended the "austerity of the Pharisees" and did not clearly violate the law of God. If an offense were only taken, and other considerations were in place, then the act could be freely engaged as a part of Christian liberty (3.19.11). If that distinction were not observed, then men would always be held captive to the opinions of others, their liberties would be severely curtailed, and confusion would arise. What was at stake, Calvin knew, was liberty of conscience, and he sought to protect it as much from the Pharisees as he did from those who were too lax.

To further bolster his theory, Calvin also offered a hierarchy of norms to help people make decisions. Matters of Christian liberty had to be subjected to the law of charity (3.19.13); by that, he meant that sometimes we must voluntarily restrict ourselves so that we do not cause others to stumble. Thus liberty is not absolute in Calvin's scheme. It is a good gift from God, but it must be kept in perspective. Moreover, just as the law of liberty must be subject to the law of charity, this norm of love is not the final test, for the law of love "must in its turn be subordinate to the purity of faith." Thus, for Calvin, a finely nuanced view of liberty and ethics valued the purity of the revealed faith to the utmost. Following that, the rule of charity trumped, and after that came Christian liberty.

Keeping things in that delicate balance—a balance that was a signature of Calvinism—would also help in periods of reform. Incremental reform is consistent with this theory. Indeed, Calvin did not condone "the intemperance of those who do every thing tumultuously, and would rather burst through every restraint at once than proceed step by step" (3.19.13). Change could come slowly and steadily in his opinion, and he did not want either Christian liberty, love, or the purity of the faith to be sacrificed in the process. Thus, he averred, "We are not at liberty to deviate one nail's breadth from the command of God" (3.19.13). Liberty thus was confined, and "consciences were exempted from human authority" that did not agree with God entirely.

This view of liberty, wherever it spread, gave citizens

confidence and protections. Within a century, the American colonies would exhibit this Calvinistic distinctive. Not incidentally one of the first law codes was named the Massachusetts Body of Liberties. So close were law and liberty that Calvin's disciples could call a law code a table of liberties. The reason was that a proper understanding of liberty is essential for any successful venture, whether it is business, civic, or religious. Calvin had seen an oppression of liberties—both in Paris as Protestants were persecuted and in Geneva in the eyes of the many Roman Catholic refugees—and he formed his view of liberties based on God's Word and in a fashion that avoided misuses.

Philanthropy and Care for the Poor

To discourage mendicancy which is contrary to good order, it would be well, and we have so ordered it, that there be one of our officials at the entrance of the churches to remove from the place those who loiter; and if there be any who give offence or offer insolence to bring them to one of the Lords Syndic.

THE PEDESTRIAN CRITICISM OF Calvin is unwarranted perhaps nowhere more so than in terms of his compassion toward the downtrodden. In reality, Calvin was a leader who knew how to help the truly needy in an effective manner.

To begin a consideration of this aspect of his leadership, we would do well to remember how Calvin reached out compassionately to thousands of homeless refugees as they traipsed through Geneva in search of a place to rest their wearied consciences. This massive immigration strapped Geneva's capacities. With the population nearly doubling in a decade because of this swelling movement, the Genevan church had to devise measures to care for the truly needy around them. One of their first steps was to analyze the problem and distinguish between those who were truly needy and those who were not.

Second, a clearer view of the heart of Calvin may be seen from his development of ways to use the officers of a private (or nongovernmental organization, NGO) agency to care for so many. Calvin believed that the church's compassion could best be expressed through its deacons. Since God had ordained that office for that function, the challenge to Calvin was to arrive at practical protocols that would care for the poor, using the mechanisms that God had already provided through these ministers of mercy.

It is an accomplishment well worth remembering that centuries ago Calvin pioneered principles and practices that were far ahead of their time. In fact, if most governmental agencies would implement some version of these principles, many people would be better off.

Jeannine Olson's able historical volume, *Calvin and Social Welfare: Deacons and the Bourse Francaise,* provided a study of Calvin's impact on Reformation culture, focusing particularly on the enduring effect of Calvin's thought on the institution of the diaconate. In her treatise, she noted that, contrary to some modern caricatures, the Reformers worked diligently to shelter refugees and minister to the poor. The Bourse Francaise became a pillar of societal welfare in Geneva;[70] in fact, this was another of Calvin's contributions to Western civilization. This diaconal ministry may have had nearly as much influence in Calvin's Europe as his theology did in other areas.

Calvin's welfare program in Geneva was contoured to fit the theological emphases of the Reformers, providing an early illustration that welfare practice was and is (and still should be) erected upon definite principles that are religious or ideological in nature. Moreover, the theology of the Reformation was the guiding force for this welfare, just as the theology of medieval Roman Catholicism had been the guiding principle for almsgiving. Ultimate principles molded welfare practices 450 years ago as they do today, which is to say, at no time is welfare truly divorced from underlying ideological values.

The activities of the bourse were numerous. Its diaconal agents were involved in housing orphans, the elderly, or those who were in any way incapacitated. They sheltered the sick and dealt with orphans and those involved in immoralities. This ecclesiastical institution was a precursor to voluntary societies in the nineteenth and twentieth centuries. But its inspiration was part of the genius of Calvin.

The Bourse Francaise was founded under his leadership sometime between 1536 and 1541 (of course, not during his Strasbourg exile). Its initial design was to appease the suffering brought onto French residents who, while fleeing sectarian persecution in France, came to Geneva. It has been estimated that in the single decade of the 1550s some sixty thousand refugees passed through Geneva, a number large enough to produce significant social stress.

Early on in the *Ecclesiastical Ordinances,* first proposed in 1541, Calvin had written a charter for the deacons, distinguishing them as one of the four basic offices of the church. This Reformation church order stipulated that among the fourth biblical office, that of the deacon, "There were always two kinds in the ancient Church, the one deputed to receive, dispense, and hold goods for the poor, not only daily alms, but also possessions, rents and pensions; the other to tend and care for the sick and administer allowances to the poor."[71] In addition, the 1541 charter prescribed, "It will be their duty to watch diligently that the public hospital is well maintained, and that this be so both for the sick and the old people unable to work, widowed women, orphaned children and other poor creatures. The sick are always to be lodged in a set of separate rooms from the other people who are unable to work. . . . Moreover, besides the hospital for those passing through which must be maintained, there should be some attention given to any recognized as worthy of special charity."[72] In the conclusion of this section, Calvin advocated "to discourage mendicancy which is contrary to good order, it would be well, and we have so ordered it, that there be one of our officials at the entrance of the churches to remove from the place those who loiter; and if there be any who give offence or offer insolence to bring them to one of the Lords Syndic."[73] Begging without honest work was an affront to the biblical Protestant work ethic. Employing both a sophistication of administration and a discrimination of root causes among physical needs, this model can still inform our practice today.

Calvin was so interested in seeing the diaconate flourish that he not only left an inheritance for his family in his will but also provided for the boys' school and poor strangers.[74] The deacons cared for a large range of needs, not wholly dissimilar to the strata of welfare needs in our own society.

In the 1541 *Ecclesiastical Ordinances,* Calvin recommended a strong role for the diaconate, especially in almsgiving. After two decades, those *Ecclesiastical Ordinances* were revised in 1561. A recent translation of the 1561 *Ecclesiastical Ordinances* shows the sophistication and refinement of the diaconate even prior to the death of Calvin.[75] The requirements of the 1561 revision make clear that ministry to the poor was significant and well ordered in Calvin's time. It was neither a low priority nor slipshod in organization. In fact, the forethought and amount of detail for such philanthropy were nearly unparalleled for the time.

The deacons actively encouraged a productive work ethic. They provided interim subsidy and job training as necessary; on occasion, they provided the necessary tools or supplies so that an able-bodied person could engage in an honest vocation. They were discriminating as they ascertained the difference between the truly needy and the indigent. If necessary, they would also suspend subsidy. Over time, they developed procedures that would protect the church's resources from being pilfered, even requiring new visitors to declare their craft and list character witnesses to vouch for their honesty.[76] Within a generation of this welfare work, the diaconate of Geneva discovered the need to communicate to recipients the goal that they were to return to work as soon as possible.

In sixteenth-century Geneva there were cases of abandonment that Calvin and others had to consider, and the bourse was frequently called upon to raise children. They supported the terminally ill, who also left their children to be supported. Special gifts were given to truly needy children. The bourse also included a ministry to widows who often had dependent children and a variety of needs.

Still, it must be noted that although the bourse resembled many other contemporary welfare funds, it had its own peculiarities. Naturally there were theological peculiarities, and these distinctives led to certain practical commitments. For example, there were no guaranteed food handouts. Furthermore, there were certain prerequisites for receiving care, including the possibility that certain moral deficiencies would nullify one's qualifications for the bourse.

The bourse was not concerned only with spiritual or internal needs. On many occasions they hired doctors to take care of the ill. Records indicate that the deacons oversaw medical care for the needy, reflecting that the full scope of diaconal ministry was not limited only to evangelism. Those who led the bourse were also prudent. By January 1581 the bourse had adopted a set of constitutional rules underscoring the need to have a vital and well-thought-out, disciplined approach to poverty amelioration.[77] Calvin and the founders of the Genevan diaconate were also realists who consulted the past and factored in Jesus's statement in Mark 14:7: "For you have the poor with you always." They lived on a cusp of a reform movement, learning from what had gone before them.

Leaders today might be better off to see what they can learn from the past rather than looking exclusively to the future. In fact, if we find ourselves advocating practices markedly different from what Calvin's bourse in Geneva did nearly five centuries ago, then it may be that our novel methods should be suspect to the extent that we deviate from earlier sound practice in the area of public welfare.

In summary, we find the following as principles of Calvin's welfare reform:

1. It was only for the truly disadvantaged.
2. Moral prerequisites accompanied assistance.
3. Private or religious charity, not state largesse, was the vehicle for aid.
4. Ordained officers managed and brought accountability.
5. Theological underpinnings were normal.
6. Productive work ethic was sought.
7. Assistance was temporary.
8. History is valuable.

Illustrative of the philanthropy of Calvin, Martin Bucer went so far as to say of the diaconate that "without it there can be no true communion of saints" [78] while simultaneously believing, "The first duty of the deacons is to distinguish between the deserving and undeserving poor, for the former to inquire carefully into their needs; the latter, if they lead disorderly lives at the expense of others, to expel them from the community of the faithful. Care, next, is to be taken for needy widows."[79]

Both as confirmation of the affinity among Reformers and of the similarity of thought that Calvin passed on to his disciples, one need look only at the communities where the seeds of Calvinism blossomed to see how this movement of philanthropy mutated. In the British Isles, almsgiving was emphasized as one means for poverty relief. John Knox, who spent several crucial years learning Calvin's Genevan model, continued this Reformation tradition of ministry to the poor in Scotland. In the *Second Book of Discipline* (1578), he established the office of deacon as a permanent function of the church.

Hence the Calvinistic tradition was settled and fairly uniform in its institutionalization of the care for the poor. It was an ecclesiological function to be carried out by spiritual officers according to biblical standards and principles. As it was carried out well, it cared for the poor, employed the church's gifts, encouraged a productive work ethic, and relieved governmental stewardship in this area. As Geoffrey Bromiley summarizes, "The able-bodied should work and support themselves. . . . The answer to poverty was still found in individual benevolence exercised either privately or through the Church."[80]

From this we can see that a number of welfare agencies began to blossom in the countryside of Western Europe following the Protestant Reformation. Indeed, the Calvinistic diaconate was a leader in its manifestation of consistent reformation of faith and life. Thus did these Reformation prototypes spread and become leaders in the sixteenth-century welfare reform. Indeed, the Reformation "left stamped upon Christendom its idea of a properly coordinated and managed care of the poor and needy as the concern of the Church and as the responsibility of the Christian community."[81]

Calvin was atypical in advancing this particular societal safety net. His philanthropy provides another instance of how his heart was compassionate toward the truly needy.

WORRY V. FAITH

He who is fully convinced that the Author of our
life has an intimate knowledge of our condition
will not entertain doubt that he will make
abundant provision for our wants. Whenever we
are seized by any fear or anxiety about food, let us
remember that God will take care of the life which
he gave us.

*W*E HAVE ALL SEEN or known leaders who are obsessed with worry. In many cases, that comes with the job. Leaders, however, can kill themselves with excessive anxiety; thus, a leader must find ways to control worry—and that is not easy. In fact, many people discover that the longer they live, the more (not less) they worry. If Calvin and Luther were two of the greatest Christians and such monumental figures in history, did they struggle with worry? Even if we grant that these and other great leaders of the past were above our normal spirituality, does that imply that they never wrestled with temptations to sin? With so much pressure on them, with persecution, threats, and temptations, did they never worry?

Calvin addressed this problem with immense clarity in his commentary on Luke. He noted that Jesus criticized "excessive anxiety" but not the inborn condition of caring about certain matters. Appropriate concern and moderate care about matters were not condemned: Christ "does not forbid every kind of care, but only what arises from distrust." What is condemned is "immoderate care" for two reasons: "either because in so doing men teaze and vex themselves to no purpose by carrying their anxiety farther than is proper or than their calling demands; or because they claim more for themselves than they have a right to do, and place such a reliance on their own industry, that they neglect to call upon God."

Certainly, Calvin admitted the calling of labor, which was not condemned in the least. He found an Aristotelian mean in the "intermediate place" between "indolent carelessness" and the needless "torments by which unbelievers kill themselves." One almost gets the feeling that Calvin viewed worry as a trait of unbelief.

He suggested that a remedy to such anxiety is to trust in the providence of God, who has not "thrown us on the earth at random." After all, Calvin reminded, "He who is fully convinced that the Author of our life has an intimate knowledge of our condition will not entertain doubt that he will make abundant provision for our wants. Whenever we are seized by any fear or anxiety about food, let us remember that God will take care of the life which he gave us." Thus the remedy is to "rely on the providence of God; for of all cares, which go beyond bounds, unbelief is the mother. The only cure for covetousness is to embrace the promises of God, by which he assures us that he will take care of us." That "providence of God is alone sufficient for us."

As he commented on Luke 12:29, Calvin noted that Christ "justly accuses us of deficiency or weakness of faith; for the more powerfully we are affected, according to our own groveling views, by anxiety about the present life, the more do we show our unbelief if every thing does not happen to our wish."

Calvin concluded his diatribe against anxiety with these words: "All those persons who are so anxious about food, give no more honor than unbelievers do to the fatherly goodness and secret providence of God."

Perfectly typical of Christian theology, he believed that Jesus's commands for our activity were tied to the character of God. God does his work, and he does it perfectly well even without our worrying. Trusting in God, thus, is the remedy for worry.

Worry means "to think in circles" or to contemplate over and over again. It could almost be translated as mentally spinning our tires. What is condemned is the nonproductive thought that stews over matters again and again. It goes nowhere but serves to paralyze us. Worry is a sinful drain on thinking and acting. It is turmoil over something we cannot fix. It is thinking dominated by anxiety.

One author put it this way: "Worry is faith in the negative, trust in the unpleasant, assurance of disaster, and belief in defeat. Worry is wasting today's time to clutter up tomorrow's opportunities with yesterday's troubles." A Swedish proverb casts things this way: "Worry often gives a small thing a big shadow."

Agreeing with Calvin, Martin Luther described the handling of anxiety as part of "the sum of this Gospel: Christians should not worry about what they are to eat; God provides for them before they think of their need." In a sermon, he observed: "In this Gospel we see how God distinguishes Christians from heathen. . . . The sum of all is, it is God's will that we serve not gold and riches, and that we be not *overanxious* for our life; but that we labor and commend our anxiety to him. Whoever possesses riches is lord of the riches. Whoever serves them, is their slave and does not possess them, but they possess him."[82]

Luther continued, "If I believe that I have a God, then I cannot be anxious about my welfare; for if I know that God cares for me as a father for his child, why should I fear? Why need I to be anxious. . . . Thus he has all things in his hand; therefore I shall want nothing, he will care for me. If I rush ahead and try to care for myself, that is always contrary to faith; therefore God forbids this kind of anxiety."[83]

Like Calvin, in associating excessive worry with a pagan unbelief, Luther noted, "Is it not a great shame that the Lord makes and presents to us the birds as our teachers that we should first learn from them? Shame on thee, thou loathsome, infamous unbelief! The birds do what they are required to do; but we not. Away with godless unbelief! God makes us to be fools and places the birds before us, to be our teachers and rule us, in that they only point out how we serve mammon and forsake the true and faithful God."[84]

Apparently, these Reformers struggled with worry. They

also found a remedy to the anxiety that can destroy by putting faith to work. Leaders must control their own anxiety, lest it control them. They would be wise to listen to the wisdom of Luther and Calvin on this challenge and let faith manage worry, not vice versa.

Adversity and Courage

*The more we are afflicted with adversity, the surer
we are made of our fellowship with Christ. Thus,
if every part of life was submitted to God's
overarching plan, then even adversity could be
seen as part of God's will.*

EARLY IN HIS MINISTRY Calvin faced and over-
came adversity. In fact, he seemed unable to
avoid it. At least three episodes show the kinds of adversity he faced and how he dealt with them.

First, he had to face opposition from Parisian Catholics.
The Roman Catholic Church and the university in Paris
had shared the authority of that polite society for years.
When the threat of reform surfaced, leaders were quickly
shunned. Some early French Protestants were persecuted,
and one of Calvin's earliest works (his preface to the *Institutes*) defended them against such persecution. The fires
of discrimination were fired so much that Calvin had to
leave Paris (which led to his settlement in Geneva). He
understood the pain of those who would later be mar-
tyred for their faith. That kind of adversity tries one's soul,

and Calvin remained faithful through all the opposition of the anti-Protestants.

Second, he encountered opposition within a short time after arriving in Geneva. He found a city council that was accustomed to ruling without interference from a popular and insightful pastor. In less than two years, things came to a head in Geneva, and Calvin was expected to sacrifice his integrity to appease an edict of the city council. Of course, he would not submit to an unlawful incursion into the territory of God's sacraments when the city council ordered him to ignore certain scriptural provisions. Calvin had to wonder why God had led him to Geneva only to have him exiled twenty-one months after his promising settlement. His experience with this humbling adversity, however, made him both a more patient and a more understanding leader. He would know that even in the face of adversity one must hold faithfully to first principles.

Third, even when Calvin returned to Geneva, his work moved with plodding speed at times, and the various works of reform were long labors of love. Even though many Genevans desired his return, some did not. Opposition both within the church and outside in the city resisted many of Calvin's proposals. Several leading families consistently opposed his ideas. Notwithstanding, Calvin knew to persevere and remain focused. He accepted adversity and did not let it deter him.

Of course, he was not removed from the other challenges of life. When his wife, Idelette, died, he experienced grief. When things went poorly, or during his own bouts with poor health, Calvin learned to rely on God. His life was fraught with adversity. On one occasion, he wrote, "The more we are afflicted with adversity, the surer we are made of our fellowship with Christ" (3.8.1). He saw affliction, in essence, as proving the genuineness of his spirituality. In his *Life of the Christian Man,* he noted that the ethical mandate for self-denial meant that believers face any adversity—ranging from death and plague to poverty and disease and affliction—as part of God's providence (3.7.10). Godly minds, taught Calvin, would apply "peace and forebearance" to "every occurrence to which the present life is subject. Thus, if every part of life was submitted to God's overarching plan, then even adversity could be seen as part of God's will.

Elsewhere in the *Institutes,* he spoke of adversity when he discussed how various rulers in the Bible had their good advice rejected (1.17.7). Calvin contended that a leader's understanding of God's providence led him toward steadiness in all things. "Gratitude of mind for the favorable outcome of things, patience in adversity, and also incredible freedom from worry about the future," he noted, "all necessarily follow upon this knowledge" (1.17.7). He advised other leaders to accept prosperity and "wholly attribute that to God" while any setbacks were also to be reconciled to God's overarching sovereignty.

Whenever adversity arose, Calvin urged his followers to follow patience and seek moderation. He warned against retaliation toward those who oppose, recommending that such things should be left in God's hands. Whatever evil our enemies afflict on us are permitted by God's providence. He also realized that God used adversity to chastise us from time to time as well.

His commentaries also reflect his consistency of tying adversity and affliction to character building. On Romans 5:3, Calvin noted that tribulations come from the "hand of a most indulgent Father," and their effect is to strengthen character. This, however, is not a work of nature but of grace. In contrast to the reaction of unbelief, which is to despise adversity, when inward meekness is "infused by the Spirit of God, and the consolation, which is conveyed by the same Spirit, succeed in the place of our stubbornness, then tribulations become the means of generating patience."

Later, his commentary on 2 Corinthians went so far as to define *patience* as "the regulation of the mind in adversity" (6:4). In fact, Calvin associated bravery with a courageous facing of affliction. Leaders, he suggested, should both pursue peace amid societal tumults and also "go forward, undaunted, through the midst of commotions, so as not to turn aside from the right course, though heaven and earth should be mingled" (his commentary on 2 Corinthians 6:5).

Qualities such as patience in adversity and courage amid opposition, Calvin wrote in his commentary on 2 Corinthians, were "indicative of a mind well established in virtue, not to be moved away from one's course by any disgrace that may be incurred—a rare virtue, but one without which you cannot show that you are a servant of God."

Leaders learn to accept adversity; it will always come. Nothing worthwhile in life is easy. Moreover, to live in denial that adversity will occur only makes it more difficult to proceed in the face of such reality. Once the reality of adversity is accepted, good leaders stick to their principles.

But the mere acceptance of adversity does not actually deal with adversity nor motivate a person to face difficulty. Something else is needed for that. And chief among the tools to combat adversity was one of Calvin's most outstanding traits: courage. Few people in history exemplify courage better than he. Calvin was willing, if need be, to face down religious authorities who had the power over life or death, entrenched civil governors, and even powerful members of his own church. Perhaps there is even a slight double entendre in his personal motto, "Here, O Lord, I offer my heart to you promptly and sincerely" (the French *coeur* is the root of the English word *courage*); Calvin also offered his courage to God sincerely and promptly. And such inspired courage would be needed to fulfill his various callings.

Characteristic of Calvinism, human virtues did not arise solely from human nature. Virtues such as courage arose for Calvin and his followers from an embrace of the power and care of God. Courage, in other words, was the logical overflow of an understanding of an all-sovereign and all-powerful God. To fail to muster courage to obey the Lord was a failure to believe. Thus it is little surprise to those who have studied Calvinism to find its faith as a prime motivator for his followers to embark on heroic acts, ranging from pioneering mission and educational endeavors to courageous political resistance and braving untamed oceans to colonize the West.

As an application of Calvin's principles, George Bancroft summarized: "The political character of Calvinism, which, with one consent and with instinctive judgment, the monarchs of that day feared as republicanism, and which Charles II declared a religion unfit for a gentleman, is expressed by a single word—*predestination.* Did a proud aristocracy trace its lineage through generations of a high-born ancestry?—the republican reformer, with a loftier pride, invaded the invisible world, and from the book of life brought down the record of the noblest enfranchisement, decreed from all eternity by the King of kings."[85]

In his *Institutes,* Calvin spoke of the need for persevering resistance on several occasions. In his final remarks (4.20.32), he called for courage not to wane. He knew that Christians could be called to resist evil rulers, and to do so would necessitate courageous perseverance. The comfort of such principled leadership, noted Calvin, would rest in obeying God even if it called for human suffering. Good leaders would rather face discomfort than forsake their principles. He would also summon leaders to "struggle manfully, to have courage" (4.15.11) and strive to please God in standing against sinful or selfish tendencies. Resisting temptation, thus, was and always is an act of courage that forms one's character.

Typical of Calvin's perspective, in one section of the *Institutes,* he mentored future leaders in combating the devil. Keenly aware that this relentless adversary stalks those who lead God's people, Calvin warned about the adversity that would come from this demonic "embodiment of rash boldness, or military prowess, of crafty wiles, of untiring zeal and haste, of every conceivable weapon and of skill in the science of warfare" (1.14.13). He prescribed that the leader not cave in to the will of the Evil One nor "be overwhelmed by carelessness or faintheartedness."

That is good advice, but his cheer is broadcast even more with these words: "But on the contrary, with courage rekindled stand our ground in combat . . . let us urge ourselves to perseverance. Indeed, conscious of our weakness and ignorance, let us especially call upon God's help, relying upon him alone in whatever we attempt, since it is he alone who can supply us with counsel and strength, courage and armor." If more leaders remembered those truths, both about spiritual warfare and the need for willful resistance and courage, their legacies might more closely resemble Calvin's.

On Government

For though tyrannies and unjust exercise of power, as they are full of disorder, are not an ordained government; yet the right of government is ordained by God for the well-being of mankind.

M OST SUCCESSFUL LEADERS CAN tell tales about how they were ambushed at some time or other by some political machine or other. When that train rolls over you, it often serves as an incentive for one to learn political formats and protocols in order either to survive or to be more effective. Calvin not only understood political order and form, he believed God had revealed certain norms in this area for all times and for all Christians. His discussion of political matters was one of the most effective ways of transmitting his faith. To the surprise of many, Calvin actually had much to say on this subject, and for centuries his advice was followed by many to the benefit of society.

The clearest single map of Calvin's political thought is found in *Institutes of the Christian Religion* (in book 4, chapter 20).[86] Calvinism is, even by critics, still credited with immense political impact.[87] Asserting that the state was not merely a necessary evil for Calvin, Lutheran scholar Karl Holl recognized that Calvinism, even more than Lutheranism, provided a theological basis to oppose unjust governments.[88] Interestingly, everywhere Calvinism spread, so did its views of both respecting government and limiting it. Calvinism, in fact, "placed a solid barrier in the path of the spread of absolutism"[89] and helped make the world safe from tyrants. Furthermore, Holl claimed, even though ancestors of human rights were found in the Middle Ages, nonetheless, their "formal acceptance into political theory is not completed until this period [Calvin's day] and only under the impact of religion. . . . The acceptance of universal human rights into the constitution was, however, not just the modification of a single point; it included in itself the transformation of the whole concept of the state."[90]

Calvin's political theory began by viewing civil government positively, as another example of how God had compassionately provided for mankind. The task of the civil ruler was to provide "that a public manifestation of religion may exist among Christians, and that humanity be maintained among men." If no civil government existed or if depraved men perceived that they could escape the consequences of their actions, they surely would opt for sin, and society would deteriorate into chaos. On one occasion, Calvin (probably with the Anabaptists in mind) likened such anarchy to living "pell-mell, like rats in straw." He argued that God does not bid persons to "lay aside their authority and retire to private life, but submit to Christ the power with which they have been invested, that he alone may tower over all." Calvin believed that "powers from God" had been appointed "for the legitimate and just government of the world. For though tyrannies and unjust exercise of power, as they are full of disorder, are not an ordained government; yet the right of government is ordained by God for the well-being of mankind."[91]

Calvin differed from some of his contemporaries in admitting that serving in political office was entirely appropriate, even going so far as to speak of civil service as the most sacred and honorable of human callings. At one point Calvin referred to civil rulers favorably as "vicars of God," describing their role as "ordained protectors and vindicators of public innocence, modesty, decency, and tranquility [whose] sole endeavor should be to provide for the common safety and peace of all." He also suggested that civil officials were "the most sacred, and by far the most honorable, of all stations in mortal life" (4.20.4) and that those who served in this "most sacred office" were "ambassadors of God" (4.20.6). Calvin's practice, thus, was neither escapist nor did it advocate an inherently negative view of human government. He was quite respectful of these offices. By early 1553 he had petitioned the magistrates of Geneva to be "the vindicators, not the destroyers, of sacred laws."[92] Civil magistrates were to be honored as superiors in keeping with the fifth commandment to honor one's superiors. Even evil rulers kept God's law to some degree, and, therefore, resistance was justified only in response to actions contrary to God's law. The task of civil government—which included the politician's employment of punishment ("the sword") as a legitimate corollary of human depravity—according to Calvin's exposition of Romans 13 was prescribed as follows:

> Magistrates may hence learn what their vocation is, for they are not to rule for their own interest, but for the public good; nor are they endued with unbridled power, but what is restricted to the well-being of their subjects; in short, they are responsible to God and to men in the exercise of their power. For as they are deputed by God and do his business, they must give an account to him: and then the ministration which God has committed to them has a regard to the subjects, they are therefore debtors to them.[93]

Calvin believed that both politics and providence were operative; indeed, he suggested that the kingdom of God was already present, but that it was not completely realized: "For spiritual government, indeed, is already initiating in us upon earth certain beginnings of the Heavenly Kingdom, and in this mortal and fleeting life affords a certain forecast of an immortal and incorruptible blessedness." He advised, "Let no man be disturbed that I now commit to civil government the duty of rightly establishing religion." It is unlikely that anyone would have been disturbed by such a statement at the time, since it was the common notion of Calvin's day that government must uphold religion. Calvin acknowledged: "All have confessed that no government can be happily established unless piety is the first concern."

Clearer still are Calvin's comments on John 18:36 in which Jesus stated that his servants did not strive for enforcement of an earthly kingdom. His view of the separation of jurisdictions, enunciated in the mid-sixteenth century, is still helpful. Discussing the conditions under which it is appropriate to defend "the kingdom of Christ by arms," Calvin wrote:

> When Kings and Princes are commanded to "kiss the son of God," not only are they enjoined to submit to his authority in their private capacity, but also to employ all the power that they possess in defending the church and maintaining godliness. I answer, first, they who draw this conclusion, that the doctrine of the Gospel and the pure worship of God ought not to be defended by arms are unskillful and ignorant reasoners; for Christ argues only from the facts of the case in hand, how frivolous were the calumnies which the Jews had brought against him. Secondly, though godly kings defend the kingdom of Christ by the sword, still it is done in a different manner from that in which worldly kingdoms are wont to be defended; for the kingdom of Christ, being spiritual must be founded on the doctrine and power of the Spirit. In the same manner, too, its edification is promoted; for neither the laws and edicts of men, nor the punishments inflicted by them, enter into the consciences. . . . It results, however, from the depravity of the world that the kingdom of Christ is strengthened more by the blood of the martyrs than by the aid of arms.[94]

Calvin wrote that if civil rulers properly understood their callings—that is, "that they are occupied not with profane affairs or those alien to a servant of God, but with a most holy office, since they are serving as God's deputies"—they would serve with more equity. Echoing Aristotle's morphology of the state and its tendency toward deterioration from monarchy to tyranny and from democracy to anarchy, Calvin advocated "a system compounded of aristocracy and democracy." He also saw a legitimate place for checks and balances, observing the need for "censors and masters to restrain his [the monarch's] willfulness."

That Calvin gave attention to a far-ranging set of civic concerns is evidenced by his discussion of the magistrate's right to tax in the *Institutes.* He recommended prudent limits, arguing that taxes should only support public necessity; "to impose them upon the common folk without cause is tyrannical extortion." Obedience was a Christian duty in this area; however, princes were not to indulge in "waste and expensive luxury" lest they earn God's displeasure. Excessive taxation was alluded to later: "Others drain the common people of their money, and afterward lavish it on insane largesse." He also declared that governors were not to tax people in order to enhance their "private chests" (4.20.12) so much as to benefit the common good.

Another major topic of discussion for Calvin was the use of the Old Testament judicial law, "the silent magistrate." Calvin believed that just as the ceremonial laws (laws regulating ritual and diet, not viewed to be as permanent as the moral law) had been "abrogated while piety remained safe and unharmed, so too, when these judicial laws were taken away, the perpetual duties and precepts of love could still remain." He admitted that different nations were free to make laws as they saw best with this qualification: "Yet these must be in conformity to that perpetual rule of love, so that they indeed vary in form but have the same purpose." On one occasion, he even called it a "Jewish vanity" (4.20.1) to confuse the specifics given to theocratic Israel with universal norms today. Elsewhere in the *Institutes,* he taught, "The Lord did not deliver [the law] by the hand of Moses to be promulgated in all countries, and to be everywhere enforced; but having taken the Jewish nation under his special care, patronage, and guardianship, he was pleased to be specially its legislator, and as became a wise legislator, he had special regard to it in enacting laws" (4.20.16).

Calvin taught that, even if all the specifics and particulars of the Mosaic judicial law were not binding, the moral principle of each continued. The moral law, which Calvin viewed as nothing other than a testimony of natural law and conscience, was never abrogated, contrary to the ceremonial and judicial codes: "Consequently, the entire scheme of this equity of which we are now speaking has been prescribed in it. Hence, this equity alone must be the goal and rule and limit of all laws. Whatever laws shall be framed to that rule, directed to that goal, bound by that limit, there is no reason why we should disapprove of them, howsoever they may differ from the Jewish law or among themselves." Since Calvin is seldom accused of laxness, his own comments must be taken seriously. Rightly interpreted in their own context, they do not call for disavowal of the equitable principles of the Old Testament judicial law; he merely called for the adaptation of aspects that were nonessential and nonmoral. It was, as

Calvin realized, possible to maintain the applicability of God's law while not necessarily advocating every cultural specific of the original Hebrew code.

Calvin was more interested in eternal values than the cultural form in politics. He advocated that any form of government, which ensured liberty, moderation, and a durable constitution (4.20.8), could be adapted. Civil servants were expected to "do their utmost to prevent liberty . . . from being impaired." Nonetheless, he was not so absolutistic as to infer that divine providence would not allow "different countries to be governed by different forms of polity" (4.20.8).

Breaking with the tradition of his day, however, Calvin knew that in some cases the lesser magistrates were justified in overturning a wicked ruler. That, nevertheless, was not to be carried out merely by private individuals. Calvin acknowledged that at times divine providence was satisfied in the overthrowing of wicked rulers, but he still preferred to allow the Lord to correct unbridled despotism. Concerning revolution, he advocated a peaceful, incremental revolution via the intermediate magistrates:

> For if there are now any magistrates of the people, appointed to restrain the willfulness of kings (as in ancient times the ephors . . .), I am so far from forbidding them to withstand, in accordance with their duty, the fierce licentiousness of kings, that, if they wink at kings who violently fall upon and assault the lowly common folk, I declare that their dissimulation involves nefarious perfidy, because they dishonestly betray the freedom of the peo-

ple, of which they know that they have been appointed protectors by God's ordinance.

The obvious exception to any of these rules, however, was that persons were not only free but also obligated to resist the magistrate who compelled ungodly activity. Calvin taught not only that there were exceptions to the considerations above but also that obedience to God was primary: "Obedience [to a ruler] is never to lead us away from obedience to Him," a good illustration of qualified absolutism.[95] He reasoned: "How absurd would it be that in satisfying men you should incur the displeasure of him for whose sake you obey men themselves!" Still, this argument is balanced with Calvin's conclusion that we should "comfort ourselves with the thought that we are rendering that obedience which the Lord requires when we suffer anything rather than turn aside from piety."

It is frequently though inappropriately implied that Calvin wished to unite church and state. In fact, he persistently advocated a difference of jurisdiction for each. Francois Wendel has noted that neither church nor state was to be annexed or collapsed into one another formally. This distinction or separation of jurisdictions "was the fountain of the entire edifice. Each of these autonomous powers, State and Church, was conceived as issuing from the Divine Will."[96] Wendel recognized that Calvin advocated the complementarity of the civil and ecclesiastical powers, even if all modern interpreters do not sense his preservation of that key distinction. Moreover, Douglas Kelly suggests that this distinction, even with a close cooperation between church and state, was an important factor in the diffusion of Calvinism.[97] Calvin himself stated the relationship succinctly in a 1538 letter: "As the magistrate ought by punishment and physical restraint to cleanse the church of offenses, so the minister of the Word should help the magistrate in order that fewer may sin. Their responsibilities should be so joined that each helps rather than impedes the other."[98] Calvin did not merge church and state into a theocratic monster.[99] He had no desire to advance the Reformation's political tradition on the back of coercion. Instead, he wished to energize the church to become a world-changing community.[100]

Despite any imperfections in his theory, one would do well to benefit from his grasp of how human communities were designed for political order. As customary, the defining ideas came from God and not man. Not only did Calvin wish to limit rulers to their divine stations, but he also wished to confine "the liberty which is promised and offered to us in [Christ] within its proper limits" (4.20.1). It would be an act of "perfect barbarism" (4.20.3) to abolish the proper roles for civil governors or for the church. Both are ordained spheres of God, and both should heed their ordained charters.

LOCAL POLITICS

If we were all like angels, blameless and freely able to exercise perfect self-control, we would not need rules or regulations. Why, then, do we have so many laws and statutes? Because of man's wickedness, for he is constantly overflowing with evil; this is why a remedy is required.

FORMER HOUSE SPEAKER TIP O'NEILL famously observed, "All politics is local." What he meant was that regardless of where leaders served, they had to face their constituency in a reelection. Thus, no matter what ideals, pragmatic concerns, or party politics, effective leaders could not run too terribly far from their local electorate.

In Calvin's case, he was a leader who was not motivated by such reelection concerns. But he did understand something profound about organization and human government: he realized that if an organizational idea were sound, it would work equally at home or abroad. The processes that developed after he came to Geneva provide a glimpse into how Calvin believed political processes should work.

The process of Genevan elections itself was a mirror of Calvin's view of human nature and the role of the state. With elections occurring on a Sunday in February, no doubt preceded by an election sermon, four chief officers were elected annually in the following manner. The longest tenured official, speaking on behalf of all four governors (called syndics), thanked the citizens for their trust and asked for forgiveness if they had been negligent in their governance. This chief syndic asked the people to whom they should pass their batons.[101] In one of the earliest organized democratic traditions, these citizens then elected four new syndics from a slate of eight for a year's term. The four with the most votes were then symbolically handed the batons.

These new syndics then convened the people the next day by the clock of St. Peter's for the election of Geneva's smallest Council of Twenty-Five (also known as the Senate). These senators were elected in groups of eight, with each nominee required to be a citizen, "born and baptized in the city of Geneva."[102] These groups formed the Council of Two Hundred and ratified the elections, with its spokesman announcing his approval or disapproval of the elections. If incumbents failed to gain a majority, they would be removed from office—a rarity since "if they have so erred, Geneva does not wait until election time to punish them, but puts them immediately into prison." Accordingly, an early method of impeachment was included. The Council of Two Hundred, thus, served as electors for the Council of Twenty-Five. An oath was then given to the Council of Twenty-Five, who proceeded to hold elections for the Council of Two Hundred in similar fashion on the following day. Only the secretary kept office for an extended period. The treasurer was elected to a three-year term.[103]

The oath taken by those elected to serve on these various councils is instructive and also reveals the imprint of Calvin. Each council member swore an oath embracing the following: first, "to live according to the Evangelical Reformation"; then to be loyal to Geneva; to preserve the laws and attend council meetings when asked; to keep confidential anything that might harm the commonweal; to keep Geneva well armed to defend the city; to remain a resident and never to desert Geneva in crisis; and finally, to foil sedition, "to neither make nor to permit any machinations or other practices against the holy evangelical Reformation, nor against the magistrates, Republic, liberties, edicts, and statutes of Geneva, but to discover, reveal, and report any such practices to Messieurs as soon as I notice them."[104] This conscientious and voluntary oath preserved Geneva's stability and morality for some time. These local politics certainly reflected Calvin's ideas and leadership.

Similarly, the oath for citizenship committed citizens to live "according to the Reformation and way of life according to the Gospel of God." Citizens pledged to support the leaders, the edicts of the city, to live in loyalty to the city and leaders, and to "pursue the good honor and profit of the city." Finally, the oath required "to neither do nor suffer to be done any practices, machinations or undertakings against the holy evangelical Reformation taking place in this city, neither against the magistrate, republic, liberties, edicts, and statutes of the city, but to discover, reveal and report to Messeigneurs as soon as you notice them."[105]

This Calvin-shaped polity, which appeared to be quite liberal or even daringly democratic for its day, provided checks and balances, separation of powers, election by the residents, specific religious norms, and elements of the federal structure that would later be copied as the finest export of Geneva. Other features of federalism, including an early appellate system, were developed by the late 1540s. Not only was Calvin's Geneva religious,[106] but it also sought the assent of the governed to a degree not previously seen, leading the world to new and stable forms of republicanism. Thus, if all politics are local, these provide good snapshots of Calvin's ideals.

Calvinism not only led to the practice of limited local government in Geneva but also led elected officials to adopt a particular view of their calling. In keeping with the teachings of Calvin,[107] elected governors perceived themselves as having a duty to God, one that compelled them to serve the public good and not to pursue personal benefit. This notion of selfless political duty owed much of its staying power to Calvin, and it soon became an integral feature of Genevan public culture.

Geneva's Calvinistic Reformation encouraged limited government in another way. Municipal officials were not full-time salaried employees in the time of Calvin, and the combination of checks and balances between the various councils required government to be streamlined and simple. Political offices in Geneva, in contrast with medieval and some modern customs, were not profitable for office-holders. Such offices were even avoided by many, requiring the threat of a fine if a citizen refused to serve after election.[108]

Thus, the pervasive influence of Calvin endured through these local political features for some time. According to one historian, Calvin was virtually "responsible for the arrival [in Geneva] of a galaxy of new talents."[109] Friend and foe alike recognize the centrality of Calvin's role in developing Geneva's political character that became a light to the New World for centuries to come.[110]

Geneva became the chief laboratory for the implementation of many of Calvin's civic ideas. As such, this brief review reminds us that the city's local political model gives clues about the character of Calvinism, complete with its tendency to limit government.

INDIVIDUAL RESPONSIBILITY

*Where princes take in less wealth, and require
only a modest amount of tribute and taxes, their
subjects overflow with personal riches.*

*P*ERHAPS NOWHERE IS THE fear of usurpation
seen more than in the sphere of civil government. Calvin argued long and hard that government
should not and could not do everything; it had to be limited in its task and scope. If it was not, it would run
aground as in the time of the prophet Samuel.

His sermons on 1 Samuel have only recently been
translated into English. Since the translation of a crucial
sermon on 1 Samuel 8 is recent and not available to all,
extracts below may be helpful to confirm Calvin's views
on individual responsibility and how citizens should not
expect centralized government to carry out all tasks or
grow excessively large.

Calvin's sermon on 1 Samuel 8 addresses one of the
most widely expounded passages about political thought
in Scripture. His 1561 exposition discusses the dangers of

monarchy, the need for proper limitation of government, and the place of divine sovereignty over human governments. It is an example of Calvinism at its best, carefully balancing individual liberty and proper government.

Calvin began his sermon on 1 Samuel 8[111] by asserting that the people of Israel were, even at the last minute prior to electing a king, still free to change their minds about seeking a king. Then Samuel warned them "that the king who will reign over them will take their sons for his own purposes and will cause much plundering and robbery." Calvin inferred from that circumstance that "the Lord does not give kings the right to use their power to subject the people to tyranny. Indeed, when the liberty to resist tyranny seems to be taken away by princes who have taken over, one can justly ask this question: since kings and princes are bound by covenant to the people, to administer the law in truest equality, sincerity, and integrity; if they break faith and usurp tyrannical power by which they allow themselves everything they want: is it not possible for the people to consider together taking measures in order to remedy the evil?"

Calvin acknowledged the complexity and unpopularity of that question. He was careful to distance himself from the Anabaptist[112] revolutionaries (who went "too far in agitating and overthrowing powers and authorities") of the day. He was consistently averse to anarchy and clung to the scriptural teaching "that God certainly punishes those who do not merit a good government by leading them into tyranny under bad princes."

He then distinguished between resistance to thieves and "the situation of leaders and superior dignitaries to whom God wills the subjects to be obedient." Calvin preached that "there are limits prescribed by God to their power, within which they ought to be satisfied: namely, to work for the common good and to govern and direct the people in truest fairness and justice; not to be puffed up with their own importance, but to remember that they also are subjects of God." Leaders were always to keep in mind the purpose (the glory of God) for which they had been providentially appointed.

The prophet Samuel, explained Calvin, warned his people about "the royal domination they will have to bear, and that their necks will have to be patiently submitted to his yoke." Calvin inferred something very significant from this: that intervening magistrates, not citizens themselves, should seek to correct abuses and tyranny. His doctrine was that "there are legitimate remedies against such tyranny, such as when there are other magistrates and official institutions to whom the care of the republic is committed, who will be able to restrict the prince to his proper authority so that if the prince attempts wrong action, they may hold him down." He counseled that, if the intervening magistrates did not free the people from tyranny, perhaps the people were being disciplined by God's providence.

In this sermon, Calvin detailed the ways in which monarchs might mistreat citizens. To some degree, he believed that shortcomings on the part of the people might well make them deserving of such oppression. Calvin also noted the long history of oppression and tyranny by "kings and princes thinking they deserve everything they want, simply because no one opposes them." Calvin recommended that the people, if faced with such tyrannical leadership, humble themselves and pray.

Even though Calvin was more permissive of monarchy than many of his successors, his calls to submit to the governor were not without limit. God established magistrates properly "for the use of the people and the benefit of the republic." Accordingly, kings also had charters to satisfy: "They are not to undertake war rashly, nor ambitiously to increase their wealth; nor are they to govern their subjects on the basis of personal opinion or lust for whatever they want." Kings had authority only insofar as they met the conditions of God's covenant. Accordingly, he proclaimed from the pulpit of St. Peter's, "Subjects are under the authority of kings; but at the same time, kings must care about the public welfare so they can discharge the duties prescribed to them by God with good counsel and mature deliberation."

Anticipating the later teaching of Theodore Beza and John Knox, Calvin taught in this sermon that lawful obedience to a ruler "does not mean that it is ever legitimate for princes to abuse them willfully. . . . This authority is therefore not placed in the hands of kings to be used indiscriminately and absolutely." In an early statement of political limitation, he claimed that private property was not "placed under the power and will of kings." Kings were to obey the laws, lest they convince themselves that they may do anything they wish. Rather, rulers should employ "all their ingenuity for the welfare of their subjects," considering themselves bound by God's law.

Rulers who did not understand the divinely circumscribed government were terribly mistaken. When they rejected divine ways, they inevitably considered their subjects as "no better than beasts." In the process, rulers were seduced to think of themselves as above the law. Yet, as Calvin had the foresight to note, "it is certain that all royal dominion is meant to be ministerial [servant oriented]." Indeed, he added, "kings are to be servants and ministers of God. Therefore it behooves them to consider themselves his commissioned legates to the people, who are to administer his affairs faithfully and are to take care of the people." Magistrates were instituted to be "ministers and servants of God and the people." More than anything, they are called to serve, not to be served.

Calvin exposed tyranny and recommended liberty as its antidote. He praised the "great gift [of] liberty, and how kindly God deals with those peoples upon whom it is poured out, where the magistrates are submitted to his laws and undertake nothing by themselves, but govern affairs by reason and counsel, for which they will at length make returns."

In addition to itemizing abuses typical of tyrannical powers, Calvin also warned against civic lethargy. He noted the following correspondence between taxation and prosperity: "Where princes take in less wealth, and require only a modest amount of tribute and taxes, their subjects overflow with personal riches."[113] Officials who ruled by will rather than reason were among the most dangerous. Such rulers became "attentive only to their own concerns, and govern the republic by personal desire alone, not by counsel and reason. . . . They devise a thousand harmful acts each day, since no one in the meantime dares to oppose them or even to utter one word." Becoming insensitive to the good of the people over time, they eschewed humility, virtue, and civic good—seeking only their own benefit—and grew "zealous not only to enlarge their authority and to confirm it more and more, but also to injure and despoil the people who are subject to them by robbery and all sorts of plundering." Naturally, Calvin said, "Their eyes and ears are closed to the calamities and miseries of suffering humanity so that their cries and groans mean nothing to them. The more they hear the groanings of their miserable subjects against their tyranny, the more out of control and ferocious they become."

This Genevan beacon, whose sermonic ideas later reached the shores of America, enumerated the ways kings abuse their power from the Samuel narrative, and he distinguished a tyrant from a legitimate prince by noting: "A tyrant rules only by his own will and lust, whereas legitimate magistrates rule by counsel and by reason so as to determine how to bring about the greatest public welfare and benefit." The king's ministers or cabinet were judged by the same standard. Calvin decried the oppressive custom of magistrates' "taking part in the plundering to enrich themselves off the poor."

He also spoke of political depravity: "God is showing that men will never do their duty unless they are drawn by some force, and when they have been raised to other ranks of more eminent dignity, they are like wild animals and beasts which no force can tame. Samuel also shows the rashness of the people which brought so much evil on themselves."

In this sermon, Calvin forewarned about the price associated with hierarchical government and warned that if

230 ~ The Character of John Calvin

political consequences resulted from poor political choices, perhaps that was an instance of God's judging a nation. If the people persisted in rejecting good government, Calvin cautioned:

> God can in his own just judgment make us blind and let us crash downwards, when we indulge our depraved and foolish desires beyond reason. . . . For it is generally the case that when we reach the stage of impudence where we prefer to follow what our own reason and lust have dictated, we will never be dissuaded from our intention by any amount of reasons, not even if we are gazing upon death itself. Such is the obstinacy of the human mind that it yields to no amount of reasoning, but with greatest arrogance sticks to its own opinion.

Neither did Calvin view Samuel's own sermon as isolated in application. Rather, he universalized: "This indeed is the outcome of all human plans which rest not on reason, but on impulse alone and on violent desires: immense unhappiness. . . . It is clear from this that once men have turned away from the right way, they make no end of sinning and are carried on to an even worse state, because they create destruction for themselves and are carried away, since they are ruled by the depraved counsels of their own passionate drives." Original sin in human beings led Calvin to call for appropriate safeguards: "Since it is this way, we must use protective remedies and measures lest we be unexpectedly overwhelmed. Experience surely teaches that this people rushed to an ever worse condition, and erred more and more from the way of righteousness, and provoked vehemently the wrath of God against themselves from having willingly repudiated the counsel of God."

Calvin did not call for rebellion, as Knox later did. However, similar sermons, along with reactions to the real depravity witnessed in the St. Bartholomew's Day massacre, demanded that Calvinistic political theory progress to the next level and more directly address the propriety of resistance to oppressive government.

The character of Calvinism is exhibited in this and other sermons that advocated limited government. Calvin was correct that individual responsibility was a good speed bump to a government taking over more than it should. Business, religious, and civic leaders would be prudent to implement similar principles.

THE ROLE OF LAW

There is always more in the requirements and prohibitions of the law than is expressed in words. . . . If this pleases God, its opposite displeases; if that displeases, its opposite pleases; if God commands this, he forbids the opposite; if he forbids that, he commands the opposite.

*I*T IS ONE THING for a person or a group to know a few basic facts about the law; it is another to have a deep and thorough appreciation for the proper use of the law. Calvin's legal education would not only serve to help him formulate local constitutions, it would also aid him in understanding the need for God's law to be applied properly.

Calvin's discussion of the law appears in book 2, chapter 8 of the *Institutes.* He begins by arguing that the law is necessary to inform us how to worship God. He also explains—and in this is contrary to some modern views— that Israel "learned from the law wherein true piety consisted" (2.8.1). Accordingly, they were "overawed by his majesty" (2.8.1) when they compared themselves to God's law. Furthermore, the law was not an external-only vehicle. To the contrary, it was an "internal law" that was "written and stamped on every heart" (2.8.1).

The law was also necessary, for even though we are created in God's image, natural law can only assist in pointing toward the right directions. While acknowledging conscience as a "monitor," Calvin knew that depravity affected each conscience and people were "immured in the darkness of error." Thus mankind was not left to natural law alone, lest it be given over to arrogance, ambition, and blind self-love. The law, then, was as gracious as it was necessary. Such a fundamentally positive view of God's law would be a distinctive feature of Calvinism.

The law also reminds us, as Calvin was quick to repeat, that we are not our own, but we have been born to serve God. It shows us how unworthy we are and leads us to "distrust our own ability" (2.8.3). Calvin frequently used phrases like "utter powerlessness" and "utter inability" to make the point that people are dependent on God's revelation if they are to do well. The law is a "perfect rule of righteousness" even though our natural minds are not inclined toward obedience.

Calvin then enunciated several principles of interpretation that should be comprehended about the law. He understood that law alone could not help but that people had to understand how to use the law. The first of those principles was that the law is spiritual (2.8.6). God speaks "to the soul not less than the body"; thus each commandment should be interpreted by its internal aim. Accordingly, Christ is the best interpreter of the mind of God on the meaning of the law, as he provided, for example, in the Sermon on the Mount.

The second principle of interpretation was the rule of implication. Calvin noted that the law is full of ramification and that it should not be limited to a few narrow applications. There is always, he wrote, "more in the requirements and prohibitions of the law than is expressed in words" (2.8.8). Each commandment also required its opposite. If one was not to steal, then he also should protect his and others' property. If one was not to lie, then he was to tell the truth, and if one was not to commit adultery, then he should support marital fidelity. Calvin believed that we must reason from the positive command to its opposite in this way: "If this pleases God, its opposite displeases; if that displeases, its opposite pleases; if God commands this, he forbids the opposite; if he forbids that, he commands the opposite" (2.8.8). Again, this would form the basis of an ethical theory that spread throughout the West, and it also shows a sophistication that was not always present in most theologies.

Third, Calvin honored the preexisting notion that the Ten Commandments (i.e., the moral law) contained two different sets of commandments (or tables). The first table of the law was commandments one through four, and those applied to God; the second table of the law (commandments five through ten) applied to our fellow beings. This provided a "complete rule of righteousness," and both indicated the duties of religion and the duties of charity (2.8.11). If ever conflicted, believers were to honor the first table over the second in priority. That would eventually become a pillar supporting a just resistance to an evil magistrate if he commanded disobedience to God.

Fourth, Calvin also identified three distinct uses for the

law. He noted that the first use was to bridle unbelievers so that they would not be as immoral as possible. God's moral law restrains unbelievers from running rampant and wreaking as much havoc as possible. If the law did not exist, it would have to be created for practical reasons alone so as to restrain evil from corrupting society. In this civil use (*usus civilis*), the law effects believer and nonbeliever alike. The second use of the law was to bring us to our knees and show us how weak and unable we are to satisfy God; in this use, the law keeps us from justifying ourselves. It provides an objective standard that we cannot avoid. Believer and unbeliever alike are condemned (*usus convictus*) by this standard. The third use of the law (and here Calvin differs with Luther) was that the law was a guide for sanctification, continually instructing us as to how God wanted us to live. Thus it provided a continuing ethical code, if rightly understood, for both believer and unbeliever alike. It maintains a teaching function; it teaches us (*usus didacticus*) how God is holy and how we are to live ethically.

To Calvin the law was a pointer. It never focused on itself but always pointed toward the Lawgiver. The "whole cultus of the Law" would "be utterly ridiculous," "vain or absurd" (2.7.1) if separated from its purpose. The three purposes of the law according to his *Institutes* were also compared to tools, which reinforced their use.

1. The convicting use was analogous to a double mirror (2.7.2,7).
2. The political, restraining use was associated with a bridle (2.7.10–11).

3. The pedagogical use was compared to a lamp to illumine God's will or whip to arouse us to obedience (2.7.12–13).

Thus the law has many practical functions, the chief of which is to guide and remind believers of God's norms.

So the moral law is spiritual, complex, and ordered. Calvin devotes the remainder of this chapter to a brief exposition of each commandment. His commentary on sexuality is less than a thousand words but ever so profound. His discussion of "thou shalt not steal" was rich with texture, calling for a person not only to avoid theft but also to "exert himself honestly to preserve his own" estate (2.8.45). These and other commentaries formed the Protestant work ethic. And when he spoke of the internal scope of the commandment that prohibited false testimony, he noted that it was "absurd to suppose that God hates the disease of evil-speaking in the tongue, and yet disapproves not of its malignity in the mind" (2.8.48). While those expositions may be brief, they are excellent and so worthy of consulting that most Protestant confessions did just that thereafter. Some of the codifications in various Puritan contexts would follow Calvin's train on the need and proper use of the law.

The reason that Calvin's teaching on this subject lasted so long was that it formed an ethos of law-abiding citizens. His followers regarded their own native abilities with such low esteem and God's revealed law in such high esteem that they became the creators and supporters of constitutionalism and law as a positive institution. Moreover, charity was the aim of law, and purity of conscience was the result. He concluded his treatise on the use of the law by affirming that this right understanding of the law "searches out and finds in all its precepts all the duties of piety and charity" and warned against any who would "merely search for dry and meager elements, as if it [law] taught the will of God only by halves" (2.8.51).

Calvinists, then, were not legalists but admirers of the perfections and wisdom of God's law, which they trusted more than themselves. Leaders who understand human nature will know the necessity of upholding law—both politically and corporately.

CONSTITUTIONALISM

The Lord does not give kings the right to use their power to subject the people to tyranny. Indeed, when the liberty to resist tyranny seems to be taken away by princes who have taken over, one can justly ask this question: since kings and princes are bound by covenant to the people, . . . if they break faith and usurp tyrannical power by which they allow themselves everything they want: is it not possible for the people to consider together taking measures in order to remedy the evil?

SHORTLY AFTER CALVIN RETURNED from exile in Strasbourg in 1541, he was appointed by the council to help revise the edicts of Geneva. Scottish historian William Naphy views Calvin as the lead drafter of Geneva's 1543 constitution. This constitution largely preserved the 1387 version, primarily substituting civil or Protestant powers for Roman Catholic authorities.[114] A century ago, historian Henri Fazy viewed the role of the Protestant church in the revision of Geneva's legal code as historic and considerable. It was first suggested that Calvin compiled the edicts for governing the people on October 4,

1541.[115] Then the council on May 15, 1542, appointed Calvin, along with Claude Roset and Fabri d'Evian, to review the previous edicts of Geneva.

These edicts were approved on January 23, 1543, and the council sent Calvin a barrel of aged wine as a token of its thanks.[116] "It is impossible," said Fazy, "to deny the role played by Calvin in the drafting of the edicts of 1543; the reformer was, if not the only, at least the principal author of the Edicts."[117] Further, Fazy reported that the 1543 edicts were "the basis of the new political system, the Calvinistic political system."[118] Marc-Edouard Chenevière, who noted that manuscripts in Calvin's own handwriting prove that he was involved in at least four drafts of this legislation, said that this work of Calvin "dominate[d] the political life of Geneva for the next two centuries."[119]

Although some scholars, such as Fazy, criticize Calvin for not being a pure democrat—it is true that he required laws to be adopted by two councils prior to final ratification—Calvin (and the councils) were seeking to initiate a balancing mechanism—an early form of separation of powers—that would preclude adopting imprudent measures because of demagoguery. Calvin's motivations, far from nefarious, were probably as simple as the Old Testament proverb that teaches that "wisdom is found in a multitude of counselors." While this was a revolutionary step, likely flowing from Calvin's pen, it was neither forced upon Geneva nor, in fact, unwise.

Many of the articles in the 1543 edicts were mundane, and some differed little from what had gone before.[120] Many of the articles included oaths of office, and numerous protocols were articulated. These primitive edicts, however, were not so much a mature constitution as a set of working procedures that functioned as a code of law.[121]

Fazy and others, however, think of Calvin as undertaking a thorough transformation of Geneva[122] both because of his earlier *Ecclesiastical Ordinances* (1541) and because of his key role in drafting these constitutional changes. The *Ecclesiastical Ordinances* and the revised edicts had as much impact on Geneva as any other documents in the century. The 1543 edicts functioned as the law of the republic during the most important days of the Protestant upheaval.

Later, in 1561, a committee revised the constitution; Calvin served in that capacity until his death. Three years after Calvin's death, the council recommended revising the edicts again and appointed a committee consisting of Bernard Chenalat, Michel Roset, Theodore Beza, and Germain Colladon. These revised edicts were first approved by the Small Council (January 26, 1568) and by the Council of Two Hundred (January 27, 1568) and then recommended to a General Council, which approved them in the early-morning hours of January 29, 1568. These edicts—compiled by Calvinist sympathizers Beza, Colladon, and Roset—remained in effect for 230 years, until 1798! These 1568 edicts introduced only minor changes, since "the Government [under Calvinistic control] had no motive for seeking any innovations." These edicts addressed Geneva's day-to-day operations, regulating the scope of civil officials (who were few in number) and certain commercial transactions.

The essential principle of Calvinism is respect for God's sovereignty, which "governs everything by his providence."[123] Calvinist citizens of Geneva thus sought to conform human government to the divine will, "safeguarding the liberties of the people protected by covenant and by divinely ordained representative government."[124] It also called for a comprehensive social, educational, economic, and political program. That comprehensiveness successfully transformed Geneva from "a frontier market-town" into "an international centre, the first Puritan commonwealth devoted to gainful vocations pursued for public purposes."[125]

Calvin's contribution to the 1543 edicts does not mention overtly religious themes, such as eternal condemnation, but retains his suggestions on "improvement in military defense, fire protection, police regulations, sewers, and weaving."[126] His impact converted a relatively isolated people into "the great Calvinistic trading peoples," eventually including Scotch, English, Dutch, and American colonists.[127] These who subscribed to Calvin's view of the sovereignty of God "deduced the moral obligation of all men to society, and a consequent devotion to production and public service as part of the service of God."[128]

These political and economic overflows of Calvin's thought bred the thrifty Yankee in New England and the clever Scot, but Calvin also required his followers to give generously to those who were needy. Calvinists, suggested Dartmouth historian Herbert Foster, were "everywhere more than theologians; they were founders of states which crystallized into practical working institutions the progressive teachings of Calvinism, social, economic, political," as well as those relating to theology.[129]

The vigorous impact of Calvin on the office of the magistrate may surprise some. He certainly labored for limited government, but he also worked equally for government to serve its God-appointed role. As strongly committed as he was to republican government, he did not labor for a pure democracy. He strengthened, if anything, the proper role of governors under the divine limitations revealed in Scripture. As such, Calvin did support a certain type of aristocracy,[130] but not an aristocracy based on wealth or privilege. He did not believe that political authority was transmitted by bloodline or status, of course. His republicanism was aristocratic in the sense that the few and the best representatives of the people were elected to serve the good of the people and the divine will. Thus Calvin both preserved some aspects of aristocracy and accelerated certain aspects of democracy. His blended republican government contained elements of both.

Marc-Edouard Chenevière's assessment, then, is apt:

> Certainly the reformer did not invent everything, certainly he abundantly helped himself to the earlier edicts, certainly he in part followed the current of aristocratic ideas that had already been born several years before his arrival on Genevan soil. But . . . if Calvin followed this current, he did not suffer through it, that is to say, he did not follow it against his will, or without attaching any importance to it. He followed it because this current was suitable to him, and that is why we can attribute to Calvin in large part the responsibility for the Edicts of 1543.[131]

These earliest constitutions of Geneva were formed under the watchful eye of original Protestant thinkers and became prototypes for republican protocols in the West. Thus the acclaim for the Reformation as the religion of liberty[132] has a long association with Calvin's constitutional revisions. His legislating activity served liberty. Good leaders know the value of good legislation to aid liberty.

Prosperity Ethic

"Thou shalt not steal" [is] to exert himself honestly
to preserve his own estate. A right understanding
of law "searches out and finds in all its precepts all
the duties of piety and charity," not "merely
search[ing] for dry and meager elements, as if it
[law] taught the will of God only by halves."

*W*ITHIN DAYS OF CALVIN'S death in 1564, his
mantle passed to Theodore Beza. Geneva
found itself on the world's stage as various groups, such as
Catholics and Anabaptists, hoped to overturn the new-
found Calvinist establishment. The crucial forty-year period between the deaths of Calvin (1564) and of Beza
(1605) determined whether or not Calvinism would be
a lasting force in Geneva, the cradle of Calvinism.[133]
William Monter attributes much of Geneva's growth and
stability during this period to the intellectual magnetism of
Calvinism.[134]

In addition, support for Calvinism in Geneva was in
part dependent on the city's prosperity. Prior to Calvin's
presence, Geneva had experienced economic hard times.
The neighboring Duke of Savoy extorted "free gifts"[135] of

massive amounts—taxation by another name—from the 1450s until 1526. In the early sixteenth century, Geneva also owed its Bernese benefactors large debts. Moreover, taxation on wine and rising property taxes in the late fifteenth century served only royalty while robbing the citizens. With Calvin, however, the patterns of taxation and income were altered. The prosperity ethic that followed is one of the wide-ranging effects of Calvin's thought and practice.

At least four significant sources of income fueled Geneva's new economic engine. First, revenue increased dramatically from 1550 to 1570 primarily due to the large number of new citizens (refugees).[136] In two years (1555–56), Calvinist refugees who flocked to Geneva contributed approximately 20 percent of the total revenue to the city coffers.[137] The popularity of Calvin's Academy[138] further boosted revenues in periods of need, and the influx of wealth continued for decades. By the 1580s many of the donors in times of crisis were people who had been refugees of the previous generation.[139] Population growth enhanced prosperity.

Second, after Calvin's arrival in 1536, Geneva retained many of the revenues formerly raised by the Catholic diocese. Parish tithes were still contributed, and, as an earlier historian wryly noted, "The last thing which a Reformed state wished to do was to abolish any Papist tax; and Messieurs knew that a preacher, even Calvin, was less expensive to maintain than a well-bred cathedral canon. . . . All in all, the Republic took in perceptibly more revenue from traditional ecclesiastical sources than it spent on Reformed ecclesiastical institutions."[140] Thus the conversion and redeployment of preexisting assets helped the local economy.

Third, Geneva surged ahead in the development of new information industries. The printing businesses of Protestant immigrants made significant fiscal contributions to the local economy.

Fourth, Geneva was successful in soliciting funds from other sympathetic Calvinistic countries. During one very difficult period (1593), Germans and other Calvinistic sympathizers contributed up to 25 percent of Geneva's budget as a result of solicitations by Beza.[141] Historian Alain Dufour summarized the sources of income: "Geneva survived principally on loans from her citizens in 1589, on foreign loans in 1590, and on collections from foreign churches in 1591."[142]

Beza also continued the political model of his mentor, favoring close interaction between the separate jurisdictions of church and state. The types and frequency of interactions between Beza and the various councils testify to the strength and longevity of Calvin's impact. Examples from the late sixteenth century[143] illustrate how this cooperative Reformation worked.[144] Beza spoke out against a 10 percent interest rate as usurious as early as 1580.[145] In 1581 city fathers consulted him about an appropriate sentence for a notorious criminal.[146] By 1588 Beza and other pastors again protested excessive usury to the Small Council.[147] In January 1596 Beza and the pastors urged the council to compensate the teachers of the Academy.[148] Beza and the pastors were frequent consultants of the council. Moreover, the types of discussions also indicate that the city governors wished to support the Reformation while not usurping the role of the ministers. Throughout 1596 the council minutes indicate close consultation between the pastors and council members on the appointment of pastors, disciplinary measures, the regulation of printing, and the search for Beza's eventual successor. On April 7, 1596, the council heard a complaint by Beza about poor church attendance, and it agreed to encourage citizens to attend. Specific pastors were approved for transfer or ordered to remain in their pulpits by the council. Geneva's separation of jurisdictions by no means erected an iron curtain between church and state. And none of this limited its growth and prosperity.

Rather, the historical record is clear: where Calvinism became thoroughly rooted, citizens saw economic growth. With the delicate combination of enhanced freedom and with opening economies, Calvin's prosperity ethic far outlived him.

CONSERVATIVE REVOLUTIONARY

For if there are now any magistrates of the people,
appointed to restrain the willfulness of kings . . . I
am so far from forbidding them to withstand, in
accordance with their duty, the fierce
licentiousness of kings, that, if they wink at kings
who violently fall upon and assault the lowly
common folk, I declare that their dissimulation
involves nefarious perfidy, because they
dishonestly betray the freedom of the people, of
which they know that they have been appointed
protectors by God's ordinance.

*I*F CALVIN WAS IN the forefront of such widespread
change, is it right to speak of him as a revolutionary? Mention that term and many envision guerrillas
or violent radicals. Most often the term *revolutionary* con-
notes violence, mayhem, ambition for power, and an unwillingness to abide by previous protocols. Calvin was
certainly none of these.

To the contrary, he was a plodding agent of change.
When he first arrived in Geneva, he did not present a manifesto to the city fathers, detailing all the changes he

wished to make. Yet, by the end of his life, after he had proved his character, he had been entrusted with some of the most important civic and diplomatic matters. Similarly, when it came to reforming the church, he called for reform five years after he'd initially arrived in Geneva. Calvin was—to the chagrin of some—far less revolutionary than some of his younger disciples wished him to be since he called for obedience to civil governors as much as possible.

He consistently argued against the use of force. Moreover, he even accepted the form of monarchy, if need be, and counseled that, in church reformation, different cultures could certainly pursue reforms at different paces. All change did not have to thump to his rhythm. The patience, perseverance, and moderation that he spoke of so often in his writings were equally exemplified in his practice. He would rather build on strong foundations than build hastily.

Like Calvin, Beza would also advise English Protestants on matters of the liturgy. Shortly before 1572, he wrote to Bishop Edmund Grindal of London, and the letter was published without Beza's consent. Excerpts from this missive below show the patience and latitude that both Calvin and Beza maintained, although many do not recognize these today.

From Beza's letter, urging Grindal to join in an international affirmation of reformed polity, the distinctives of the Puritan Presbyterianism of the day were supported. But he did not call for the abolition of bishops, averring:

> I know there are two opinions concerning the Reformation of Churches. For there be some of opinion, that

nothing at all should be added to the simplicity of the Apostolic church, and therefore that (without exception) all things are to be done by us which the Apostles did, and whatever the Church that succeeded next after the Apostles has added to the former things, they think they must be abolished at once. Contrariwise, there are some others, who think that certain of the old ceremonies moreover, are partly to be held still as profitable and necessary; and partly to be born with for concord's sake, although they are not necessary.

While Beza contended that "the Doctrine of the Apostles was most perfect in all points," it was equally clear from this gracious letter that he advocated reformed polity, even if it must be gradually introduced "for concord's sake." The primary goal of this tract was to point out the obvious contrast between the apostolic church and the present practice of the Episcopalian form of government. But he could wait for Protestantism to mature in England rather than call for a bloody revolution. This is an example of Calvinism rightly understood: it could patiently wait for persuasion to take root rather than incite coercive measures.

After all, if Calvin's disciples understood his work, they would realize that God would sovereignly create societal change in his own time. As such, violent upheavals were shunned. Calvin and Beza learned, as Luther did before them, that revolutionary anarchy rarely yielded positive or lasting results. These Reformers knew that change took time. They accepted that enduring social order was worth building slowly and on strong foundations.

Thus Calvin was a revolutionary only in this sense: he worked for incremental change that did not destroy the delicate balance of the preexisting social order, and he was a conservative revolutionary in the sense that he sought to return institutions to their original (and God-designed) charters. Rather than creating a new order for the ages, Calvin wished to return the family, the church, and the government back to their pristine biblical states. He was, thus, profoundly dystopian (not looking for a utopia of any sort), and his changes were characterized by patience and deliberation. He would sooner depend on methodical change through the existing officeholders and institutions than to completely overthrow all institutions and start all over.

Leaders in many different sectors would do well to remember this, whether they inherit a bloated bureaucracy or whether the tools of the trade need upgrading. Sometimes, as Calvin knew, the way change arrives is as important as what change brings.

PRAYER

"Prayer is the chief exercise of faith . . . by which we daily receive God's benefits." In it, we must realize "how completely destitute man is of all good, how devoid of every means of procuring his own salvation."

OST LEADERS KNOW THAT leadership roles often lead to loneliness, at times frequently reminding leaders of their need to turn to God in prayer. Calvin not only knew the value of prayer; he also wrote about it for the benefit of generations of ministers. One of the original chapters of his first edition (1536) of the *Institutes* focused on prayer.

The apex of his instruction on Christian living is reached in book 3, chapter 20 (if not already in chapters 6–10) on the subject of prayer, which is a means of grace for all Christians. Calvin assigned to prayer the elevated function of being "the chief exercise of faith . . . by which we daily receive God's benefits" as the chapter title suggests. Thus, having given prayer the highest priority for daily Christian living, Calvin embarked on a seventy-page exposition of the Christian's communication with God. In this, the longest single chapter in the *Institutes,* Calvin provided much information. Contrary to certain customary stereotypes, he was not only interested in horrible decrees or philosophical matters beyond the grasp of normal people. Rather, he extensively discussed a vital discipline and a benefit of grace. In keeping with his previous notions, before we can appreciate prayer, we must see "how completely destitute man is of all good, how devoid of every means of procuring his own salvation" (3.20.1). After a preamble (paragraphs 1–3) stating his beginning considerations, Calvin set out to establish four rules for prayer that benefit any person who prays.

1. The first rule (3.20.4–5) was that our minds should not be distracted by human concerns but oriented toward reverence according to God's majesty. As he put it, one must have his "heart and mind framed as becomes those who are entering into convers[ation] with God." That determines the parameters of prayer.

2. The second rule (3.20.6–7) was that prayers should originate with our own insufficiency according to our true need.

3. The third rule (3.20.8–10) followed from that position of inadequacy: in humility we should cast off our own worth and seek God's mercy alone. In order to pray, Calvin suggested that one "must divest himself of all vainglorious thoughts, lay aside all idea of worth; in short, discard all self-confidence, humbly giving God the whole glory, lest by arrogating anything, however little, to himself, vain pride

cause him to turn away his face." Such a submissive posture "casts down all haughtiness."

4. The fourth rule (3.20.11–14) suggested that our prayers could be made in confidence, knowing that God will answer them. A true practice of prayer leads one to "assuredly understand that God cannot be duly invoked without this firm sense of the Divine benevolence."

Amid these healthy rules for prayer, though, one should not think that Calvin required perfection. He understood that these "rules" were suggested attitudes, key to approaching God. They were not "so rigorously enforced" that God would not answer prayers that did not follow these precise rules (3.20.16).

Various other practical queries are then dealt with concerning prayer, such as:

1. Will God hear prayers when offered by one who is less than pleasing to him? (3.20.15)
2. Can deceased saints be intercessors? (3.20.21–27)
3. Of what value is private prayer? (3.20.28) or public prayer? (3.20.29)
4. Should prayer be in the vernacular? (3.20.33)
5. Is the Lord's Prayer a binding form? (3.20.48–49)
6. Should we have regular times of prayer? (3.20.50–51)
7. Are there unheard prayers? (3.20.52)

Calvin's detailed exposition of the Lord's Prayer was part of the original 1536 edition of the *Institutes.* He intentionally expounded material already familiar to the average churchgoer. Because of its catechetical history, Calvin explained the Lord's Prayer following the traditional division. After his exposition of the ascription in book 3, chapter 20 (paragraphs 36–40), he expands on the first three God-ward petitions (paragraphs 41–43) and then elaborates the last three earthly petitions (paragraphs 44–47). Would anything less than a godly, practically concerned, nonspeculative theologian devote so much of his crucial life and the print of his magnum opus to prayer? Calvin devotes such a lengthy chapter to prayer because he knew that the cogs of prayer are behind and beneath the overt wheels of history and industry.

PART 3

THE LEGACY OF JOHN CALVIN

The political character of Calvinism, which, with one consent and with instinctive judgment, the monarchs of that day feared as republicanism, and which Charles II declared a religion unfit for a gentleman, is expressed by a single word— predestination. *Did a proud aristocracy trace its lineage through generations of a high-born ancestry?—the republican reformer, with a loftier pride, invaded the invisible world, and from the book of life brought down the record of the noblest enfranchisement, decreed from all eternity by the King of kings.*

—GEORGE BANCROFT

CALVIN TO THE NEW WORLD

*B*Y THE END OF the sixteenth century, Calvin's Geneva had become an exporter of ideas, including groundbreaking democratic innovations that would kindle New World experiments in government. Later, Puritans would build on these foundations. Various dissenting groups explored additional initiatives and formulations for the respective powers of rulers, ministers, and citizens. These Puritan descendants of Calvin carried on his legacies as founders of the strongest democracies in history.

These antimonarchical Calvinists sketched the contours for much modern political innovation. Without Calvin and his disciples, the growth of liberty and stability in societies would have been stunted. Only when Calvin's followers implemented scriptural models of government did limited government and popular sovereignty become firmly planted. Although the exact cause-and-effect relationships may be debated, the historical sequence is clear. William Dunning, for instance, tracked the parallel trajectories of ecclesiastical and civil reform, noting: "As [Jean] Gerson and the conciliar party sought to destroy the autocracy of the Pope, and substitute the sovereignty of the General Council, so [Hubert] Languet [the likely author of the *Vindiciae*] and [George] Buchanan [disciples of Calvin] and the rest sought to destroy the autocracy of the king and substitute the sovereignty of the Estates of the Realm. . . . As the conciliar party had consciously sought to establish a government by the great prelates, so the antimonarchic party sought to establish a government by secular nobles."[1] An internal logic seemed to connect both reforms, providing a coherent matrix for church and state in the New World.

The tenacious roots of many freedoms, which most of us take for granted, extend back to—and seldom before—Calvin's religious foundations. But those roots would not remain confined only in Geneva, for the New World colonists packed these transcendent insights as they moved westward to establish their new communities. Indeed, those new polities became laboratories for the application of these theories without the hindrance of local traditions or preexisting authority. A genie of liberty had been released and would not easily be placed back in its bottle.

The evolution from Luther and Calvin to the New World of John Cotton and Samuel Adams eliminated the tired presumption that absolute submission to an illegitimate ruler was divinely mandated. Moreover, post-

Reformation Calvinists agreed, "The law and the contract intervene between God and the monarch." Even royal acts, they agreed, were subject to conditions. "Despotism had no sanction from heaven," and Protestants began to deny that secular rulers were immune from evaluation based on divine principles merely because of some divine right.[2] Dunning assessed the contributions of the Calvinistic thinkers, who were happy to leave behind a monarchy: "They sought and in a measure achieved certain concrete ends, but it was left for a series of thinkers who could bring more of philosophy and less of passion to the task to formulate with precision the definitions and dogmas which were of the highest significance in the political theory of the times."[3]

By the time of Calvin's death, Geneva had become a force in European politics independent of Paris, Rome, or Vienna. Supporting widely extensive Calvinistic efforts, Geneva "contributed in material ways to the Huguenot armies in France. Calvin's community encouraged the sending of small groups of men, large sums of money, and substantial quantities of gunpowder to the forces fighting for the Calvinist faith. And the spiritual leaders of the city were actively involved in these activities." As Robert Kingdon succinctly noted, "Geneva became an arsenal of Calvinism."[4]

Kingdon also noted that the development of ecclesiastical consistories and synods paved the way for other more secular democratic and federal structures. If these innovations could work in the church, they were workable in the state as well. Calvin's disciples soon were spreading the political message to Germany, with Rhineland students regularly training at the Genevan Academy, especially after Philipp Melanchthon's time. Kingdon reported that the Polish Diet was controlled by a majority of Protestants for a season in the mid-sixteenth century and Calvinism "remained perhaps the strongest form of Protestantism there, even after the re-establishment of traditional Catholic authority. Calvinism also penetrated deeply into Hungary. Even Catholic Spain produced a small group of Calvinists."[5]

Meanwhile, in Holland, William the Silent (1533–84) led the second Calvinistic republic into being by suggesting that covenants could be annulled between rulers and the ruled when the sworn conditions had been broken. As if laying the foundation for an American declaration two centuries later, the Dutch Declaration of Independence in 1581 gave full vent to this essential Calvinistic impulse: "A prince is constituted by God to be ruler of a people to defend them from oppression. . . . God did not create the people slave to their prince, to obey commands, whether right or wrong, but rather the prince for the sake of subjects."[6] Whenever such princes violated the covenant, the people ought—consistent with the ideas of Calvin, Knox, Beza, and Peter Martyr Vermigli—to resist him as a tyrant and defend the liberties of others. If resistance to tyrants was not uniquely invented by Genevans, the "Calvinist provided a method of resistance that was at once definite, legal, and practicable."[7]

Various European communities were weaning themselves from monarchy and replacing that top-down system with local autonomy, self-direction, and federal structures. The Western world would not be the same afterward.

Calvin's political tradition became the fountainhead for what became a broad stream of popular pamphlets, missionaries, educated clergy, loans, and even arms.

The political teachings of Calvin, Beza, and Johannes Althusius would spread to parts of Great Britain en route to America. There John Knox and other Scots would sow new fields with the message of freedom from tyranny. The popularity of Calvin's and Beza's disciples ensured that the ideas of Calvin would be exported to the New World. The movement begun by Calvin and originally centered in Geneva during his life became a radiating movement, expanding dramatically over the century after his death.

His legacies in education, church reform, and the doctrine of vocation were all encapsulated in these political liberties.

CALVIN IN THE PUBLIC SQUARE

*W*ITH A MISSIONARY ENTHUSIASM characteristic of the American founders, Samuel Rutherford, the author of *Lex Rex,* preached in 1640, "Who knows but this great work which is begun in Scotland now when it is going into England, and it has taken some footing there, but the Lord He will make it to go over sea?"[8] Indeed, it was such Puritan preaching, in part, which led to the colonization of the New World. This is reflected in the Mayflower Compact, which opened with a decidedly Calvinistic tone, as did the 1639 Fundamental Orders of Connecticut. After the preamble of that first written constitution in the New World, the Connecticut colonists covenanted to hold two general assemblies per year to elect a governor and (at least six) magistrates for no more than a year, who were to "administer justice according to the Laws here established, and for want thereof, according to the Rule of the Word of God." Such political novelties could be traced as a part of Calvin's legacy.

Features such as limited terms, balance of powers, citizen nullification, interpositional magistracies, and accountability to the church authorities were at the heart of New World government—these became megaphones for Calvinism. Moreover, all of these political concepts were established step-by-step during the late Middle Ages and the Reformation. Many were translated into political specifics in England during the early and middle seventeenth century.

Prior to that, however, rights were neither well defined nor clearly expressed in written charters. Before Calvin, there had been only halting surges toward popular sovereignty. Principled formulation for limited government, however, would not be accepted by a broad majority until after the Reformation was launched in and from Calvin's Geneva.

Many ideas that began with Calvin's Reformation in Geneva and later became part of the fabric of America were cultivated and crossbred in seventeenth-century London. Not only did the British Puritans introduce new twists in areas, but they also served as a conduit for many of Calvin's ideas. Customs now taken for granted— freedoms of speech, assembly, and dissent—were extended as Calvin's British and Scottish disciples refined these ideas.

The newfound right to dissent and freedom to publish (aided considerably by revolutionary advances in printing technology and distribution, so well exploited by Calvin's cadre of publishers) were extremely important for the broad dissemination of Puritan ideas. To be sure, Puritans and dissenters sought to extend reformation beyond the walls of the cathedrals, if only by demanding a new level of freedom of speech. While these disciples of Calvin may not have intended to push their revolution into the public square, nonetheless, with unforeseen rapidity, pulpit liberty was suddenly achieved after 1640, and governmental interference with sermons virtually disappeared. Puritan preachers, who originally sought freedom in the pulpit, "found themselves free as they had never been before to expound the Word in confident expectation that the long awaited reformation of the English church was at last to be accomplished and that reformation in England would lead to the reformation of the church throughout the world."[9] Such freedom is one of Calvin's legacies.

This trajectory of greater civic participation, William Haller noted, also led to freedom of the press. Haller concluded, "There had been revolutions in England before this but never one in which the press had been at so many men's command. And never one in which so many men found themselves so full of ideas concerning the nature of man and the structure of human society."[10] The fires of the American Revolution were fueled as well by this new freedom of the press and, in particular, by the publication of Calvinistic sermons.

Beginning with the revolutionary thought of the likes of John Knox, Christopher Goodman, and George Buchanan, the Puritans (Scottish and English) became a force for an ever widening idea of liberty. One sure effect of the Puritan[11] movement was to advance the discussion of limited government from theory and theology to the point of actually bringing courts and even crowns to accountability. What began as a courageous stand for the freedom of the pulpit laid the foundation for freedom of the press, freedom to assemble, and numerous other civic advances. Had the story ended with Calvin, the American Bill of Rights might have seemed a civic non sequitur. But the principles of Calvin, Beza, and Samuel Rutherford were in fact elaborated and practiced, and the Puritan experiments in England resulted in a truly momentous and much broader application of such ideas in America.

These British Calvinists' ideas were certainly compatible with Calvin's thought. These early choristers would inspire others, who would denounce kings and preach that "Government by a single Person [was] liable to Inconveniencies and aptest to degenerate into Tyranny, as sad and long Experience has taught us."[12] Thus Englishmen rebelled against the Crown on Calvin's covenantal principles a century before the American Revolution. Moreover, with a strong groundswell of presbyterianism, the 1689 Scottish Claim of Right appealed to Beza's "fundamental law" in an attempt to bring the Scottish government back to the people and back to its rightful limitations. Calvinists in Scotland, Ireland, and England a century after Calvin's death were still invoking this doctrine of resistance, which would be copied a century later by Americans who made good use of both the British and the Calvinistic arguments for revolution.

Later, England as well as America would develop a tradition of government-recognized fast days. Preaching, as in Geneva in Calvin's time, proved to be a potent source of communication and education in Puritan England, influencing government with its moral precepts. Freedom to preach became a symbol for wider freedom. Should hierarchical bishops oppose truth in preaching, they would necessarily be resisted in that small but hotly contested arena. "Obedience to God's Word, whether in print or on the lips of his prophets," said William Haller, "might thus come to require disobedience not only to bishops but to princes and magistrates."[13] Preaching of the Word thus was emblematic for resistance to tyranny and a higher loyalty to transcendent norms. Calvinist Puritans, in Old England and alike in New England, believed that preaching could change hearts and society.[14]

With Calvinistic preachers calling for reform, the press did not lag far behind. The logic of emancipation from prelatical control readily transferred into the political realm. The principles of Calvin, articulated and renewed a century later by British Puritans, would eventually take root in New England.

The 1647 Agreement of the People, which embodied the Puritan thought of London at that time and which was later enshrined in Oliver Cromwell's military regime, argued that the English Parliament could hold the king accountable. This Agreement of the People was in fact a draft for the constitution of Cromwell's commonwealth that never went into effect.[15] Even though aborted, it portended an advance for participatory democracy led in large part by Westminster Calvinists. Cromwell's army insisted that Parliament members were representatives of the people, elected every two years by local districts. In terms later made familiar by the American Constitution, this mid-seventeenth-century document also contained a bill of rights that allowed free expression of religion, protection against bills of attainder, and the security of private property.[16] Such rights guaranteed that individuals would not be harmed by the government. This agreement also conferred on the people the right of resistance against an unjust government. In addition, in words that would be imitated a century later, such rights were "fundamental to our common right, liberty, and safety." American Calvinists remembered and followed the formulations of these earlier British Calvinists. Yet it is hard to imagine these notions having the following they did apart from Calvin's pioneering work.

Hilaire Belloc may have exaggerated slightly, but only slightly, when he wrote, "No Calvin, No Cromwell."[17] Without Calvin's thoroughgoing reforms that converted Geneva to a laboratory for democratic freedoms, Cromwell and later developments would have been unthinkable. Cromwell himself, after all, was familiar with the work of George Buchanan.[18]

We are probably warranted also in claiming: No Calvin, No Cromwell, No Washington. The strongest democracy of the West was founded on the platform of Calvin. Not only was that true in political matters but in education as well.

MATHER ON HARVARD

*F*OR THE FIRST HUNDRED years of American colonial history, the best-seller list would have featured (1) the Bible, the Genevan version; (2) the Bay Psalm book (an Anglicized version of Calvin and Clement Marot's translation of the Psalter into the vernacular); and (3) the Westminster Shorter Catechism. All three works formed a core of cultural literacy for early Americans, and all three were legacies of Calvin. Furthermore, most of the greatest and earliest educational ventures in America bloomed from Calvinistic seeds.

Harvard became one of the most enduring names from the colonizing of America to independence. John Harvard (1607–38) had been educated at Emmanuel College, Cambridge, then a Puritan and Calvinistic stronghold within Anglicanism. A beautiful stained-glass window still commemorates the Harvard family in an ornate cedar-paneled hall of that once-Puritan college. Harvard responded to the call to assist the colonists in the New World, and by 1636 he had almost single-handedly established Harvard College. It was to become an important part of America's Reformation heritage, and its development under able Puritan hands was swift. The faith needed educated ministers. And the entire culture benefited from the education offered by Calvinist pedagogues.

Diary entries indicate that as soon as homes, churches, and civil governments were established, the next institution on the colonists' agenda was a college to "advance learning and perpetuate it to posterity; [we dread] to leave an illiterate ministry to the churches, when our present ministers shall lie in the dust."[19] Harvard's first class graduated in 1642, and by 1643 the General Court ordered that the civil rulers and the teaching elders of the six nearest churches be appointed "to be forever governors of the college."

Since educating future ministers was a priority, Harvard's earliest presidents were usually Puritan ministers who viewed themselves as followers of Calvin. Indeed, not only in early American academia, but also in several great European universities, such as those in the Netherlands and Switzerland by the 1650s, "Calvinism was firmly established as a leading academic movement."[20] Calvin's views are reflected in Harvard's 1646 Rules and Precepts. Among its Reformation-style provisions were, "Every one shall consider the main end [a paraphrase of the first question in the Westminster Shorter Catechism, "What is the *chief end* of man?"] of his life and studies to know God and Jesus Christ which is eternal life. . . . Every one shall so exercise himself in reading the Scriptures twice a day that they be ready to give an account of their proficiency therein, both in theoretical observations of languages and in practical spiritual truths."[21]

Cotton Mather reiterated his familiarity with Calvin in the opening discussion of his history of Harvard College. He spoke of Harvard as an "academy" and also repeated that ours was a "protestant and puritan country," zealous for a university like those in "reformed Belgium."[22] In his discussion of the origin of Harvard, Mather emphasized the connection between Calvinists on both sides of the Atlantic when he mentioned that Governor John Winthrop traveled to Holland to try to recruit renowned Dutch Calvinist Johannes Commenius to be the college's first president.[23]

That the Mather family and other founders of Harvard saw themselves as continuing the Calvinism of Geneva is evident from a review of references that Mather made in his history without great elaboration. In his story of Harvard, Mather referred to (and assumes his readers' acquaintance with) "the black [St.] Bartholomew day" and assumed that the notes in the Geneva Bible were authoritative.

Mather's *History of New-England* clearly viewed Calvin's Reformation in Geneva as the model that New England should follow and extend. At one point in his history of the college, Mather referred to the Reformation of Geneva and Scotland as a "larger step, and in many respects purer than" the British Reformation.[24] Mather believed that the main reason for Calvin's unpopularity was that he empowered the church to enforce moral behavior.[25]

Of the close agreement of New England churches with Continental Calvinism, Mather stated that the churches in early America "took all the occasions imaginable to make all the world know that in the doctrinal part of religion, they have agreed entirely with the reformed churches of Europe."[26] As proof, he cited the large number of catechisms produced by New England divines. He also informed his readers that when the time came for Puritan settlers to adopt their first confession of faith (in September 1648), they approved what had become an icon of Calvinism, the Westminster Confession of Faith, as "very holy, orthodox and judicious, in all matters of faith."[27]

This connection remained remarkably durable. A generation later, with Increase Mather presiding, an ecclesiastical synod at Boston on May 12, 1680, publicly endorsed the Westminster Confession "with a few variations" as their own belief system. Calvinism in Boston in 1680 was "what was agreed by the reverend assembly at Westminster, and afterwards by the general assembly of Scotland." The 1680 endorsement came only after the confession was twice "publickly read," then debated, and after small amendment (in church government only). "After such collations, but no *contentions,*" that chief Calvinistic pillar was "voted and printed as the *faith of new-England.* But they chose to express themselves in the words of those assemblies."[28] The New England version of the Westminster Confession also altered the role of the civil magistrate, shrinking his power to regulate religion since the original confession (reflecting its Anglican roots) authorized a governor to call a synod.

By 1696 Mather's list of ministers in New England confirmed his claim that churches were "erected in an American corner of the world on purpose to express and pursue the Protestant Reformation."[29] To Mather, the earliest historian of the America's earliest college, Harvard was clearly the American incubator of Calvinistic Puritanism, much as Cambridge had been a century earlier in England and Calvin's Academy had been even earlier. By 1696 its influence is seen in this fact: 100 of the 126 New England ministers were graduates of Harvard.[30] This college would nourish a wide range of infant political movements. Like the Geneva Academy before it, Harvard became both a preserver of culture and "the physician of the state."[31]

Harvard students attended daily chapels, which featured an exposition of Scripture by the president (always a Calvinist minister in the seventeenth century), and they devoted the Sabbath to catechism recitals and worship. Each day, students attended morning and evening prayer. The original college seal was a strong reflection of the Puritan faith, displaying the simple words *In Christi Gloriam.*[32] John Harvard, in fact, established the college to teach students to "know God and Jesus Christ." The founding Harvards hoped to replicate Calvin's Academy as much as possible. At Harvard the political ideas of Calvin echoed for decades, even as the college departed its original orthodoxy. Consider the following thesis topics—each of which had been a controverted topic in Calvin's Geneva—the century following Harvard's founding:

- Joseph Green (1729) denied that the New Testament advocated unlimited obedience to rulers.

- Samuel Adams (1743) defended his thesis that resistance against the supreme magistrate was lawful "if the Commonwealth cannot otherwise be preserved."
- Between 1743 and 1762 at least five graduates defended the proposition that civil government originates from compact.
- John Adams (1758) argued that civil government was an absolute necessity for society.
- Elbridge Gerry (1765) argued against the magistrate's restriction of free commerce.
- John Hunt (1769) defended the thesis that citizens are the "sole Judges of their Rights and Liberties."
- In 1770, Thomas Bernard's thesis answered the query, "Is a Government tyrannical in which the Rulers consult their own interest more than that of their Subjects?"
- Increase Sumner asserted that a "Government [was] despotic in which the People have no check on the Legislative Power."[33]

The seeds sown by Calvinist ministers in the 1640s were still in full flower in America by the eighteenth century. When Yale College was founded in 1701, it was for purposes similar to those of Harvard. Yale shared much of the same religious heritage. A recent study indicates that at least up to 1742, an older, classic Calvinism was dominant there. This strong brand of Calvinism was still present at Yale in 1753, when President David Clapp prohibited students from attending Anglican services.[34] Yale students and faculty alike could have fit in easily at Calvin's Academy in Geneva. The religion of Calvin—complete with all its political, educational, and social implications—was alive and well at America's foundation, especially in the early colonial colleges.

Americans also esteemed Calvin's colleagues and followers. The views expressed in the Solemn League and Covenant thrived in America in the late seventeenth century and may have been growing stronger, in fact, than in Scotland or Continental Europe. The Great Awakening of the 1730s and 1740s should be seen as one of a series of Calvinistic revivals rather than as an exception to slow a purported cultural and spiritual decline.[35] The Great Awakening, writes historian Marilyn J. Westerkamp, "represented neither innovative religious behavior nor a statement of challenge to the establishment. Rather, that revivalism, first observed in the colonies during this time, was actually part of the Scots-Irish religiosity, a tradition that flourished under the encouragement afforded by the colonial ministers."[36] It is not accidental, Westerkamp noted, that "outbreaks of revivalism in Pennsylvania and New Jersey followed directly after large-scale migration from Ireland, nor that the awakening spread to Virginia and the Carolina back country during the years when the Scots-Irish moved south." Indeed, the influx of Calvin's stepchildren bolstered the Calvinistic worldview of the colonies from 1660 to 1760.[37] It is even possible that what was founded as a Calvinistic colony with congregational government morphed into a Calvinistic nation as the number of Presbyterian immigrant pastors and settlers increased.

Calvinism was disseminated in America through three chief sources: (a) its ministers, (b) the earliest colleges, and (c) written materials. To roughly approximate the media monopoly of Calvinism in colonial America at its founding, imagine a country with no strong central government and the majority of its nonvisual communications *all* trumpeted the same religious and philosophical approach. Thus was Calvinism an enormous influence on education in the West, and it also was sown and cultivated for decades through those educational paradigms such as Harvard, Yale, and the College of New Jersey (later known as Princeton).

A statistical token of the pervasiveness of Calvinism in early America reveals the disproportionate number of colleges founded by Calvinistic groups. Of the 207 colleges founded prior to the Civil War, 49 were begun by Presbyterians.[38] Such was one aspect of the educational legacy commenced at Calvin's Academy.

LIMITED GOVERNMENT

*E*VEN WITH STRONG INDEPENDENT strains, cove-
nantalism or Calvinistic federalism under-
girds many American developments in the seventeenth
century. One of the clear legacies of Calvinism is its vision
for limited government. William Dunning noted, "The
Mayflower Compact, the Fundamental Orders of Connecticut, and the Newport Declaration expressed without
disguise or reservation the democratic principles that
were only latent in the Scottish National Covenant of
1638."[39] Puritan founders of Massachusetts established a
system that shared much of the "character of Calvin's
regime in Geneva" despite the unsuccessful lobbying of
Roger Williams.

The Puritan founders of America did not harbor grand
illusions about human potential, and they did not embrace
the enlightened dogmas of the innate goodness of man or

the inevitability of human progress. According to historian Gregg Singer, "Complete realism characterized their view of man and every sphere of his activity on earth. Their political, social, and economic philosophies were beholden to the doctrine of total depravity as much as they were to the sovereignty of God. Both the nature and functions of government were articulated by Puritan writers in the light of the fact that man is a sinner."[40] Even if many modern historians are dogmatically opposed to recognizing this strain of thought and its pervasive influence, research easily establishes its ubiquity during the colonial era. Early American Puritanism "was the rugged Calvinism of Calvin, Knox, and the Westminster divines who brought it to a new home in a new land."[41] The new environment, of course, permitted both preservation of Calvinism without interference by the monarch and innovation springing from the novelty of a totally new environment.

Gregg Singer observed, "The first product of the [American] Puritan theology was a Puritan philosophy of government." The British context itself necessitated or "induced the leaders of the exodus to the New World to set up a state which would conform to the dictates of the Puritan theology."[42] Moreover, the modern idea that the state was not subject to divine norms would have been abhorrent to a seventeenth-century Puritan.

It may appear to some moderns, at least to those not attuned to the nuances from previous centuries, that there was little or no separation of church and state in the early seventeenth century on North American shores. But a consideration of the thought of Calvin, Beza, Knox, Rutherford, and Althusius should disabuse readers of that notion. American Puritans, who were all too familiar with the dangers of blurring the ecclesiastical and political spheres, wanted nothing to do with a theocracy or an ecclesiocracy—neither did Calvin nor Zwingli, despite numerous superficial attempts to cast them as advocates of theocracy. The heart of their rejection of theocracy was that they wanted government limited so that it could not dictate to or impede an individual's conscience.

Following the tides of Calvin's thought, these Puritans wanted a separation of jurisdictions and energetically encouraged each sphere of government—family, church, and civil—to perform its own functions. Puritans, whether in Old or New England, recognized the Calvinistic pattern of differing and legitimate roles for both ministers and magistrates. It was possible, at least in their minds, for a lawful separation of jurisdictions to exist without hindering either church or state in its proper sphere.

Early American Puritans expected the state and the governor to support eternal moral and religious norms without transgressing on either conscience or the role of the church. The state had no power over religion or the soul but was to support the due exercise of the ministry. One modern Calvinist summarized: "Both church and state had their own spheres of action and neither was to transgress the domain of the other."[43]

Even the most sympathetic scholars of Puritanism admit that perfect separation was impossible to achieve, and the Puritans were certainly imperfect, both in Boston and Geneva, in their application of the theory. Yet, if their own testimonies are accepted, in principle, they consistently held to the jurisdictional separation of church and state.

Puritan ideas did not develop in a vacuum. American political experiments would be carried out in the context of strongly theological assumptions. Much of the prehistory of the American founding was rooted in Calvinism, even if much of that has long since been jettisoned. This Calvinistic idea was so dominant in the colonial mind "that it continued to guide even those who had come to regard the Gospel with indifference or even hostility."[44] As surely as this Calvinism was the root of the American oak of democracy, the waning of the Puritan experiment is also associated with the later demise of Calvinism.

Still, Calvinism's unique contribution was too potent to be ignored, lest one misunderstand the rehearsals leading up to the events of 1776. Calvin's political beliefs, embraced by the Puritans, were the seeds that grew into the vast luxuriance of the American founding. Historian Gregg Singer summed up the unique contributions flowing from the Calvinistic tradition of political life by stating that no government should transgress its charter.

The beginning of New England did not occur merely in 1607 or 1620. John Adams would later explain how the revolution of 1776 did not begin instantaneously; so too the *idea* of New England sprang from earlier religious impulses. The liberation of religion from clerical domination in the sixteenth-century Reformation, aided by the democratizing of literature by mass publishing, spawned the real seeds of the New England settlement. Nineteenth-century historian Carlos Martyn explained that, while New England began in physical terms at Plymouth Rock, in reality it was "cradled in the pages of the first printed copy of the English Bible."[45] New England, in fact, represented a development originating in the revolutionary faith of the Genevan Reformation. And New England Puritanism was thoroughly Calvinistic.[46]

Many governors and leading thinkers of the colonial era (1607–1700) left lengthy paper trails of their sentiments, which are strikingly compatible with those of influential writers and thinkers in John Calvin's Geneva and John Knox's Scotland. Most of these settlers invoked "providence" at the drop of a Puritan hat, and their understanding of providence was much closer to that of Calvin's *Institutes* or the Westminster Assembly's Confession of Faith (1648) than to latter-day Deism. Indeed, providence had long been a guiding light for these Calvinists, and these Puritans were unambiguously committed to that religion of providence.

RELIGION AND EARLY AMERICA

*I*F THE IDEAS FORGED by Calvin in the fires of sixteenth-century Europe were shared by American Puritans and New England Calvinists at the founding of America, it should not be a surprise that such views were reflected in the proclamations adopted near the American Revolution. In 1776, Americans continued to reiterate the views and rights developed by the previous centuries of Puritans and Calvinists. A survey of social norms and religious practices just before the Declaration of Independence reinforces that observation. Approximately three out of four Americans attended church services regularly, near an all-time high for America. Recent studies have noted that the Revolutionary period saw Christianity flourishing with an almost revivalistic fervor, as many of the sermons of the period indicate.[47] Religion played a leading role in the American Revolution. The first order of the

Continental Congress in September 1774 was to find a minister to lead in prayer. Jacob Duche, a Philadelphia minister, served informally as that spiritual mentor until after the Declaration was adopted. Five days after the Declaration's adoption, he was formally elected as a chaplain to the Congress.[48] This same Congress called for a day of public prayer and fasting in July 1775, similar to the British parliamentarians four generations earlier. When this Congress commissioned a seal, the committee consisting of Franklin, Jefferson, and Adams returned with an illustration largely derived from the book of Exodus, with George III caricatured as a latter-day Pharaoh and featuring a Calvinistic motto that equated rebellion against tyrants with religious duty.

Congress on several occasions called for public fasts and days of humiliation. One such notable day, approved on March 16, 1776, urged united hearts to make "sincere repentance and amendments of life" and to appease the righteous displeasure of "the Lords of Hosts, the God of armies" and "through the merits and mediation of Jesus Christ" to "obtain his pardon and forgiveness."[49]

Two months later, in May, Congress invoked another fast day. This time, the representatives requested that ministers publicly read the proclamation, similar to the distribution method for the *Magna Carta* and other ancient documents that had been circulated to churches. Another fast day, a fortnight after the promulgation of the Declaration (July 20), featured sermons by prominent Philadelphia clergy—Chaplain Duche (whose church featured a stained-glass window containing the motto "The Church and Magna Carta") and Presbyterian patriarch Francis Alison. Of this occasion, John Adams observed, "Millions will be on their Knees at once before their great Creator, imploring His forgiveness and Blessing, his Smiles on American Councils and Arms."[50] Several scholars have noted that the language of this July 20, 1776, proclamation (and others) was riddled with the covenant theology of the Swiss Reformation. "As old as the Reformation itself," noted historian James Hutson, this common faith "was embraced by all of the major Protestant groups who settled America, although it has become known as one of the signature statements of the New England Puritans."[51]

Such fiery preaching, coupled with such unambiguous theological conviction, occurred regularly in early congressional fast and Thanksgiving services. James Hutson also commented that, for a decade, from the first proclamation of a national fast on June 12, 1775, to August 3, 1784, "Congress adopted and preached to the American people the political theology of the national covenant, the belief that the war with Britain was God's punishment for America's sins and that national confession and repentance would reconcile Him to the country and cause Him to bare His mighty arm and smite the British. . . . Covenant theology had legitimized this approach for generations."[52]

Congress formally endorsed the following Reformation notions, either in its annual fast day proclamations in March or by its Thanksgiving Day proclamations in November: God's overruling providence (1776); God's judgment on the people's sins (1780); the need for confession and repentance to "appease his righteous displeasure" (1776, 1781); a call to pursue national reformation of religion (1776); a call for God to bless "the means of religion for the promotion and enlargement of that kingdome which consisteth 'in righteousness, peace and joy in the Holy Ghost'" (1777); and an invitation to Americans to "join the penitent confession of their manifold sins . . . and their humble and earnest supplication that it may please God, through the merits of Jesus Christ, mercifully to forgive and blot them out of remembrance."[53] Most of these pleas could have been offered equally by the Westminster Assembly–influenced Long Parliament in London's 1640s or the Council of Two Hundred in Calvin's Geneva in the 1540s.

In 1782 Congress approved a Bible for America's citizens—one that was more akin to the 1560 Geneva Bible than to the Englishman's King James Version.[54] As James Hutson observed, the sanction of certain religious initiatives by the federal Congress (plus an even wider latitude for state legislatures) meant that both

> politicians and the public held an unarticulated conviction that it was the duty of the national government to support religion, that it had an inherent power to do so, as long as it acted in a nonsectarian way without appropriating public money. What other body, after all, was capable of convincing a dispersed people that a "spirit of universal reformation among all ranks and degrees of our citizens," would "make us a holy, that so we may be a happy people"? The conviction—that holiness and virtue were prerequisites for happiness, that religion was, in the words of the Northwest Ordinance, "necessary to good government and the happiness of mankind"—was not

the least of the Confederation's legacies to the new republican era that began with Washington's inauguration in 1789.[55]

Moreover, Hutson confirmed the high pitch of religiosity at the time: "Perhaps only Cromwell's Parliaments can compare to [the Continental] Congress in the number of deeply religious men in positions of national legislative leadership."[56] Among those were Charles Thomson, the recording secretary of the Continental Congress, who, after his retirement, translated New Testament Greek texts into a four-volume Bible commentary with notes; John Dickinson, a member of Congress from Delaware who helped draft the first version of the Articles of Confederation;[57] Presbyterian minister John Zubly, a Calvinist from Switzerland; Henry Laurens, president of Congress (1777–78)—well known for holding regular religious devotions for his family; John Jay, president of Congress (1778–79) and first chief justice of the Supreme Court, who became president of the American Bible Society after his public service; and Elias Boudinot, president of Congress (1782–83) and director of the Mint, who wrote numerous tracts and served as the original president of the American Bible Society.[58]

That so many Calvinists occupied prominent roles in the early stages of the American republic may help explain why many Baptists, including Ezra Stiles, feared that the American Revolution was "a Presbyterian War."[59] Many Founding Fathers continued to expect legislators or rulers to approximate "nursing fathers"[60]—just as Calvin had taught.

The early colonists of Virginia believed that religious consensus was necessary for social cohesion. In 1784 they advocated that "the aid of religion will be the more necessary and its influence more decisive" since the new country had no monarchies and little tradition.[61] Subsequent to the Declaration of Independence, the following states restricted office holding to those who believed in eternal life: Pennsylvania (1776), Delaware (which, along with Pennsylvania, also required belief in the inspiration of the Scriptures—Old and New Testaments), Vermont (1777), South Carolina (1778), and Tennessee (1796).[62]

For a while, Georgia (1777), Massachusetts (1780—which stated that good government depended on "piety, religion, and morality")—and Maryland (1785) taxed their citizens to support ministers of the gospel. Virginia was on the verge of supporting such a measure, with John Witherspoon and Patrick Henry narrowly missing that accomplishment, due to last-minute tactics from James Madison and Thomas Jefferson. South Carolina (1778) ordered "the Christian Protestant Religion" to be established, and Maryland (1784) affirmed, among other things, that the order and preservation of civil government, as well as the happiness of its citizens, "essentially depended upon morality, religion, and piety."[63] In addition, twelve of the original thirteen states had some sort of religious test for holding office.

Many others have set forth cogent and convincing arguments for the Christian orientation and belief of many of the Founding Fathers. Rather than humanism or Deism holding ideological preference among those who were the political heirs of the Reformation, the Christian doctrines flowing from Calvinism remained at the forefront during the formation of America. These were the essential beliefs at about 1750 that have been lost to many citizens. Also lost has been an understanding that a particular theology influenced the politics of the day. Theological principles and the political themes that flowed naturally from them were proclaimed from pulpits with regularity and vigor.

Consequently, the Declaration of Independence and the Constitution of the United States reflect Calvin's hearty skepticism about human abilities to create anything approaching perfection on earth. One result was that no individual would be given unlimited power because human nature, including human reason, was fallible. Another safeguard was the belief that states were governed best with the active involvement of the people, guided by fixed constitutional principles. At first, the unique American Constitution stood alone in the world. In time, many other nations would come to follow aspects of this model so rooted in Scripture and a particular view of the nature of man and his limited abilities. Today, even though many mutations have occurred, the religion of Calvinism still proffers some of the most liberating political advances.

In 1773 the theological argumentation developed earlier by Calvin, and advanced by the Puritans, trumpeting that "Supreme or unlimited Authority can with Fitness belong only to the Sovereign of the Universe" was still sounded, especially in America.[64] The logic of that theology had remarkable consequences for Western political thought. Founding Father John Adams credited the Reformation for tumbling monarchical claims, and it should not be surprising to note that opposition to Britain's monarchical claims arose first from Calvinists, who believed that absolute sovereignty belonged exclusively to God[65] and who had also opposed the Anglican hierarchy.

Jonathan Clark has shown that, at the founding of America, references to scriptural ideas were employed until the end of the seventeenth century.[66] American orators during the Revolutionary period still identified America with the "New Israel."[67] Far from being a secular errand in the wilderness, as some have claimed, the great preponderance of colonial Americans saw God's providence in daily events. Hardly based on pluralistic models, they had a strong religious identity that even superseded the rights of Englishmen.[68]

CALVIN AND MADISON AND ADAMS

*M*ANY LEADERS AT THE founding of America betrayed their own Calvinistic context. James Madison—one of the early graduates of the Presbyterian college that became Princeton—asserted that fixed laws and constitutions were necessary to constrain human ambition. Human depravity, that innate tendency toward sinfulness and the exploitation of others, required that governmental power be circumscribed. To Madison, it was but "a reflection on human nature, that such devices should be necessary to control the abuses of government." He reflected the thought of John Knox—who was mentored in the Calvinistic politics of Geneva and transported these ideas to his native Scotland and ultimately to America—when he wrote: "But what is government itself, but the greatest of all reflections on human nature? *If men were angels, no government would be necessary.* If angels were to govern men, neither external nor internal controls on government would be necessary" (Federalist No. 51). Had Madison derived his view from human experience alone, this reference would merit little comment. But it appears remarkably similar to a particular theological formulation from several centuries earlier and derived from a common well.

More than two centuries prior to the publication of Madison's Federalist paper in American newspapers, John Calvin had preached a very similar message from the book of Galatians to his Genevan audience, observing: "*If we were all like angels, blameless and freely able to exercise perfect self-control, we would not need rules or regulations.* Why, then, do we have so many laws and statutes? Because of man's wickedness, for he is constantly overflowing with evil; this is why a remedy is required."[69] The similarity between these two comments two centuries apart is both striking and deserving of explanation.

Had this been the sole instance of nearly identical phrasing, one might consider coincidence a possible explanation. When, however, other American founders repeat similar mantras, it is more difficult to chalk up the parroting of Calvinistic phrases to mere accident. As early as 1760, John Adams entered a comparable thought in his diary with an even more pointed application, reflecting a Calvinistic view of human nature: "Lawyers live upon the sins of the people." Then, sounding like both Calvin and Madison, he added: "If all men were just, and honest, and pious, and religious, etc., there would be no need of lawyers. . . . [I]t may be said, with equal truth, that all magistrates and all civil officers and all civil government are founded and maintained upon the sins of the people. *All armies would be needless if men were universally virtuous.*"[70] Adams also believed that economics and manufacturing were affected by these tendencies toward depravity.

At the time of the American Revolution, Adams esteemed the tiny republic of Geneva as the "first Puritan state," and wrote of it: "Let not Geneva be forgotten or despised. Religious liberty owes it much respect."[71] He understood the contribution of Calvin and also attributed the best morality and political wisdom to the Bible, which he called "the most republican book in the world."

It is difficult to ignore the similarity of substance, if not the virtually identical vocabulary, between these written sentiments separated by centuries. Several other passages in the Federalist Papers and numerous other writings from America's founding period have a distinctively Calvinistic flavor as well. Many American leaders, both during the colonial founding period and at the time of independence, explicitly referred to Calvinistic political ideas and ideals.

Even late into the nineteenth century, English historians still referred to Geneva's Christian republic. John Richard Green noted, "It is into Calvinism that the modern world plunges its roots. For it is Calvinism which first reveals the dignity and worth of man. Called of God, heir of heaven, the merchant in his shop and the peasant in his field suddenly become the equal of noble and king."[72] At the very least, one should acknowledge "the rather striking correlation, both in time and in place, between the spread of Calvinist Protestantism and the rise of democracy."[73]

Up to the time of the American Revolution, even Calvin's adversaries, not to mention his followers, recognized his vast contribution to Western political culture. Praise for Calvin from those who marched to a different drumbeat can be seen in Thomas Jefferson. Why did he, a man more closely associated with French Revolutionary *philosophes* than with Calvin's Reformation thought, join with Ben Franklin in recommending an official seal for the United States emblazoned with biblical imagery from the book of Exodus and encircled by the motto "Rebellion Against Tyrants Is Obedience to God"?

That motto, with historically Calvinistic associations, did not have its origin in the New World. The tyrants for New Englanders to overthrow were mainly distant ones, and the upstart revolutionary army eventually disposed of those troops. Moreover, the remaining biblical symbolism first proposed by Jefferson alluded to Moses, complete with a depiction of the Red Sea deluging the pursuing British army under the command of Pharaoh George III. The symbolism was likely Jefferson's mature reflection on a principle that stemmed from the Protestant Reformation. Calvin's disciples were the ones (Theodore Beza after 1572 in Switzerland and John Knox in Scotland) who taught that it was not only permitted for Christians to oppose a tyrannical regime but also that, in some cases, *it was required.* It was merely living out the Golden Rule to do so, they argued. Jefferson apparently concurred that this was the irreducible minimum of good government, placarding "Rebellion to Tyrants Is Obedience to God" as a lasting imprint of the enduring Calvinistic philosophy of government.

Many earlier observers, who did not have the recent biases of secularism, realized the value of Calvin's political contribution. Near the time of the ratification of the American Constitution, the great historian of Switzerland, Johannes von Muller, referred to Calvin as a genius, an indefatigable lawgiver, and a font for advancing human culture and knowledge. Von Muller further extolled him for promoting free inquiry while at the same time refining government to curtail the worst of human passions.[74]

The limitations placed on governors in both Madison's America and Calvin's Switzerland share an organic similarity that has been frequently noted by both historians and politicians. John Adams referred to the Swiss republic, which perpetuated many of Calvin's political legacies, as a model for the American republic. In his 1787 *Defense of the Constitution,* Adams noted the benefits of a well-regulated militia and advocated the same right to vote on laws and possess arms as the citizens of the Swiss cantons enjoyed. Adams also noted the value of the decentralized cantonal spheres (already operative in the time of Calvin) and the courage to resist tyranny. Adams believed these decentralized spheres provided an apt model for the American government in "fix[ing] the sacred rights of man." American Founding Fathers George Mason, Patrick Henry, and others lauded the preservation of independence fostered by the Swiss republics, a form of government that would not have endured without Calvin's strong commitment to limited government.

John Adams later paid tribute to several of Calvin's disciples. American theologian Stanley Bamberg noted that Adams commended Calvinist theorist John Ponet for promulgating "all the essential principles of liberty, which were afterward dilated by Sidney and Locke." Later Adams specifically endorsed several other works from the Calvinistic tradition, including those by John Milton and the *Vindiciae Contra Tyrannos,* among others. These (plus the works of Algernon Sidney and John Locke), he thought, should be "preserved as the most precious relics of antiquity, both for curiosity and use."[75] Stanley Bamberg concluded that "Adams' justification of revolution and the arguments propounded in *Vindiciae* demonstrate a basic agreement as well as Adams' acceptance of the social contract theory of government found in the Calvinist work." The arguments Adams employs bear striking similarities to the *Vindiciae Contra Tyrannos,*"[76] written nearly two centuries before the peak of the Enlightenment. Moreover, it is clear from Adams's *Discourses on Davila* that he was also very familiar with Reformation and Huguenot political history—and he was specifically acquainted with the contributions of Theodore Beza, Peter Martyr Vermilly [Vermigli], and "others who came from Geneva."[77]

Bamberg confirmed "that Adams was closer to the tradition of *Vindiciae,* Rutherford's *Lex Rex,* and Ponet than to some of his own contemporaries." This recent research also demonstrates that Adams's definition of tyranny and his views on the legitimacy of revolt are closer fits with the earlier Calvinist tracts than with Enlightenment sources. Adams, wrote Bamberg, like other Founding Fathers, "took ideas and phrases from whatever source they deemed helpful. . . . Adams, like other American Whigs, derived his theory from the English

Civil War tradition which was itself informed by *Vindiciae.*" He also recognized that, in his providence, God "raised up the champions who began and conducted the Reformation." Moreover, by 1681, John Locke himself owned a copy of the *Vindiciae Contra Tyrannos* and most other Calvinistic resistance tracts.[78] From the earliest settling of America, a full century and a half before the Revolutionary War, Calvinistic thought suffused the political ruminations of the entire colonial period.

The Legacy and Decline of Calvinism

*T*HE LATE ERIK VON KUEHNELT-LEDDIHN once observed, "If we call the American statesmen of the late eighteenth century the Founding Fathers of the United States, then the Pilgrims and Puritans were the grandfathers and Calvin the great-grandfather. . . . [T]hough the fashionable eighteenth century Deism may have pervaded some intellectual circles, the prevailing spirit of Americans before and after the War of Independence was essentially Calvinistic."[79]

Presbyterians were the most rapidly growing segment of American religion in the early eighteenth century; and in Pennsylvania, Virginia, and in both Carolinas, they were the largest distinctive ideological group.[80] Most of the leading politicians and officers from the North Carolina militia were Presbyterian (and Calvinistic) elders. On an even larger scale, approximately two-thirds of the colonial population at the time of the Revolution was dominated by dissenting groups who retained little affection for Anglicanism or any other hierarchical structure.[81]

This explains, in part, why some of the revolutionary militia from New York called themselves the "Presbyterian *Junto*" and accounts for the fear that, with such a visible cadre of Calvinist participants in the Revolution, "rumors were very rife that projects were on foot to make Presbyterianism the religion of the new republic."[82] As the Reverend William Jones observed: "This has been a Presbyterian war from the beginning as certainly as that in 1641."[83] In 1776 this same Jones wrote about the wide influence that these dissenters, mainly the Presbyterian children of Calvin, were having in America. He accused them of supporting the government when convenient or insofar as it agreed with their views, but never failing "to oppose it, if its establishment is of service to any party but themselves."[84]

This strong Calvinistic support of the Revolution is evident from both secular and ecclesiastical records in the mid-1770s. For example, a group of Virginians protested against "unlimited and unconstitutional power" in 1775. Later, the near "complete uniformity of Presbyterian clergy"[85] in support of the war may be seen from their support of Gen. George Washington in various synodic resolutions. Harking back to their Scottish and Ulster roots, these Presbyterians viewed themselves as continuing the Calvinistic tradition of removing kings if they violated their covenant, "setting aside bigotted Princes," rather than as creating a new theo-political doctrine.[86]

On the eve of the Revolution, Presbyterians, still echoing Beza and Rutherford, were arguing against taxation and confiscatory reprisals. To seize one's money or property without consent was "unjust and contrary to reason and the law of God, and the Gospel of Christ; it is contrary to *Magna Carta* . . . and the Constitution of England; and to complain, and even to resist such a lawless power is just and reasonable and no rebellion."[87]

At the time of the Revolution, one British soldier wrote of the continuing influence of Calvin on popular support for independence. Capt. Johann Heinrichs wrote to a friend in Hessia: "Call this war, dearest friend, by whatsoever name you may, only call it not an American Rebellion, it is nothing more or less than an Irish-Scotch Presbyterian Rebellion."[88] Heinrichs went on to compare the conflict to earlier French Huguenot wars, except this time the Calvinists were the victors, and they viewed religion and liberty as inextricably intertwined. Heinrichs was not alone in observations such as these.

Presbyterian ministers showed no hesitation in taking on political roles. They did so with vigor and had great impact in the political arena. It was in no way unusual, therefore, that in addition to John Witherspoon, Presbyterian Jacob Green (Ashbel Green's father) was a member of the provincial Congress of New Jersey. John J. Zubly (a Swiss native) was one of Georgia's delegates to the Continental Congress. Many others served in state provincial congresses at the formation of the union.[89]

Another author noted: "When Cornwallis was driven back to retreat and ultimate surrender at Yorktown, all the colonels in the Colonial Army but one were Presbyterian elders. More than one-half of all the soldiers and officers of the American Army during the Revolution were Presbyterians." Presbyterian pastor Charles Thomson doubled as a secretary of the Continental Congress and earned John Adams's praise as "the life of the cause of liberty."[90]

Not only did Presbyterian convictions fuel the Revolution, the faith's underlying Calvinism is also reflected in many of the official documents between the Revolution and the ratification of the Constitution. Primary documents confirm the thesis: the Declaration of Independence, acts of the Continental Congress between 1776 and 1787, and the Constitution all bear the impress of two centuries of Calvinistic thinking. *The Federalist Papers,* the original constitutions for the states, and other popular discourse also spell out the heritage of the Reformation as well. Even if fading in some respects and transformed in others, Calvin's ideas were still vital during this final act of the founding period.

If Calvin's ideas were so strong, did they continue in force? It is a fact that, by the time of the American Revolution, Calvin's sun was setting even in lands where it once burned brightly. Europe grew in secularism as the Enlightenment took root. In one of the more egregious examples of early-modern humanism, the French Revolution sought unbridled liberty. While few Americans gravitated to those Jacobin sentiments, many others in Europe were more enamored with liberty and egalitarianism—not to mention secularism.

If the 1789 French Revolution is the epitome of modernity, the American Revolution was fundamentally different. But even the Calvinism that fueled much of the American experiment began to diminish after that revolution in some sectors of society. By the time of Jefferson's death (1826), the climate permitted more skepticism about the salutary effect of religion in general and Calvinism in particular. And Jefferson was by no means alone. Many other public leaders would join to renounce the Protestantism of Calvin as too confining and seek greater liberty from constraint.

Between the Declaration of Independence and the Civil War, Calvinism began a swift decline in America. Numerous causes for its demise can be cited.

First, as the Enlightenment spread in educational and intellectual quarters, those who held the franchise became more willing to seek a type of consistency. If a citizen could vote for his civic representatives, then, he reasoned, why could he not vote on his choice for or against God, or, for that matter, creed and church? With the rise of American democracy, most Westerners began to believe—later to presuppose—that all men, created equal, were also capable of choosing the good and expressing their franchise for God . . . or not. Freewill blood began to pulse through Western veins, and it was only a matter of time before Calvinism became known as an enemy of that unbridled liberty.

Second, Unitarianism and Transcendentalism presented philosophical alternatives to the erstwhile Protestant worldview. These thoroughly humanistic thought systems—one of which focused on reason, the other on idealism—rooted themselves in New England and migrated southward and westward. In time, these alternatives conquered many universities and institutions.

Third, the Industrial Revolution began to alter the traditional communal structure of American life and families.

An inchoate urbanism started to undermine certain cultural aspects of the family. Instead of small businesses and tightly knit communities, large factories dotted the landscape. Church attendance began, slowly at first, to give way to the gospel of materialism. As Western democracies became affluent, more of its citizens felt less need to rely on God or his providence.

Fourth, by the mid-nineteenth century, Darwinism added a more corrosive effect to the shrinkage of Calvin's influence. It would not take long for this worldview to influence the thinking of generations to come. If, as presumed, humans only evolved and there was no Creator, then morality was also up to individuals. Similarly, it was possible for humans to define their own values and to live for this life totally instead of for the world to come.

Finally, evangelical religion itself contributed to the demise of Calvinism. With the rise of revivals and with the growing popularity of Arminian denominations, Calvinism became less popular among churchgoers in America. The rugged individualism necessary for survival on the frontier seeped into the walls of churches, and the expectations of congregants changed rapidly.

By the end of the nineteenth century, America—the last bastion of Calvinism—was leaving the moorings of its founding. Universities became the incubators of twentieth-century humanism. By the end of the world wars in the twentieth century, society became increasingly secular. The sacred could not be empirically demonstrated, and in a scientific or nuclear age, truth became subject to laboratories or to those who formulated the experiments. God was conveniently left out, and with the rise of statism in formerly Calvinist lands, a once-robust movement was largely laid to rest. This American pattern was similar to but lagging behind the earlier decline of Calvinism in Europe. The grandchildren of Calvin outgrew their own genes, and swift was the mutation of life and thought thereafter.

One painful result, of course, was the absence of a principled force to resist the various tyrannies of the twentieth century. Millions of people were sacrificed on the altars to Nazism, Communism, various genocides, and numerous oppressive regimes. Diminishing resistance to tyrants, once the signature of thinkers ranging from Knox to Madison, was also decoupled from obedience to God. Indeed, without duty to God, society and politics were the weaker and less free.

But the remains of Calvin need not remain buried.

Epilogue

*A*s we have sought to prove, few thinkers with a lineage as ancient as Calvin's have as much future promise. Calvin set forth both the positive necessity for well-ordered government as well as the limitations of its scope. His Reformed theology compelled government to be limited to the role of servant of the people; his political insights helped restrain the leviathan. Today, when individuals frequently act as if centralized government agencies can provide lasting solutions to a wide range of social and individual problems, Calvinistic realism is one of the few substantial intellectual traditions that cogently warns against the danger of accumulated government power.

Of all theologies, Calvinism has made the most significant contribution to democracy. One summary of political Calvinism reduced Calvin's ideas to five points that may be of continuing validity. Herbert Foster noted the following as hallmarks of Calvin's political legacy,[1] and most are exhibited by the works we have surveyed above:

1. The absolute sovereignty of God entailed that universal human rights (or Beza's "fundamental law")

should be protected and must not be surrendered to the whim of tyranny.

2. These fundamental laws, which were always compatible with God's law, are the basis of whatever public liberties we enjoy.

3. Mutual covenants—as taught by Beza, Hotman, and the *Vindiciae*—between rulers and God and between rulers and subjects were binding and necessary.

4. As Ponet, Knox, and Goodman taught, the sovereignty of the people flows logically from the mutual obligations of the covenants above.

5. The representatives of the people, not the people themselves, are the first line of defense against tyranny.[2]

The preceding testimony unites to underscore this message: at least an elementary grasp of Calvin is essential to any well-informed self-understanding of Western democracy—indeed, for modernity itself. Unfortunately, many remain unaware of the signal contribution that the leadership of Calvin has made to open societies. We may even credit Calvin's Reformation with aiding the spread of participatory democracy. An understanding of this political heritage is necessary as we enter a new millennium, even if this heritage no longer holds a place of honor in our textbooks and in our public tradition. What the foregoing pages illustrate is simply this: we owe our Calvinistic forefathers a large debt of gratitude for their efforts to establish limited government and personal liberty grounded in virtue. A single man with heart aflame changed the world.

Recently, Supreme Court Justice Antonin Scalia estimated the paramount political accomplishment of the millennium as law established by elected representatives instead of by the king or his experts. His candidate for the *fin-de-millénaire* award was "the principle that laws should be made not by a ruler, or his ministers, or his appointed judges, but by representatives of the people. This principle of democratic self-government was virtually unheard of in the feudal world that existed at the beginning of the millennium. . . . So thoroughly has this principle swept the board that even many countries that in fact do not observe it pretend to do so, going through the motions of sham, unopposed elections."[3]

"We Americans," continued Scalia, "have become so used to democracy that it seems to us the natural order of things. Of course it is not. During almost all of recorded human history, the overwhelming majority of mankind has been governed by rulers determined by heredity, or selected by a powerful aristocracy, or imposed through sheer force of arms. Kings and emperors have been always with us; presidents (or their equivalent) have been very rare." It should be noted here that Scalia is describing the kind of republicanism pioneered by Calvin and his disciples—a republic grounded in the eternal truth of morally ordered liberty.

Even during the twentieth century, intellectuals certainly remained aware of Calvin. In fact, in the words of contemporary theologian Douglas Kelly, Calvin's legacy continues and is "perhaps the stronger and deeper for the very fact that its roots are largely unperceived." Huge segments of political thought have often embraced such forward-looking Calvinistic concepts as respecting fixed limits on governing power and permitting people the rights to resist oppression with little awareness of their genesis.[4] Calvin's original formulation of these ideas was eventually "amplified, systematized, and widely diffused in Western civilization. . . . Thus modified, it would prevail across half of the world for nearly half a millennium."[5]

Calvin should certainly be acknowledged for his overall contribution to the legacy of freedom and openness in democratic societies. It is undeniable that he had a large influence on the American Founding Fathers who had absorbed much more Calvinism, particularly in their views of the nature of people and the need for limited government, than some realize.

John Calvin was much more than a theologian, and his influence extended far beyond churches.[6] He inspired the cultural changes that gave rise to the political philosophy of the American founders, a truly extraordinary development in world history. Founding Fathers such as George Washington, James Madison, Samuel and John Adams, Patrick Henry, and Thomas Jefferson[7] stand on the shoulders of some of the greatest philosophers in all history, not the least of whom was a pastor from Geneva hundreds of years ago. That we may still look to him as a leader in action indicates that the character of his thought was so robust and sturdy as to leave a lasting legacy for generations.

The Lessons of Leadership

∽ A leader doesn't avoid the huge task.

∽ A leader stands on the shoulders of others.

∽ A leader absorbs all the good that is around him.

∽ A leader faces rejection—and recovers.

∽ A leader is oriented toward usefulness.

∽ A leader knows the value of instruction and education.

∽ A leader finds ways to multiply his values.

∽ A leader keeps his eye on the target.

∽ A leader understands the mind.

∽ A leader understands human nature and how to deal with it.

∽ A leader acts in humility, even when he is called to great causes.

∽ A leader keeps the long-range horizon near; eternity defines the present.

∽ A leader changes what he can and accepts God's providence.

- A leader ennobles enterprise by his vision of calling, work, and labor.

- A leader appreciates history.

- A leader plans for succession by training future leaders.

- A leader responds to tragedy by proposing better measures.

- A leader inspires colleagues and builds friendships.

- A leader uses the collective wisdom of many counselors.

- A leader helps the truly needy.

- A leader controls his anxiety and walks in faith.

- A leader faces adversity with courage.

- A leader knows the value of individual responsibility.

- A leader wants to understand how things really work.

- A leader is a man of prayer.

NOTES

Full bibliographical data can be found in the bibliography.

PART 1: THE LIFE OF JOHN CALVIN

1. That was my conclusion, when comparing the likes of Calvin, Thomas Jefferson, Gutenberg, and others in my *The Genevan Reformation and the American Founding* (2003).

2. See Schaff, *History of the Christian Church,* 8:264.

3. Ibid., 8:522.

4. Cited in Kingdon, *Calvin and Calvinism,* xiii. The original citation is from Bancroft, *A History of the United States,* 1:464.

5. Cited in Kingdon, *Calvin and Calvinism,* 7.

6. D'Aubigne, *The History of the Reformation in Europe,* 3:vi–vii.

7. The other normal candidates for most influential theologian prior to Calvin include Augustine, Thomas Aquinas, Martin Luther, and Desiderius Erasmus. Of those suggested afterward, the names of John Wesley and Jonathan Edwards (albeit largely restricted to American influence) are often mentioned. But none of these affected more areas of thought for a greater period of time than did Calvin. Of interest and worth debating, Matthew Burton noted that perhaps Pelagius, the grandfather of freewill theory, was more influential than any Christian thinker in history.

8. Cited by McGrath, *Life of John Calvin,* 247.

9. Barnes, "Event-Maker in the White House."

10. Augustine, *City of God,* 454.

11. See Schaff, *History of the Christian Church,* 8:539.

12. Custance, *Sovereignty of Grace,* 27.

13. Augustine, *City of God,* 99.

14. Ibid., 103.

15. Ibid., 74.

16. For a fuller commentary on this, see Hall, "In a Meadow Called Runnymede," 6–9.

17. Another important force in undermining excessively centralized governments was the Conciliar movement. Beginning with the Councils of Pisa (1409) and Constance (1415) and leading up to the Reformation, various ecclesiastical trends, such as the Conciliar movement, either reflected or led the incipient decentralizing tendencies.

18. I have provided a fuller description of the other major Reformers in *The Genevan Reformation and the American Founding.* Rather than repeat those studies here, I refer the interested reader to that work.

19. Martyn, *Pilgrim Fathers of New England,* 29.

20. Breed, *Presbyterians and the Revolution,* 6.

21. D'Aubigne, *History of the Reformation of the Sixteenth Century,* 4:261.

22. Griffin, *Revolution and Religion,* 4.

23. McCrackan, *Rise of the Swiss Republic,* 263.

24. Walton, *Zwingli's Theocracy,* 106.

25. D'Aubigne, *History of the Reformation of the Sixteenth Century,* 3:338.

26. Bonnet, *Letters of John Calvin,* 2:25, a letter to Peter Viret on October 24, 1545. See also Wiley, "Calvin's Friendship with Guillaume Farel," 187–204.

27. Schaff, *History of the Christian Church,* 8:237.

28. Beza, *Life of John Calvin,* 1:lxxvii.

29. Heyer, *Guillaume Farel,* 82.

30. Ibid., 83.

31. McCrackan, *Rise of the Swiss Republic,* 277.

32. This terminology reflects the thesis of my doctoral dissertation:

"The Calvinistic Political Tradition, 1530–1790: The Rise, Development, and Dissemination of Genevan Political Culture to the Founders
of America Through Theological Exemplars" (2002). Portions of this
chapter have been taken from that.

33. Bouwsma, *Calvin,* 1.

34. Robert Kingdon has cautioned against forming an incomplete
notion of Calvinism by focusing on some artificially limited *part* of his
written corpus other than the *Institutes,* or on the *Institutes* themselves, or on what his disciples did, or on what Calvin did regardless of
what he wrote. This work prefers a holistic approach, as does the work
of Kingdon, e.g., in *Calvin and Calvinism,* vii–xii.

35. Beza idiosyncratically dates his birth at July 27, 1509. See Beza,
Life of John Calvin, 1:lvii.

36. Bouwsma, *Calvin,* 9.

37. Cited in D'Aubigne, *History of the Reformation of the Sixteenth Century,* 3:474. See Beza, *Life of John Calvin,* vol. 1.

38. Some historians see a common pedagogical strain, insofar as it is
likely that Calvin, John Knox, and George Buchanan were all students
of Major. See McNeill, "Calvinism and European Politics in Historical
Perspective," 15. Douglas Kelly sees Major's *History of Great Britain* as
especially influential on Knox and Buchanan.

39. McGrath, *Life of John Calvin,* 34. For a recent evaluation of the
place of Calvin, see also McGrath, "Calvin and the Christian Calling,"
31–35.

40. McGrath, *Life of John Calvin,* 45.

41. The humanism of the day emphasized the classics. *Ad fontes,*
or "back to the sources," became the rallying cry of the new educational model at that time.

42. McGrath notes that an inscription on the facade of the Biblio-
theque Sainte-Genevieve in Paris lists Calvin, along with Erasmus and
others, as an intellectual leader (McGrath, *Life of John Calvin,* 21).

43. Hopfl, *Christian Polity of John Calvin,* 16.

44. Beza called Calvin's teacher at Orleans, Peter de L'Etoile, "the

keenest jurisconsult of all the doctors of France" (cited in Kelly, *Emergence of Liberty in the Modern World,* 8).

45. All citations from Calvin's self-testimony about his spiritual conversion are taken from Calvin's *Commentaries,* vol. 4.

46. Cited in Bouwsma, *Calvin,* 11.

47. Ibid., 18.

48. McGrath, *Life of John Calvin,* 15.

49. Still, Calvin was more private than Luther, less colorful, in general timid about autobiography, and there are certainly gaps in our knowledge about him.

50. McGrath, *Life of John Calvin,* 73.

51. Ibid., 76.

52. Schaff, *History of the Christian Church,* 8:3222.

53. Beza, *Life of John Calvin,* cxxxvi.

54. Ibid., cxxxviii.

55. Roney and Klauber, *Identity of Geneva,* xiii. There is some slight discrepancy over the date of the formal proclamation, with Beza setting the date of deliverance from the "yoke of Antichrist" (and the Duke of Savoy) by Genevan Senate proclamation at July 20, 1537. See Beza, *Life of John Calvin,* lxviii. McGrath sets the dates at May 19, 1536, for the Council of Twenty-five, with ratification by the public assembly on May 25, 1536. See McGrath, *Life of John Calvin,* 94. But Geneva's own monuments and self-testimony have long dated the decisive vote declaring themselves a Protestant community as May 26, 1536. The wording of the resolution, committing Genevans to live according to "this holy evangelical law and the Word of God," is contained in Foster, *Collected Papers,* 22.

56. McGrath, *Life of John Calvin,* 96–97.

57. William Naphy suggests that part of the 1538 disruption was due to the fact that Genevans did not wish to offend their protectorally Bern by adopting a confession of faith that may have been viewed as a threat to Bern. Thus some felt that Calvin's reform was moving too rapidly or could alienate the Bernese, on whom some Genevans

believed their freedom depended. See Naphy, *Calvin and the Consolidation of the Genevan Reformation,* 28.

58. Heyer, *Guillaume Farel,* 59.

59. Ainsworth, *Relations Between Church and State,* 15, reports that the unrest began with a minister denouncing the political government from the pulpit, which led to his arrest.

60. Heyer, *Guillaume Farel,* 60.

61. Beza, *Life of John Calvin,* 1:lvii, lxxi–lxxii.

62. McGrath, *Life of John Calvin,* 86.

63. Beza, *Life of John Calvin,* lxxv.

64. Ibid., lxxvi.

65. McGrath, *Life of John Calvin,* 101.

66. Schaff, *History of the Christian Church,* 8:368.

67. At the time, Farel was settled in Neuchatel and was reluctant to return. He persuaded Calvin of the need. On September 13, 1541, Calvin reentered Geneva. See McGrath, *Life of John Calvin,* 103.

68. Wallace, *Calvin, Geneva and the Reformation,* 41.

69. Schaff, *History of the Christian Church,* 8:431.

70. The first Consistory in 1542 was comprised of twelve elders (elected annually by the magistrates) and nine ministers. The number of ministers grew to nineteen by 1564. The Consistory met each Thursday to discuss matters of common interest and church discipline (see McGrath, *Life of John Calvin,* 111). Since Calvin insisted so strongly on this institution after his Strasbourg period, some believe that he imitated the practice of Martin Bucer (see ibid., 113).

71. Roney and Klauber, *The Identity of Geneva,* 3.

72. Several studies detail Calvin's Geneva. Among the best are Monter, *Calvin's Geneva;* Duke, Lewis, and Pettegree, *Calvinism in Europe;* McNeill, "John Calvin on Civil Government," 22–45; Dunning, *History of Political Theories,* 26–33; Graham, *Constructive Revolutionary;* and Naphy, *Calvin and the Consolidation.* Two recent biographies also add to our understanding: Bouwsma, *John Calvin,* and McGrath, *Life of John Calvin.*

73. Roney and Klauber, *Identity of Geneva*, 7.

74. See Olson, "Social Welfare and the Transformation of Polity in Geneva," 155–68.

75. Naphy, *Calvin and the Consolidation*, 224.

76. Monter, *Calvin's Geneva*, 72. The 1541 *Ecclesiastical Ordinances* were approved by the Genevan magistrates (ibid., 127).

77. Schaff, *History of the Christian Church*, 8:464. A later revision of Genevan law codes was undertaken in 1560 in consultation with Germain Colladon (ibid., 464).

78. Monter, *Calvin's Geneva*, 72. In 1542 the General Council adopted this proviso: "Nothing should be put before the Council of Two Hundred that has not been dealt with in the Narrow Council, nor before the General Council before having been dealt with in the Narrow Council as well as the Two Hundred" (translation by Kim McMahan).

79. Monter, *Calvin's Geneva*, 99.

80. Cited in Duke, Lewis, and Pettegree, *Calvinism in Europe*, 48.

81. See Baird, *Beza*, 200.

82. Naphy, *Calvin and the Consolidation*, 160.

83. Calvin, *Institutes of the Christian Religion*. Unless otherwise referenced, all quotations in this section from the *Institutes*, book 4, chapter 20, are from this edition.

84. Skinner, *Foundations of Modern Political Thought*, 192, suggests that by 1559 Calvin had begun to change his views, permitting at least a discussion of the propriety of active resistance.

85. Hancock, *Calvin and the Foundations of Modern Politics*, 62–81, provides an excellent summary of Calvin's political thought from the *Institutes*.

86. Kingdon, *Calvin and Calvinism*, 37. The sermon referred to by Foster is a 1663 sermon by British minister Robert South, who referred to Calvin as "the great mufti of Geneva." See Foster, *Collected Papers*, 116.

87. Kingdon, *Calvin and Calvinism*, 37. Other historians argue that the Puritanism of New England was "patterned after the Westminster

Catechism and embodied the type of Calvinistic thought current in all of New England at that time." See De Jong, *Covenant Idea in New England Theology,* 85. Foster, *Collected Papers,* 79, lists the numerous Americans who owned copies of Calvin's *Institutes.* Patricia Bonomi has also firmly established that the majority of seventeenth-century Americans followed "some form of Puritan Calvinism, which itself was divided into a number of factions." See Bonomi, *Under the Cope of Heaven,* 14.

88. See Edwards, *Christian England,* 146. In "A Translation Fit for a King, *Christianity Today,* October 22, 2001, David Neff argues how powerfully biblical translation aided the flow of liberty. "Logically," he notes, "it is a fairly short step from the biblical language of liberty to the secular politics of Liberty." For more, see: http://www.christianitytoday .com/ct/2001/013/6.36.html.

89. Kingdon, *Calvin and Calvinism,* 40.

90. Foster, *Collected Papers,* 93.

91. Cited in Charles Arrowood, posted at: http://www.visi.com/~ contra_m/ab/jure/jure-chapter3.html.

92. Mather, *Magnalia Christi Americana,* 428. Following that, he continued to cite Calvin (from his Latin) as an authority calling for an austere lifestyle among ministers.

93. Fisher, *Albion's Seed,* 795.

94. The most recent history of the university recounts several abortive efforts, including one in 1420 under Roman Catholic authority and in 1429 by Francois de Versonnex. See Marcacci, *Historie de L'Universite de Geneve,* 17. For a prehistory of the Genevan Academy, see also Naphy, "The Reformation and the Evolution of Geneva's Schools," 190–93. Until recently, Borgeaud's *Historie de l'Universite de Geneve* was the standard history.

95. See Marcacci, *Historie de L'Universite de Geneve,* 20.

96. Under Beza, Geneva was known as a Christian state or a "bibliocentric Republic" (ibid., 23). The pastors and the students played a large role in supporting the city and liberty.

97. Monter, *Calvin's Geneva,* 112. The *schola privata* began classes in the fall of 1558, and the *schola publica* commenced in November 1558 (Marcacci, *Historie de L'Universite de Geneve,* 17).

98. Public records for January 17, 1558, refer to the establishment of the college with three chairs (theology, philosophy, Greek). Notice was also given commending the college as a worthy recipient of inheritance proceeds. See Baird, *Beza,* 104.

99. See Kelley, *Francois Hotman,* 270.

100. See Naphy, *Calvin and the Consolidation,* 142.

101. Baird, *Beza,* 106, 113.

102. Monter, *Calvin's Geneva,* 113.

103. See Bouwsma, *Calvin,* 14–15.

104. See Duke, Lewis, Pettegree, *Calvinism in Europe,* 218.

105. The later history of this educational institution is a noble one as well. As early as 1708, Jean Robert Chouet called for a transition from the Academy to a "university" (Marcacci, *Historie de L'Universite de Geneve,* 42). Numerous chairs of science were added in the 1700s, while the once-stalwart theological faculty began to tend toward rationalism. The school, however, was still called the "Academy" in the 1750s, and many patrician children received an excellent education at the Academy throughout the eighteenth century. It was first known as a university in 1798 and was moved to its present location in 1868.

106. Kingdon lists Thomas Cartwright as a missionary, along with thirteen students from the Genevan Academy, seven other teachers, and seven Genevan pastors between 1564 and 1572. See Kingdon, *Geneva and the Consolidation of the French Protestant Movement,* 203–8. See also Monter, *Calvin's Geneva,* 135.

107. McGrath, *Life of John Calvin,* 183.

108. The Marian Exiles were Protestants who fled England during the reign of Queen ("Bloody") Mary when she attempted to reverse the emergence of Calvinism in that country.

109. Monter, *Calvin's Geneva,* 138.

110. McGrath, *Life of John Calvin,* 184.

111. See Wallace, *Calvin, Geneva and the Reformation,* 36.

112. Jefferson's distaste for Calvinism is clear, e.g., when he spoke of Calvinists as fanatics who taught "a Counter-religion made up of the deliria of crazy imaginations" and "the blasphemy and absurdity of the five points." See Olasky, *American Leadership Tradition,* 36. Jefferson also caricatured the Calvinists of his day as intolerant and tyrannical, once referring to the New Englanders' God as "a daemon of malignant spirit" (cited by Bonomi, *Under the Cope of Heaven,* 102). Olasky believes that Jefferson saw the descendants of Calvin as a grave threat and sought to marginalize them by building up democratic groups like the Connecticut Baptists, to whom he wrote in 1803, creating the phrase "wall of separation" (ibid.).

113. The Huguenots were French Calvinists who resisted hierarchies in both state (monarchy) and church (Roman Catholic). Many fled to Geneva during the 1560s and particularly after the 1572 St. Bartholomew's Day massacre, during which thousands of Calvinists were killed and nearly two thousand churches were eradicated in France.

114. Hutson, *Sister Republics,* 68–76, tells this fascinating story and is the source for all quotations in this section.

115. The children's book *Poor Richard in France* has Franklin's grandson saying, "I'm going to have to go to school in Switzerland— because they don't have any kings there. Grandfather says we aren't going to have any kings in America, either, after we win this war!"

116. Hutson, *Sister Republics,* 76.

117. For a recent and accurate study on Jefferson's religious sentiments, see Dreisbach, *Jefferson and the Wall of Separation.* Cf. also Dreisbach's earlier study that provides essential perspective and corrective to earlier imbalances, "Thomas Jefferson and the Mammoth Cheese," http://www.acton.org/publicat/randl/02may_jun/article2 .html.

118. Duke, Lewis, Pettegree, *Calvinism in Europe,* 201.

119. Schaff, *History of the Christian Church,* 8:851.

120. Monter, *Calvin's Geneva,* 181.

121. Reid, "The Battle Hymns of the Lord," 36–54, speaks of the Psalms as the battle hymns of "one of the earliest modern resistance movements." He also describes Calvin's view of church music as a via media between Luther's liberal embrace of contemporary music and Zwingli's elimination of music at the Grossmunster.

122. Ibid., 43, 45. Reid comments: "Whether one thinks of the fourteen martyrs of Meaux who sang the 79th Psalm, the five scholars of Lausanne in Lyon who sang Psalm 9, or others who turned to other parts of the Psalter as they went to their deaths, one can see how in the last great struggle of faith, the psalms indeed were true battle hymns" (ibid., 46). These psalms, once ingrained, fit "every occasion and form of resistance."

123. McGrath contrasts Calvin's success with that of Zurich Reformer Joachim Vadian and identifies Calvin's "extensive publishing programme" as one of the differences (McGrath, *Life of John Calvin*, 124–26).

124. Monter, *Calvin's Geneva,* 179.

125. Robert Kingdon explains that the number was likely more since some were co-opted by others. In 1562, neighbors complained that paper mills were running round the clock. See Kingdon, *Geneva and the Coming Wars of Religion in France,* 94. Jean Crespin even contracted to purchase bales of paper from outside Geneva (ibid., 95).

126. Naphy, *Documents,* 87.

127. Kingdon, *Geneva and the Coming Wars of Religion in France,* 97. This may explain why Calvinism's publishing headquarters were Genevan shops. Yet Kingdon avoided the theocratic association by noting, "Censorship was the chief duty of the Commission." Even some of Calvin's friends were fined, and some printers had to cease operations (ibid., 98).

128. Ibid., 101.

129. Monter, *Calvin's Geneva,* 182. Kingdon noted that the books were so well circulated that as early as 1560 the cardinal of Lorraine had successfully collected twenty-two pamphlets that had criticized

him (Kingdon, *Geneva and the Coming Wars of Religion in France,*
103). Another historian in 1561 reported the spread to Paris of Beza's
Psalter, catechisms, and popular Christian books, "all well bound in
red and black calf skin, some well gilded" (ibid., 103).

130. Monter, *Calvin's Geneva,* 182.

131. Duke, Lewis, and Pettegree, *Calvinism in Europe,* 57.

132. McGrath, *Life of John Calvin,* 12. See also Droz, "Fausses
adresses typographiques," 380–86, 572–74.

133. Monter, *Calvin's Geneva,* 101.

134. Ibid., 169. McGrath notes that population, reflecting this massive immigration, surged from 13,100 to 21,400 between 1550 and
1560 (McGrath, *Life of John Calvin,* 121).

135. See Naphy, *Calvin and the Consolidation,* 53–79, for a study of
the impact of Calvin in attracting a new cadre of pastors.

136. Monter, *Calvin's Geneva,* 174.

137. Ibid., 170.

138. Ibid., 173.

139. Ibid., 172.

140. Ibid., 85.

141. Naphy notes, "French power in the city grew substantially after
1555 and in later years as well. In 1574, the Petit Conseil contained
six senators (24 percent) who were connected by marriage to French
refugee families. But by 1605, this number had risen to at least ten
senators (40 percent), half of whom were related to the French by
marriage while the other five senators were sons of French immigrant
bourgeois" (Naphy, *Calvin and the Consolidation,* 226).

142. Monter, *Calvin's Geneva,* 89. Monter also notes that, from
1555 on, Geneva was less dependent on Bern, even though Bern had
contributed much, and more dependent on Calvin's ideas, which
would in time support Bern and other Swiss cities.

143. Beza, *Life of John Calvin,* 1:cxxv.

144. Ibid., cxxxviii.

145. Beza refers to this Little Council as the "senate." See ibid., cxxii.

146. See http://capo.org/premise/99/jan/p990110.html.

147. Doumergue, *Character of Calvinism,* 173.

148. Bungener, *Calvin,* 5.

149. McGrath, *Life of John Calvin,* 109.

150. Linder, *Political Ideas of Pierre Viret,* 113, notes that Calvin and Viret both became citizens (*bourgeois*) of Geneva on the same day: December 25, 1559.

151. McNeill, "The Democratic Element in Calvin's Thought," 165.

152. Ibid., 166.

153. Duke, Lewis, Pettegree, *Calvinism in Europe,* 27–28.

154. Michael Servetus, a Spanish medical doctor by training, challenged the Genevan orthodoxy by denying the Trinity and infant baptism. After a trial, he was sentenced by the city council of Geneva to death.

155. See a related discussion in Schaff, *History of the Christian Church,* 8:766–68. Shortly afterward, the contest for political power came to a head, and the Perrinists were no longer competitive after 1555.

156. McGrath, *Life of John Calvin,* 180.

157. See Doumergue, *Character of Calvinism,* 168.

158. Cited in McGrath, *Life of John Calvin,* 116. See Thomas Aquinas, *Summa Theologica,* 154, IIa IIae, q. 11 a. 3. Kelly, *Emergence of Liberty in the Modern World,* 27, also notes that the Justinian Code approved of capital punishment for heretics. Robert Linder even notes that Luther, after 1529, approved of capital punishment for Anabaptists (Linder, *Political Ideas of Pierre Viret,* 144). See also Schaff, *History of the Christian Church,* 8:702–8. William Naphy concurs that the Servetus case "is certainly of interest . . . but there is no basis for treating the case as though it were as important in the Genevan context as the Ameaux, Trolliet, Berthelier, or the Perrin-Meigret cases" (Naphy, *Calvin and the Consolidation,* 231).

159. Hall, "The Calvin Legend," 124–25.

160. One of the most recent surveys of the possible reasons for oppo-

sition to Calvin is Naphy, "Baptism, Church Riots, and Social Unrest in Calvin's Geneva," 87–97.

161. Hughes, *Register of the Company of Pastors,* 7.

162. The contemporary record of this trial—the record with the least after-the-fact interpretation—may be found in ibid., 223–84.

163. Monter's numbers, of course, may be challenged. It is possible that records were kept better after 1536, which could explain some of the rise of the merchant class (*Calvin's Geneva,* 5). However, even should that be established, the astronomic rise of printers and nobility is certain. Nobles, mainly from France, fled to Geneva because adhering to Protestantism at home could have meant their deaths.

164. Monter, *Calvin's Geneva,* 15.

165. Ibid., 57.

166. Ibid., 58.

167. Roney and Klauber, *Identity of Geneva,* 3.

168. Naphy, *Calvin and the Consolidation,* 5. Noting that the sermons were a prime medium of mass communication, Naphy urged scholars to "rescue Geneva and Calvin's work there from Calvin's all-pervasive grasp and examine them for their own sake, thereby providing the historical context for Calvin's work as a theologian and leader of the wider Reform movement" (ibid., 6). In making this clear, Naphy asserted that input must come not only from Calvin, nor exclusively from his adversaries, but from a mosaic of sources contemporaneous with Calvin.

169. See Hall, *Savior or Servant?* ii.

PART 2: THE CHARACTER OF JOHN CALVIN

1. Calvin, *Institutes of the Christian Religion,* 3.

2. Ibid., 4.

3. Ibid., 4–5.

4. For other references to Calvin's concept of the *seed* or *sense* of divinity, see ibid., 43–47, 51–52, 55, 57, 192, and 277.

5. For other illustrative descriptions of depravity, see ibid., book 2, chap. 1, paragraphs 3–4, 8–9.

6. See ibid., 42. More recently Baker has reprinted these chapters in ninety-nine pages as *The Golden Booklet of the Christian Life.*

7. Kelly, *Emergence of Liberty in the Modern World,* 133.

8. See "The Parliamentary Background of the Westminster Assembly" in Carson and Hall, *To Glorify and Enjoy God,* 267–300, for the pertinent petitions and bills to Charles I (1640–44).

9. Clark, *Language of Liberty,* asserts that the "consent of the governed" idea is properly derived from the covenant theology of the late sixteenth century.

10. Kelly, *Emergence of Liberty in the Modern World,* 135.

11. I am indebted for the quote in this paragraph to Olasky, *American Leadership Tradition,* 7.

12. McCrackan, *Rise of the Swiss Republic,* vi.

13. Cited by Sproul, *Chosen by God,* 46.

14. Duke, Lewis, and Pettegree, *Calvinism in Europe,* 34.

15. Olson, *Calvin and Social Welfare,* 139.

16. Calvin, *Commentaries,* 21:355.

17. McKee, *Diakonia in the Classical Reformed Tradition and Today,* 54.

18. Thomas, "Calvin's Exposition of the Book of Job," 13 (emphasis added).

19. This section is taken from Hall, "Hermeneutics: *With* History or *With* Hubris," first submitted to the John M. Templeton Foundation in 1994 and later reprinted in Hall, *The Arrogance of the Modern.*

20. Cited in Tyrrell, *Conservative Crack-Up,* 280, as one definition of a conservative, in tandem with Abraham Lincoln's famous definition of conservatism as "adherence to the old and tried, against the new and untried."

21. Paul T. Fuhrmann, among others, locates the departure point for the development of resistance theory after Calvin and with Beza (Fuhrmann, "Philip Mornay and the Huguenot Challenge to Absolutism," 47, 49).

22. Schaff, *History of the Christian Church,* 8:849–50.

23. Gerstner, *Idelette,* 160.

24. For a recent study of Viret's political thought, see Berthoud, *Pierre Viret.*

25. In his 1899 biography of Beza, Henry Martyn Baird noted that, with Beza's transfer to Geneva, Lausanne "lost its great opportunity of permanently possessing the school for the training of the Christian athletes who were to achieve wonders in the cause of French Protestantism" (Baird, *Beza,* 102).

26. For information about Beza's voluminous correspondence with Puritans in England (e.g., John Jewell, Edmund Grindal), see ibid., 254–58.

27. Unfortunately, sometimes those who have not read Beza's works carefully depict him as calcifying Calvinism into a Draconian orthodoxy, a caricature that must be discarded if the broad scope of his life and work is considered.

28. McNeill, "John Calvin on Civil Government," 24.

29. Cited in ibid.

30. Cited by Fuhrmann, "Philip Mornay and the Huguenot Challenge to Absolutism," 50.

31. An abridgement of this 1572 work was published in Franklin's *Constitutionalism and Resistance in the Sixteenth Century.*

32. See Ainsworth, *Relations Between Church and State,* 30–40, for an informed discussion of Beza's influence on church and state concerns in Geneva.

33. Schaff, *History of the Christian Church,* 8:870.

34. Baird identified Beza as Geneva's "first citizen," with each appeal to foreign dignitaries invoking his authorization or seal (Baird, *Beza,* 333).

35. Ibid., 326.

36. Ibid., 353.

37. For centuries, Genevans have remembered Beza more kindly than Calvin. Beza is still remembered in anniversary celebrations of the December 12, 1602, *Escalade* in which the Duke of Savoy was finally

defeated by Geneva. Following a surprise night attack by the duke, at the conclusion of the victorious fighting, the octogenarian Beza led Genevans in the singing of Psalm 124 (which he had put to meter while Calvin was still living). See Reid, "The Battle Hymns of the Lord," 53.

38. Baird, *Beza,* 348. Baird also includes an obituary for Beza from October 13, 1605, commending him as a pastor and professor at the Academy.

39. Cited in Schaff, *History of the Christian Church,* 8:519.

40. For a survey of other Huguenot political tracts, see Skinner, *Foundations of Modern Political Thought,* 303–7.

41. Harold Laski avers that this massacre was the critical turning point in Calvinistic thought. See Brutus, *A Defense of Liberty Against Tyrants,* 10–18.

42. This 1572 effort to purge Protestants from France eventually resulted in the Edict of Nantes in 1598.

43. Monter, *Calvin's Geneva,* 210. McGrath among others also identifies this massacre as the transformation point (McGrath, *Life of John Calvin,* 187).

44. Foxe, *Foxe's Book of Martyrs,* 83.

45. Of interest, many of these cities were the exact locales where Geneva sent missionaries between 1564 and 1572. See Kingdon, *Geneva and the Consolidation,* 203–8.

46. Foxe, *Foxe's Book of Martyrs,* 84. In one locale, Augustobona, all Protestants were killed. *Christian History* 20, no. 3, includes numerous articles on the massacre, leading figures from the French Reformation (including a short essay on Viret), and other helpful information on the subject.

47. Francois Hotman stated that the death toll was 50,000. See Kelley, *Francois Hotman,* 219. Another contemporary, John Foxe, cited similar numbers (Foxe, *Foxe's Book of Martyrs,* 83–84). Later, Jonathan Edwards set the level of disaster even higher, noting that within one generation France lost 39 princes, 148 counts, 234 barons,

147,518 gentlemen, and 760,000 common people to genocidal persecution (cited in Cox, "The Standards and Civil Government," 287).
See also Kingdon, *Geneva and the Consolidation.*

48. Beza, *Grounds and Principles of Christian Religion,* 262.

49. Beza qualified the duty to rebel against the civil magistrate, re-
stricting such duty by the following notions: (1) "no one in private station is allowed to set himself in open violence against a tyrant"
(Question 6); (2) "that the tyranny must be undisguised and notorious"; (3) "that the recourse should not be had to arms before all other
remedies have been tried"; and (4) "Nor yet before the question has
been thoroughly examined, not only as to what is permissible, but also
as to what is expedient, lest the remedies prove more hazardous than
the very disease" (Question 7); See Beza, *Concerning the Rights of
Rulers over Their Subjects;* Patrick S. Poole, ed. *Reformation Political
Tracts* (forthcoming).

50. This document is available at Patrick S. Poole's "Reformation
Political Works," http://fly.hiwaay.net/~pspoole/Beza1.htm.
Searches for the citations may be keyed to phrases on that page. Modern editions of this work are Sturm, *De Iure Magistratuum,* and Kingdon, *De Droit des magistrats.*

51. Although some of the churches were no doubt small, the existence of 1,785 Consistories in France by 1562 reveals the magnitude
of this Huguenot explosion (McGrath, *Life of John Calvin,* 184). The
1852 edition of Calvin's commentary on Daniel claims that Beza had
up to 40,000 followers near Paris, that each of the 2,150 churches had
its own pastor, and that the Huguenots were nearly one-third as numerous as the Catholic population.

52. Earlier, an abridgement of Beza's *Concerning the Rights of
Rulers* was available in Franklin, *Constitutionalism and Resistance in
the Sixteenth Century.*

53. Stauffer, *Humanness of John Calvin.*

54. Ibid., 9.

55. Ibid., 19.

56. Emile Doumergue wrote a 1923 French work on *The Character of Calvinism* that highlighted the following as distinguishing attributes, among others, of Calvin's character: vivacity, joyishness, affection (Fr. *mignardise,* preciousness), nobility, and a concern to pitch his written style for common understanding. At one point (ibid., 55), Doumergue notes, "Le style c'est l'homme." He also credited Calvinism with the "exaltation of the individual" and attributed to it "the perfection of truth" (ibid., 131). He also viewed the very fabric of the church under Calvin's reforms as epitomizing these three aspects of his own character: the church was a (1) constitutional, (2) representative, and (3) democratic society (ibid., 141–42). Correspondingly, Doumergue noted that the state had a similar character, distinguishing, nonetheless, the state as "elective (not hereditary) in place of representative" (ibid., 149).

57. Stauffer, *Humanness of John Calvin,* 47.

58. Ibid., 51.

59. Kelly, *Emergence of Liberty in the Modern World,* 37.

60. Ibid., 40–44, provides a summary of Hotman and a variety of Huguenot political tracts.

61. D'Aubigne, *History of the Reformation of the Sixteenth Century,* 3:416.

62. Stauffer, *Humanness of John Calvin,* 57.

63. Duke, Lewis, and Pettegree, *Calvinism in Europe,* 200. This internationality, to some degree, blunts the suggestion by Hopfl that Geneva was unique in applying Calvinism because it was a relatively small political space in which the laws could be easily enforced. See Hopfl, *Christian Polity of John Calvin,* 56–57.

64. Duke, Lewis, and Pettegree, *Calvinism in Europe,* 200.

65. Stauffer, *Humanness of John Calvin,* 71.

66. See McNeill, "Calvin and Civil Government," 272.

67. Hopfl, *Christian Polity of John Calvin,* 112, 162, 164, 165, 166.

68. Ibid., 171. In this and other sections, Hopfl notes "a very clear

but imperfect homology" between church government and civil polity in Calvin.

69. Foster, *Collected Papers,* 65–66.

70. Olson, *Calvin and Social Welfare,* 11–12.

71. Calvin, *Theological Treatises,* 64.

72. Ibid., 65.

73. Ibid., 66.

74. Cited by Bromiley, "The English Reformers and Diaconate," 113.

75. Cf. Crumpacker, "Ecclesiastical Ordinances, 1561," 148–49.

76. Olson, *Calvin and Social Welfare,* 39–40.

77. Ibid., 104–6.

78. Hall, "Diaconia in Martin Butzer," 94.

79. Ibid.

80. Bromiley, "The English Reformers and Diaconate," 113.

81. Atkinson, "Luther," 88.

82. Luther, *Sermons,* 5:109; see http://www.orlutheran.com /mlsemt624.html.

83. Ibid., 112.

84. Ibid., 115.

85. M'Clure, *Lives of John Wilson, John Norton and John Davenport,* 2:219.

86. Calvin, *Institutes of the Christian Religion,* book 4, chap. 20.

87. Hancock, *Calvin and the Foundations of Modern Politics,* classifies the Protestant Reformation as "an essentially modern movement that . . . laid the foundations for our modern openness."

88. Holl, *Cultural Significance of the Reformation,* 65–66.

89. Ibid., 68.

90. Ibid., 72–73.

91. Calvin, *Commentary on Romans,* 479.

92. Beza, *Life of John Calvin,* 1:c.

93. Calvin, *Commentary on Romans,* 481.

94. Calvin, *Commentary on John,* 210.

95. "Qualified absolutism" is the term I use in *Savior or Servant?* See also Keen, "The Limits of Power and Obedience in the Later Calvin," for a good harmonization between the earlier and later statements by Calvin on the propriety of resistance.

96. Wendel, *Calvin,* 79.

97. Kelly, *Emergence of Liberty in the Modern World,* 14.

98. Cited in ibid., 15.

99. William G. Naphy raises three key points to rebut the idea that Calvin was a repressive theocrat. First, he notes that the Genevan ministers focused on religious issues and did not seek to gain the civil magistrate's sword to punish crime. Second, the theoretical ideal for church government was not always followed, even at the height of Reformist zeal. Third, he suggests that, by the 1570s, the influence of the church had begun to wane. See also Duke, Lewis, and Pettegree, *Calvinism in Europe,* 15.

100. See Kelly, *Emergence of Liberty in the Modern World,* 23.

101. Bonivard recorded an instance of an attempt to tyrannically seize a syndic's baton, which was met with this reply—indicative of the *Vindiciae Contra Tyrannos* ethos: "This staff has been given me not by you but by God and the people, to whom I shall return it and not to you" (cited in Foster, *Collected Papers,* 83).

102. Others could serve on other councils (the Council of Sixty or the Council of Two Hundred).

103. This account is taken from the 1555 description by former Castle d'Chillon prisoner Francis Bonivard, recorded in Monter, *Studies in Genevan Government,* 85–88. Naphy describes the process of Senate (Petit Conseil) election: "These senators were elected by having the senators of the previous year's Petit Conseil stand for election with eight new nominees; the new Petit Conseil was elected from this group" (see Naphy, *Calvin and Consolidation,* 176). Herbert Foster asserts that the Little Council (of twenty-five) was the most powerful, and that it included four syndics from the previous year, plus the four newly elected syndics (all eight elected by the General Assembly), and

the treasurer and sixteen other assemblymen elected by the Council of Two Hundred (see Foster, *Collected Papers,* 42).

104. Monter, *Studies in Genevan Government,* 89–90.

105. I am indebted to Kim McMahan for her translation of this oath, taken from Kelley, *Francois Hotman,* 346. Students at the Academy also pledged to obey the magistrats and support the "Republicae" as well as the rules of the "School of Geneva."

106. As in early Massachusetts, church attendance was sanctioned. Absenting oneself from church in Reformed Geneva drew a fine. See Monter, *Studies in Genevan Government,* 79.

107. Monter observed that Calvin did not so much purpose to instruct the existing magistrates "as to show others what magistrates are and for what end God has appointed them" (ibid., 58).

108. Ibid., 57.

109. Ibid., 118.

110. Monter goes so far as to claim, "In Genevan history, all roads eventually lead to Calvin" (ibid., 118).

111. Quotations in this section are from Douglas Kelly's translation, see Kelly, "Sermon XXIX." Used with permission.

112. The Anabaptists of Calvin's and Luther's time were frequently associated with an anti-intellectual bent. They were not the spiritual parents of Baptists but were more organically related to Quakers, Mennonites, and some Pentecostals. They initially embarrassed the Protestant movement with their fanatical Peasants' Rebellion in Germany in 1525. Luther and Calvin were both overtly critical of the movement.

113. In his first edition of the *Institutes,* Calvin commented on taxation: "Taxes are not so much private revenues as the treasury of the whole people, or rather the blood of the people and aids of public necessity; to burden the people with which without cause would be tyrannical rapacity" (cited in Foster, *Collected Papers,* 70).

114. Hopfl asserts that Calvin also drew upon the *Corpus Juris Civilis* for "models of contract, property law and judicial procedure." See Hopfl, *Christian Polity of John Calvin,* 6.

115. Calvin was a well-trained lawyer—a rare profession in Geneva at the time—and the council asked him to devote his talent to this area. Still, he may have been as much a redactor of civil code as a legislator. See Naphy, *Calvin and Consolidation,* 83, 85.

116. Chenevière, *La Pensee Politique de Calvin,* 211; Hopfl, *Christian Polity of John Calvin,* 201.

117. Fazy, *Les Constitutions de la Republique de Geneve,* 48.

118. Ibid., 55.

119. Chenevière, *La Pensee Politique de Calvin,* 197. Moreover, Calvin was also asked to complete the final draft of the edicts, at times filling in blank spaces where other coeditors could not read his handwriting (ibid., 216). Chenevière also traced direct phrases and exhortations from Calvin that appear in these drafts.

120. Chenevière states that the edicts were not a de novo constitution but rather primarily sought to improve the existing codes. The brevity of the work (which he dates from an order to create a commission on September 15, 1542, to the council's approval of such on October 2, 1542) supports his argument that Calvin was not a radical revisionist. Another interesting part of Chenevière's study is that he refused to follow Fazy's bias (which viewed Calvin as the inventor of aristocracy in Geneva) or Amedee Roget's bias (who saw Calvin as a mere mouthpiece of the reigning patrician families). He states that it is "absolutely certain . . . that this introduction [of aristocratic elements] had begun a number of years before Calvin's arrival in Geneva" (ibid., 205). Among the reasons to view Calvin as conserving, rather than creating, much of Geneva's extant tradition are: (1) the near impossibility of Calvin being a mouthpiece; (2) his stated admiration for the existing Genevan political tradition (although he did not always favor the persons in office); and (3) his comments in his *Institutes* that express favor for aspects of aristocracy as long as blended with other features of republicanism. Chenevière observed: "There is every reason to think that Calvin sought to conserve what he admired, improving it in a direction that was dear to him, that is to say, in an aristocratic direction" (ibid., 207).

121. An English translation of these was made by Robert Fills as early as 1562. Of these, Fills said that, without such constitution, "a common weale can no more be ruled than the body live without the soul . . . and they are ye statutes of Geneva, a Citie counted of all godly men singularly well ordered, as well for good policie, as also for the government of the church in all estates and vocations" (cited in Hopfl, *Christian Polity of John Calvin,* 6). Hopfl also cautions that Genevan politics, after Calvin's return from Basel, did not "unequivocally endorse" republicanism exclusively (ibid., 156).

122. Fazy, *Les Constitutions de la Republique de Geneve,* 55.

123. Cited in Foster, *Collected Papers,* 112.

124. Ibid., 113.

125. Ibid.

126. Ibid., 114.

127. Ibid., 115.

128. Ibid.

129. Ibid., 117.

130. Some theological assessments of the major forms of church government even describe the three main options as monarchy (an episcopal arrangement), democracy (congregational forms), or aristocracy (meaning representation by the few). As such, Calvin might have pleaded guilty as charged in advocating a certain kind of aristocratic form. It must be remembered, however, that he never advocated the divine right of kings.

131. Chenevière, *La Pensee Politique de Calvin,* 220–21.

132. Fazy, *Les Constitutions de la Republique de Geneve,* 55.

133. The definitive study of the impact of Calvinism in this period is Choisy, *L'etat Chretien Calviniste a Geneve au Temps de Theodore de Beze.*

134. Arthur David Ainsworth examined "The Relations Between Church and State in the City and Canton of Geneva," in his 1964 dissertation at the University of Lausanne (see Ainsworth, *Relations Between Church and State,* esp. 30–45, for his discussion of Beza's tenure).

135. Monter, *Studies in Genevan Government,* 11.

136. Estimations of French Huguenot sympathy in the period range from 10 to 25 percent of the entire French population. Douglas Kelly sets the range at 5 to 25 percent (Kelly, *Emergence of Liberty in the Modern World,* 38). Other projections estimate that up to 2 million of France's 20 million population at the time were Huguenot.

137. Monter, *Studies in Genevan Government,* 25. William G. Naphy, *Calvin and the Consolidation,* 24, 216, charts the revenue to Geneva from Bourgeois admissions during the period from 1536 to 1556.

138. Monter notes that the cost of the Academy was borne by selling off the estates of exiled enemies (Monter, *Studies in Genevan Government,* 25).

139. Ibid., 40. Monter believed it "an interesting commentary on the Calvinist conscience" to note that Beza, Calvin's nephew, and theology professor Antoine de la Faye were also able to contribute during times of need (ibid., 43).

140. Ibid., 20.

141. Ibid., 48.

142. Ibid., 42.

143. Beza's role was viewed as so important by Jesuits from Germany and France that they called for his assassination in October 1597.

144. Lest these Calvinists be seen as overly ascetic, a June 5, 1598, act should be considered: "M. de Bèze having received from l'Hôpital a barrel of light red wine that was too young, Syndic Favre is asked to deliver to him a half-barrel of older wine." Calvinists were not easily cheated out of good wine.

145. Monter, *Studies in Genevan Government,* 37.

146. Ibid., 37.

147. Ibid., 109.

148. References to the *Registry of the Company of Pastors,* 1596, are taken from Kim McMahan's translation published at http://capo.org/premise/98/FEB/p980209.html.

PART 3: THE LEGACY OF JOHN CALVIN

1. Dunning, *History of Political Theories,* 77.

2. Ibid., 78–79.

3. Ibid., 80.

4. Kingdon, *Geneva and the Coming Wars of Religion in France,* 124.

5. Ibid., 128.

6. Cited in Kingdon, *Calvin and Calvinism,* 42.

7. Cited in ibid., 44.

8. Maclear, "Samuel Rutherford," 83.

9. Haller, *Liberty and Reformation in the Puritan Revolution,* xii.

10. Ibid., xii–xiii.

11. William Dunning characterizes Puritanism as containing "an unmistakable Calvinistic leaven" (Dunning, *History of Political Theories,* 209). In addition, he averred: "The heroes of French and Scottish and Dutch Calvinism could not receive their due meed of veneration from their English admirers without communicating in turn to the Englishmen that anti-monarchic doctrine which glowed on every page of Buchanan, Althusius, and the *Vindiciae.*"

12. Cited in Clark, *Language of Liberty,* 229.

13. Haller, *Liberty and Reformation in the Puritan Revolution,* 26.

14. Citations from ibid., 27–31.

15. Dunning, *History of Political Theories,* 238.

16. Ibid., 239.

17. Cited in Wallace, *Calvin, Geneva and the Reformation,* 186. This original essay is Belloc, *Characters of the Reformation,* 280–92.

18. Skinner, *Foundations of Modern Political Thought,* 348.

19. Arthur S. DeMoss Foundation, *Rebirth of America,* 41.

20. McGrath, *Life of John Calvin,* 208.

21. Arthur S. DeMoss Foundation, *Rebirth of America,* 41. This work estimates that half of Harvard's graduates from 1638 to 1699 became pastors.

22. Mather, *Magnalia Christi Americana,* 2:6.

23. Ibid., 10.

24. Ibid., 65.

25. Ibid., 60.

26. Ibid., 155.

27. Ibid.

28. Ibid., 156.

29. Ibid., 86.

30. Harvard, in its early years, had a close connection to Britain's Puritan fortress, Cambridge. Harvard's first eight presidents (including Urian Oakes, John Rogers, Increase Mather, and Samuel Willard) were ministers and left behind election sermons in Massachusetts, that are clearly indicative of their views. See Morison, *Three Centuries of Harvard,* 1.

31. Martyn, *Pilgrim Fathers of New England,* 364.

32. Morison, *Three Centuries of Harvard,* 24–25.

33. Ibid., 90–91.

34. See Geissler, *Edwards to Burr,* 50, 60.

35. Westerkamp, *Triumph of the Laity,* 10–11.

36. Ibid., 14.

37. On February 14, 1642, a fast was observed for "our native country and Ireland," as well as for Massachusetts (Winthrop, *Journal,* 387).

38. Leyburn, *The Scotch-Irish,* 321.

39. Dunning, *History of Political Theories,* 231.

40. Singer, *Theological Interpretation of American History,* 11.

41. Ibid., 12.

42. Ibid., 13.

43. Ibid., 15.

44. Ibid., 326.

45. Martyn, *Pilgrim Fathers of New England,* 18.

46. De Jong, *Covenant Idea in New England Theology,* 9, 15, 79.

47. Hutson, *Religion and the Founding of the American Republic,* 33.

48. Ibid., 51.

49. Ibid., 52.

50. Ibid.

51. Ibid., 53.

52. Ibid.

53. Ibid., 53–54.

54. Ibid., 57. A committee of Congress approved either the printing of twenty thousand copies of the Bible or the importation of the same number from Holland, Scotland, or elsewhere (Arthur S. DeMoss Foundation, *The Rebirth of America,* 39).

55. Hutson, *Religion and the Founding of the American Republic,* 58.

56. Ibid.,49.

57. James Hutson notes that Dickinson's early draft of the Articles of Confederation, in style befitting the Massachusetts Bay Colony's Puritanism, sought to require church attendance of citizens (ibid., 54).

58. Ibid., 49–50.

59. Clark, *Language of Liberty,* 378.

60. As described in Isaiah 49:23.

61. Hutson, *Religion and the Founding of the American Republic,* 61.

62. Ibid., 62. Moehlman, *American Constitutions and Religion,* 38–55, assembles the pertinent articles treating religion from state charters from 1776–91. His collection (ibid., 56–61) also indicates that religious themes, and in some cases (e.g., Mississippi in 1817) limited religious tests, continued into the nineteenth century.

63. Hutson, *Religion and the Founding of the American Republic,* 63–64.

64. Clark, *Language of Liberty,* 106.

65. Ibid., 112.

66. Ibid., 56.

67. Ibid., 58.

68. Ibid., 154.

69. Calvin, *Sermons on Galatians,* 313 (emphasis added).

70. Koch and Peden, *Selected Writings of John and John Quincy Adams,* 9. Emphasis added to illustrate the substantial similarity in the quotes above.

71. Cited by Herbert Foster in Kingdon, *Calvin and Calvinism,* 39.

72. John Richard Green, cited in ibid., 5.

73. Ibid., vii.

74. Schaff, *History of the Christian Church,* 8:281–82.

75. Bamberg, "A Footnote to the Political Theory of John Adams," 10.

76. A helpful summary of this volume is provided by Bamberg (ibid.).

77. Adams, *Works,* 6:345, 358. Adams noted, "Beza explained his doctrines with great pomp of eloquence" (ibid., 358).

78. Ashcraft, *Revolutionary Politics,* 295.

79. Cited in Wilkins, *America,* 46. Kuehnelt-Leddihn also commented as early as 1972, "The history of the United States is that of a battle between the two Johns of Geneva, John Calvin and Jean-Jacques Rousseau, and it seems that Rousseau is winning" (cited in Brown, "Unfettered Individualism," 2).

80. Clark, *Language of Liberty,* 353.

81. Wilkins, *America,* 71.

82. Breed, *Presbyterians and the Revolution,* 15.

83. Clark, *Language of Liberty,* 357.

84. Ibid., 358.

85. Ibid., 358–59.

86. Ibid., 360.

87. Cited in ibid., 360.

88. Ibid., 362. David Ramsay also confirms that the Scottish-Irish Presbyterians were a natural constituency to support the revolution on theological grounds. "The presbyterians and independents, were almost universally attached to the measures of Congress. Their religious societies are governed on the republican plan. From independence

they had much to hope, but from Great Britain if finally successful, they had reason to fear the establishment of a church hierarchy" (Ramsay, *History of the American Revolution,* 2:626.

89. Breed, *Presbyterians and the Revolution,* 29–30, gives a helpful summary.

90. Boettner, *Reformed Doctrine of Predestination,* 384, cited in Wilkins, *America,* 70.

EPILOGUE

1. Foster, *Collected Papers,* 163–74. I have summarized the five points of political Calvinism slightly differently, referring to: Depravity as a perennial human variable to be accommodated; Accountability for leaders provided via a *collegium;* Republicanism as the preferred form of government; Constitutionalism needed to restrain both the rulers and the ruled; and Limited government, beginning with the family as foundational. The resulting mnemonic device, DARCL, though not as convenient as TULIP, seems a more apt summary if placed in the context of the political writings of Calvin's disciples.

2. Ibid., 174. Besides Calvin, this idea was reiterated in Buchanan, Beza, Peter Martyr, Althusius, Hotman, Daneau, *Vindiciae,* Ponet, William the Silent, and others.

3. Scalia, "The Millennium That Was."

4. Kelly, *Emergence of Liberty in the Modern World,* 4, 27.

5. Ibid., 32.

6. Some of the foregoing work was also contained in my dissertation, "The Calvinistic Political Tradition, 1530–1790: The Rise, Development, and Dissemination of Genevan Political Culture to the Founders of America through Theological Exemplars."

7. A recent article further corroborates Jefferson's ease with religion. See "What Would Jefferson Do?" *Wall Street Journal,* March 9, 2001. That editorial contains a finding by Kevin Hasson, to wit: "The Framers did not share the suspicion that religion is some sort of allergen in the body politic. Quite the contrary, they welcomed public

expression of faith as a normal part of cultural life." It is also noted that, in Jefferson's day, the Treasury Building was used for a Presbyterian communion, Episcopal services were held in the War Office, and as the Library of Congress exhibition states, "The Gospel was also preached in the Supreme Court chambers." That America today doesn't know its own history here is a reflection of the larger revisionism that today portrays the churches, synagogues, and mosques that crisscross the country not as bulwarks of freedom but as incipient threats to the American way of life. The editorial concludes by suggesting that if future Supreme Court justices are hostile to the free expression of religion, "They'll have to do it without Jefferson."

Bibliography

Adams, John. *The Works of John Adams, Second President, of the United States.* 10 vols. Boston: Little, Brown, 1851–65.

Ainsworth, Arthur David. *The Relations Between Church and State in the City and Canton of Geneva.* Atlanta, GA: Stein Printing, 1965.

Anonymous. *Monument International de la Reformation a Geneve.* Geneve: Imprimerie Atar, 1917.

Arthur S. DeMoss Foundation. *The Rebirth of America.* [Bala Cynwyd, PA]: Arthur S. DeMoss Foundation, 1986.

Ashcraft, Richard. *Revolutionary Politics & Locke's Two Treatises of Government.* Princeton, NJ: Princeton University Press, 1986.

Atkinson, James. "Luther." In *Service in Christ: Essays Presented to Karl Barth on His 80th Birthday.* Edited by James I. McCord and T. H. L. Parker. London: Epworth Press, 1966.

Bailyn, Bernard. *The Ideological Origins of the American Revolution.* Cambridge, MA: Belknap Press of Harvard University Press, 1967.

———, ed. *Pamphlets of the American Revolution, 1750–1776.* vol. 1. Cambridge, MA: Belknap Press of Harvard University Press, 1965.

Baird, Henry Martyn. *Theodore Beza: The Counsellor of the*

French Reformation, 1519–1605. New York: G. P. Putnam's Sons, 1899.

Baker, J. Wayne. *Heinrich Bullinger and the Covenant: The Other Reformed Tradition.* Athens: Ohio University Press, 1980.

Baldwin, Alice M. *The New England Clergy and the American Revolution.* Durham, NC: Duke University Press, 1928.

Bamberg, Stanley. "A Footnote to the Political Theory of John Adams: *Vindiciae contra tyrannos.*" *Premise* 3, no. 7 (August 1996): 10.

Bancroft, George. *A History of the United States, From the Discovery of the American Continent.* 10 vols. Boston: Little, Brown, 1834–75.

Barnes, Fred. "Event-Maker in the White House." *Wall Street Journal,* February 2, 2005.

Belloc, Hilaire. *Characters of the Reformation.* London: Sheed and Ward, 1936.

Berthoud, Jean-Marc. "Pierre Viret: The Apologetics and Ethics of the Reformation." Lecture, Westminster Conference, London, December 12, 1995.

Beza, Theodore. *The Christian Faith.* Translated by James Clark. East Sussex: Christian Focus, 1992.

———. *Concerning the Rights of Rulers over Their Subjects and the Duty of Subjects Towards Their Rulers.* Translated by Henry-Louis Gonin. Cape Town, South Africa: HAUM, 1956.

———. *The Grounds and Principles of Christian Religion.* Edinburgh: Robert Waldegrave, 1591.

———. *Life of John Calvin.* In John Calvin, *Tracts and Treatises on the Reformation of the Church.* Grand Rapids, MI: Eerdmans, 1958.

Boettner, Lorraine. *The Reformed Doctrine of Predestination.*

1932. Reprint, Philadelphia: Presbyterian and Reformed, 1973.

Bonnet, Jules, ed. *The Letters of John Calvin.* 4 vols. Philadelphia: Presbyterian Board of Publication, 1858.

Bonomi, Patricia U. *Under the Cope of Heaven: Religion, Society, and Politics in Colonial America.* New York: Oxford University Press, 1986.

Borgeaud, Charles. *Historie de l'Universite de Geneve.* Geneva, 1900.

Bouwsma, William J. *John Calvin: A Sixteenth-Century Portrait.* New York: Oxford University Press, 1988.

Breed, W. P. *Presbyterians and the Revolution.* 1876. Reprint, Decatur, MS: Issacharian Press, 1993.

Bromiley, Geoffrey. "The English Reformers and Diaconate." In *Service in Christ: Essays Presented to Karl Barth on His 80th Birthday.* Edited by James I. McCord and T. H. L. Parker. London: Epworth Press, 1966.

Brown, Harold O. J. "Unfettered Individualism." *The Religion and Society Report* 16, no. 9 (September 1999).

Brutus, Junius [Hubert Languet]. *A Defense of Liberty Against Tyrants.* Translated by Harold J. Laski. 1924. Reprint, Gloucester, MA: Peter Smith, 1963.

Bungener, Felix. *Calvin: His Life, His Labours, and His Writings.* Edinburgh: T. and T. Clark, 1863.

Buscarlet, Daniel. *International Monument of Reformation: A Short Outline.* Geneva: Editions l'Eau Vive, 1966.

Butler, Jon. *The Huguenots in America: A Refugee People in New World Society.* Cambridge, MA: Harvard University Press, 1983.

Calvin, John. *Commentaries.* 22 vols. Reprint, Grand Rapids, MI: Baker Book House, 1979.

————. *Institutes of the Christian Religion.* Edited by John T. McNeill. Translated by Ford Lewis Battles. 2 vols. Philadelphia: Westminster, 1960.

————. *Sermons on Galatians.* Edinburgh: Banner of Truth Trust, 1996.

————. *Theological Treatises.* Translated by J. K. S. Reid. Philadelphia: Westminster Press, 1954.

————. *Tracts and Treatises on the Reformation of the Church.* Grand Rapids, MI: Eerdmans, 1958.

Carson, John L., and David W. Hall, eds. *To Glorify and Enjoy God.* Edinburgh: Banner of Truth Trust, 1994.

Chenevière, Marc-Edouard. *La Pensee Politique de Calvin.* Geneva: Editions Labor, 1937.

Choisy, E. *L'etat Chretien Calviniste a Geneve au Temps de Theodore de Beze.* Geneva, 1902.

Clark, Jonathan C. D. *The Language of Liberty, 1660–1832.* Cambridge: Cambridge University Press, 1994.

Cox, William M. "The Standards and Civil Government." In *Memorial Volume of the Westminster Assembly, 1647–1897.* Richmond, VA: Presbyterian Committee of Publication, 1897.

Crumpacker, Mary. "Ecclesiastical Ordinances, 1561." In *Paradigms in Polity.* Edited by David W. Hall and Joseph H. Hall. Grand Rapids, MI: Eerdmans, 1994.

Custance, Arthur. *The Sovereignty of Grace.* Phillipsburg, NJ: Presbyterian and Reformed Publishing Co., 1979.

D'Aubigne, J. H. Merle. *The History of the Reformation in Europe in the Time of Calvin.* 8 vols. 1863–78. Reprint, New York: R. Carter, 1870.

————. *The History of the Reformation of the Sixteenth Century.* 5 vols. New York: American Tract Society, 1849–53.

De Jong, Peter Y. *The Covenant Idea in New England Theology, 1620–1847.* Grand Rapids, MI: Eerdmans, 1945.

Doumergue, Emile. *The Character of Calvinism: The Man, His System, the Church, the State.* 1923. Reprint, Neuilly [Seine]: La Cause, 1931.

Dreisbach, Daniel L. "Thomas Jefferson and the Mammoth Cheese." *Religion and Liberty* 12, no. 3 (May–June 2002).

———. *Thomas Jefferson and the Wall of Separation Between Church and State.* New York: New York University Press, 2002.

Droz, E. "Fausses adresses typographiques." *Bulletin of Historical Research* 23 (1961): 380–86, 572–74.

Duke, Alistair, Gillian Lewis, and Andrew Pettegree, eds. *Calvinism in Europe, 1540–1610: A Collection of Documents.* Manchester: Manchester University Press, 1992.

Dunning, William A. *A History of Political Theories: From Luther to Montesquieu.* New York: Macmillan, 1919.

Edwards, David L. *Christian England: From the Reformation to the Eighteenth Century.* Grand Rapids, MI: Eerdmans, 1983.

Fazy, Henri. *Les Constitutions de la Republique de Geneve.* Geneva and Basel: H. George, Libraire-Editeur, 1890.

Fisher, David Hackett. *Albion's Seed: Four British Folkways in America.* New York: Oxford University Press, 1989.

Foster, Herbert D. *Collected Papers of Herbert D. Foster.* N.p.: privately printed, 1929.

Foxe, John. *Foxe's Book of Martyrs.* Edited by Marie Gentert King. Old Tappan, NJ: Spire Books, 1978.

Foxgrover, David, ed. *Calvin Studies Society Papers.* Grand Rapids, MI: 1995, 1997.

Franklin, Julian H., ed. *Constitutionalism and Resistance in the Sixteenth Century.* New York: Pegasus, 1969.

Fuhrmann, Paul T. "Philip Mornay and the Huguenot Challenge to Absolutism." In *Calvinism and the Political Order,* edited by George L. Hunt. Philadelphia: Westminster Press, 1965.

Garnett, George, ed. *Vindiciae, Contra Tyrannos.* Cambridge: Cambridge University Press, 1994.

Geissler, Suzanne. *Jonathan Edwards to Aaron Burr, Jr.: From the Great Awakening to Democratic Politics.* New York: Edwin Mellen Press, 1981.

Gerstner, Edna. *Idelette: A Novel Based on the Life of Madame John Calvin.* 1963. Reprint, Ligonier, PA: Soli Deo Gloria Publications, 1992.

Graham, W. Fred. *The Constructive Revolutionary: John Calvin and His Socio-Economic Impact.* Richmond, VA: John Knox Press, 1975.

Griffin, Keith L. *Revolution and Religion: American Revolutionary War and the Reformed Clergy.* New York: Paragon House, 1994.

Hall, Basil. "The Calvin Legend." *The Churchman* 73, no. 3 (September 1959): 124–25.

———. "Diaconia in Martin Butzer." In *Service in Christ: Essays Presented to Karl Barth on His 80th Birthday.* Edited by James I. McCord and T. H. L. Parker. London: Epworth Press, 1966.

Hall, David W. *The Arrogance of the Modern: Historical Theology Held in Contempt.* Oak Ridge, TN: Calvin Institute, 1997.

———. "The Calvinistic Political Tradition, 1530–1790: The Rise, Development, and Dissemination of Genevan Political Culture to the Founders of America Through Theological Exemplars." PhD diss., Whitefield Theological Seminary, 2002.

————, ed. *Election Day Sermons.* Oak Ridge, TN: Kuyper Institute, 1996.

————. *The Genevan Reformation and the American Founding.* Lanham, MD: Lexington Press, 2003.

————. "In a Meadow Called Runnymede." *Religion and Liberty* 10, no. 4 (July–August 2000): 6–9.

————, ed. *Jus Divinum Regiminis Ecclesiastici, or, The Divine Right of Church-Government.* Dallas, TX: Naphtali Press, 1995.

————. *Savior or Servant? Putting Government in Its Place.* Oak Ridge, TN: Kuyper Institute, 1996.

————, and Joseph H. Hall, eds. *Paradigms in Polity.* Grand Rapids, MI: Eerdmans, 1994.

Haller, William. *Liberty and Reformation in the Puritan Revolution.* New York: Columbia University Press, 1955.

Hancock, Ralph C. *Calvin and the Foundations of Modern Politics.* Ithaca, NY: Cornell University Press, 1989.

Heyer, Henri. *Guillaume Farel: An Introduction to His Theology.* Translated by Blair Reynolds. Lewiston, NY: Edwin Mellen Press, 1990.

Holl, Karl. *The Cultural Significance of the Reformation.* Translated by Karl Hertz, Barbara Herta, and John H. Lichtblau. New York: Meridian, 1959.

Hopfl, Harro. *The Christian Polity of John Calvin.* Cambridge: Cambridge University Press, 1982.

Hughes, Philip E., ed. *The Register of the Company of Pastors in the Time of Calvin.* Grand Rapids, MI: Eerdmans, 1966.

Hutson, James H. *Religion and the Founding of the American Republic.* Washington DC: Library of Congress, 1998.

————. *The Sister Republics: Switzerland and the United*

States from 1776 to the Present. 2nd ed. Washington DC: Library of Congress, 1992.

Keen, Ralph. "The Limits of Power and Obedience in the Later Calvin." *Calvin Theological Journal* 27, no. 2 (November 1992): 252–77.

Kelley, Donald R. *Francois Hotman: A Revolutionary's Ordeal.* Princeton, NJ: Princeton University Press, 1973.

Kelly, Douglas. *The Emergence of Liberty in the Modern World: The Influence of Calvin on Five Governments from the 16th Through 18th Centuries.* Phillipsburg, NJ: Presbyterian and Reformed Publishing, 1992.

———. "Sermon XXIX on First Samuel (1 Samuel 8:11–22)." Davidson (Columbia) Calvin Conference Papers. Davidson College Presbyterian Church, 1982.

Kingdon, Robert M. *Calvin and Calvinism: Sources of Democracy.* Lexington, MA: D. C. Heath and Co., 1970.

———, ed. *De Droit des magistrats.* Geneva: Librairie Droz, 1971.

———. *Geneva and the Consolidation of the French Protestant Movement, 1564–1572.* Madison: University of Wisconsin Press, 1967.

———. *Geneva and the Coming Wars of Religion in France, 1555–1563.* Geneva: Librairie Droz, 1956.

Knox, John. *On Rebellion.* Edited by Roger A. Mason. Cambridge: Cambridge University Press, 1994.

Koch, Adrienne, and William Peden, eds. *The Selected Writings of John and John Quincy Adams.* New York: Knopf, 1946.

Kuyper, Abraham. *Lectures on Calvinism.* 1898. Reprint, Grand Rapids, MI: Eerdmans, 1953.

Laski, Harold, ed. *A Defense of Liberty Against Tyrants.* Gloucester, MA: Peter Smith, 1963.

Leyburn, James G. *The Scotch-Irish: A Social History.* Chapel Hill: University of North Carolina Press, 1962.

Linder, Robert Dean. *The Political Ideas of Pierre Viret.* Geneva: Librairie Droz, 1964.

Luther, Martin. *The Sermons of Martin Luther.* Edited and translated by F. A. Klug. 5 vols. Grand Rapids, MI: Baker Books, 1983.

Maclear, J. F. "Samuel Rutherford: The Law and the King." In *Calvinism and the Political Order: Essays Prepared for the Woodrow Wilson Lectureship of the National Presbyterian Center.* Edited by George L. Hunt. Philadelphia: Westminster, 1965.

Marcacci, Marco. *Historie de L'Universite de Geneve 1558–1986.* Geneva: University of Geneva, 1987.

Martyn, W. Carlos. *The Pilgrim Fathers of New England: A History.* New York: American Tract Society, 1867.

Massachusetts Sabbath School Society. *Lives of the Chief Fathers of New England.* 6 vols. Boston: Massachusetts Sabbath School Society, 1846–49.

Mather, Cotton. *Magnalia Christi Americana: The Great Works of Christ in America.* 2 vols. 1702. Reprint of the 1853 edition, Edinburgh and Carlisle, PA: Banner of Truth Trust, 1979.

McComish, William. *The Reformation: Many Men with One Idea.* Geneva: Foundation of Les Clefs de Saint-Pierre, 1985.

McCoy, Charles S., and J. Wayne Baker. *Fountainhead of Federalism: Heinrich Bullinger and the Covenantal Tradition.* Louisville: Westminster–John Knox, 1991.

McCrackan, W. D. *The Rise of the Swiss Republic.* 2nd ed. 1901. Reprint, New York: AMS Press, 1970.

M'Clure, A. W. *The Lives of John Wilson, John Norton and John Davenport.* Vol. 2, *Lives of the Chief Fathers of New England.* Boston: Massachusetts Sabbath School Society, 1846.

McGrath, Alister. "Calvin and the Christian Calling." *First Things* 94 (June–July 1999): 31–35.

———. *A Life of John Calvin: A Study in the Shaping of Western Culture.* Oxford, UK, and Cambridge, MA: Basil Blackwell, 1990.

McKee, Elsie. *Diakonia in the Classical Reformed Tradition and Today.* Grand Rapids: Eerdmans, 1989.

McNeill, John T. "Calvin and Civil Government." In *Readings in Calvin's Theology.* Edited by Donald McKim. Grand Rapids, MI: Baker, 1984.

———. "Calvinism and European Politics in Historical Perspective." In *Calvinism and the Political Order,* edited by George L. Hunt. Philadelphia: Westminster Press, 1965.

———. "The Democratic Element in Calvin's Thought." *Church History* 18, no. 3 (1949): 165.

———. "John Calvin on Civil Government." In *Calvinism and the Political Order,* edited by George L. Hunt, 22–45. Philadelphia: Westminster Press, 1965.

Moehlman, Conrad H. *The American Constitutions and Religion.* Berne, IN: n.p., 1938.

Monter, E. William. *Calvin's Geneva.* New York: John Wiley & Sons, 1967.

———. *Studies in Genevan Government, 1536–1605.* Geneva: Librairie Droz, 1964.

Morison, Samuel E. *Three Centuries of Harvard, 1636–1936.* Cambridge, MA: Harvard University Press, 1936.

Naphy, William G. "Baptism, Church Riots, and Social Unrest in Calvin's Geneva." *Sixteenth Century Journal* 226, no. 1 (1995): 87–97.

―――. *Calvin and the Consolidation of the Genevan Reformation.* Manchester, UK: Manchester University Press, 1994.

―――, ed. *Documents on the Continental Reformation.* New York: St. Martin's Press, 1996.

―――. "The Reformation and the Evolution of Geneva's Schools." In *Reformations Old and New,* edited by Beat Kumin, 190–93. London: Scolar Press, 1996.

Olasky, Marvin. *The American Leadership Tradition: Moral Vision from Washington to Clinton.* New York: Free Press, 1999.

Olson, Jeannine E. *Calvin and Social Welfare: Deacons and the Bourse Francaise.* Cranbury, NJ: Susquehanna University Press. 1989.

―――. "Social Welfare and the Transformation of Polity in Geneva." In *The Identity of Geneva: The Christian Commonwealth, 1564–1864.* Edited by John B. Roney and Martin I. Klauber, 155–68. Westport, CT: Greenwood Press, 1998.

Ozment, Steven E., ed. *The Reformation in Medieval Perspective.* Chicago: Quadrangle Books, 1971.

Poole, Patrick S., ed. *Reformation Political Tracts.* (Forthcoming.)

Ramsay, David. *The History of the American Revolution.* Edited by Lester H. Cohen. 2 vols. 1789. Reprint, Indianapolis: Liberty Classics, 1990.

Reid, W. Stanford. "The Battle Hymns of the Lord: Calvinist Psalmody of the Sixteenth Century." *Sixteenth Century Journal* 2, no. 1 (1971): 36–54.

Roney, John B., and Martin I. Klauber, eds. *The Identity of*

Geneva: The Christian Commonwealth, 1564–1864. Westport, CT: Greenwood Press, 1998.

Scalia, Antonin. "The Millennium That Was: How Democracy Swept the World." *Wall Street Journal.* September 7, 1999.

Schaff, Philip, ed. *The Creeds of Christendom.* 3 vols. 1877. Reprint, Grand Rapids, MI: Baker Bookhouse, 1983.

————. *History of the Christian Church.* 8 vols. 1859–67. Reprint, Grand Rapids, MI: Eerdmans, 1979.

Shain, Barry A. *The Myth of American Individualism: The Protestant Origins of American Political Thought.* Princeton, NJ: Princeton University Press, 1994.

Shimitzu, J. J. *Conflict of Loyalties, Politics, and Religion in the Career of Gaspard de Coligny, Admiral of France, 1519–1572.* Geneva: Librairie Droz, n.d.

Singer, C. Gregg. *A Theological Interpretation of American History.* 3rd ed. 1964. Reprint, Greenville, SC: A Press, 1994.

Skinner, Quentin. *The Foundations of Modern Political Thought.* Vol. 2, *The Age of Reformation.* Cambridge: Cambridge University Press, 1978.

Sproul, R. C. *Chosen by God.* Wheaton, IL: Tyndale, 1986.

St. Augustine. *The City of God.* Translated by Gerald G. Walsh. Garden City, NY: Image Books, 1958.

Stauffer, Richard. *The Humanness of John Calvin.* Translated by George H. Shriver. New York: Abingdon, 1971.

Sturm, Karl, ed. *De Iure Magistratuum.* Neukirchen, 1965.

Thomas Aquinas. *The Summa Theologica of St. Thomas Aquinas.* London: R. & T. Washbourne, 1912–25.

Thomas, Derek. "Calvin's Exposition of the Book of Job." *The Banner of Truth,* 366 (March 1994): 13.

Tyrrell, R. Emmett, Jr. *The Conservative Crack-Up.* New York: Simon and Schuster, 1992.

Wallace, Ronald S. *Calvin, Geneva and the Reformation: A Study of Calvin as Social Reformer, Churchman, Pastor, and Theologian.* Edinburgh: Scottish Academic Press, 1988.

Walton, Robert C. *Zwingli's Theocracy.* Toronto: University of Toronto Press, 1967.

Wendel, Francois. *Calvin: The Origins and Development of His Religious Thought.* Translated by Philip Mairet. London: Collins, 1963.

Westerkamp, Marilyn J. *Triumph of the Laity: Scots-Irish Piety and the Great Awakening, 1625–1760.* New York: Oxford University Press, 1988.

Wiley, David N. "Calvin's Friendship with Guillaume Farel." In *Calvin Studies Society Papers.* 187–204. Edited by David Foxgrover. Grand Rapids, MI: Calvin Studies Society, 1998.

Wilkins, J. Steven. *America, The First 350 Years.* Forest, MS: Covenant Publications, 1988.

Winthrop, John. *The Journal of John Winthrop, 1630–1649.* Edited by Richard S. Dunn, James Savage, and Laetitia Yeandle. Cambridge, MA: Harvard University Press, 1996.

INDEX